BEDE

A HISTORY
OF THE
ENGLISH
CHURCH
AND
PEOPLE

✳

Translated and with an Introduction by
Leo Sherley-Price

PENGUIN BOOKS

Penguin Books Ltd, Harmondsworth, Middlesex
U.S.A.: Penguin Books Inc., 3300 Clipper Mill Road, Baltimore 11, Md
AUSTRALIA: Penguin Books Pty Ltd, 762 Whitehorse Road,
Mitcham, Victoria

—

This translation first published 1955
Reprinted 1956, 1960

Made and printed in Great Britain
by R. & R. Clark Ltd
Edinburgh

CONTENTS

Contents

Contents

BOOK TWO

Contents

Contents

BOOK THREE

Contents

Contents

Contents

Contents

Contents

INTRODUCTION

THE LIFE OF BEDE

BEDE (Baeda) was probably born in the year of the Council of Hertford (A.D. 673) on lands that were shortly afterwards granted by King Egfrid of Northumbria to S. Benedict Biscop's new monastery of Saint Peter at Wearmouth. He himself tells us (v. 24) that when he reached the age of seven, his parents – of whom we know nothing – placed him under the care of Abbot Benedict for his education and upbringing. But when the monastery of Saint Paul was established as a joint-foundation at Jarrow in the year 682, Bede seems to have been transferred to the care of its first abbot, Ceolfrid, and to have remained a monk there for the remainder of his life.

To have served under abbots of such learning and ability as Benedict and such holiness as Ceolfrid (whose biographies Bede was to write in his *Lives of the Abbots*) can have had no small influence on Bede's own life and activities, and his own inborn love of learning and devotion to the spiritual life must have received constant stimulation and encouragement. A touching incident which almost certainly refers to Bede's boyhood is preserved in the anonymous *Life of Abbot Ceolfrid*, which tells how the plague of 686 attacked Ceolfrid's monastery and swept away all the choir monks capable of maintaining the regular services of the Church 'with the exception of the Abbot himself and one boy reared and educated by him, who is now a priest of the same monastery and commends the Abbot's admirable doings both verbally and in writing to all who desire to learn them. Greatly distressed by this catastrophe, the Abbot decided to discontinue their usual practice, and to recite and sing all the psalms without antiphons except at Vespers and Matins. But when they had done this for a week with great sorrow and regret, he could bear it no longer and directed that the psalms and their antiphons were to be restored in their appointed course. So with the help of all [survivors], he and the aforesaid boy carried his decision with no little trouble until such time as he could either train or procure from elsewhere sufficient numbers to assist at the Divine Office.' Only a boy as naturally scholarly and devout as Bede would have been capable of performing the duties of a choir-monk in this way, and the story almost certainly refers to him. This early training endowed Bede with a deep and lasting love for the Church's regular Hours of worship, and in a letter written by Alcuin to the Wearmouth community, he says in reference to Bede's latter years: 'It is told how blessed Bede, our master and your patron, said "I know that the angels are present at the canonical Hours, and what if they do not find me among the brethren when they assemble? Will they not say, Where is Bede? Why does he not attend the appointed devotions with his brethren?' "

Benedict Biscop, who founded and ruled both Wearmouth and Jarrow, was of noble birth, and a man of wide learning and culture. He had been trained at Lérins, and had accompanied Archbishop Theodore and Abbot Hadrian from Rome in 669, when the former had been consecrated to the Archbishopric of Canterbury. His learning and artistic knowledge was to influence all England, and greatly enriched both Church and national life. Not only was he a Greek and Latin scholar, and taught theology, astronomy, art, and music, but he also made many visits to the Continent and Rome, from which he brought back treasures for the English churches – books, altar-vessels, paintings, and vestments – which had no small influence on native standards. He also brought stone-masons and glaziers from Gaul to build and furnish the churches, and in order that they might teach their crafts to the English, who had hitherto built almost exclusively in timber. Further, with the approval of Pope Agatho, he brought John, the Arch-cantor of Saint Peter's, to teach his monks the liturgical chant *sicut ad sanctum Petrum Romae agebatur* (IV. 18), a visit that had widespread influence on the development of English church music, since many monasteries sent monks to Wearmouth to receive instruction from him, while others invited him to visit them for the purpose.

Bede tells us that he was made deacon at the age of nineteen by Bishop John of Hexham (later known as Saint John of Beverley). And since canon law laid down the age of twenty-five as the norm for admission to the diaconate, Bede's scholarship and devotion must have been recognized as exceptional for him to have been presented by Abbot Ceolfrid six years early. He was advanced to the priesthood by Bishop John eleven years later, and tells us that 'from the time of my receiving the priesthood until my fifty-ninth year, I have worked, both for my own profit and that of my brethren, to compile extracts from the works of the venerable Fathers on holy scripture, and to make commentaries on their meaning and interpretation.' During all these years, Bede was doubtless gathering material for his *History*, which he completed in 731.

Both in his *History* and in his *Lives of the Abbots* Bede gives us much valuable information about the daily life of a monastery in Saxon times, as well as many illuminating character-sketches. From abbot to lay-brother, all took an active share in the well-ordered day of work and prayer, and Bede tells how Abbot Eosterwin, a former King's Thane, 'remained so humble that he loved to thresh and winnow, milk the cows and ewes, and occupied himself obediently in the bakery, garden, kitchen, and all the work of the monastery.' At the same time, this humble and democratic abbot 'corrected offenders with regular discipline' and exercised unquestioned authority. Apart from any specialized work that monks were directed to undertake in accordance with their knowledge and capabilities, whether writing, copying and illuminating manuscripts, cooking or care of the infirm, the life of the whole community centred around its church, with the offering of Mass and the maintenance of the regular Hours of prayer, beginning with Matins and Lauds in the early hours of the morning, and closing with Compline as darkness ended the activities of the day. A post of considerable importance under the Abbot and Prior (*Praepositus*) was that of Guestmaster, for there was a constant coming and going between monasteries, while persons of all walks of life from king to peasant were assured of simple hospitality in a monastery when on their travels. Among visitors of interest Bede certainly met Adamnan, abbot of the Celtic monastery of Iona (v. 15) who came to visit King Alfrid and to 'observe the rites of the Church canonically performed'; which visit resulted in his adoption of the Roman usages. Thanks to the artistic tastes of Abbot Benedict and his journeys to the Continent and Rome, the church in Bede's own monastery was built of stone, and well furnished with service-books, vestments, relics, and pictures. Bede describes these latter in his *Lives of the Abbots* as 'vividly portraying the relationship of the Old and New Testaments, such as Isaac carrying the wood for his own sacrifice, and our Lord carrying the cross on which He was to suffer.'

Bede's life centred on his own monastery of Jarrow, and it does not seem likely that he left it very frequently, although he paid visits to other monastic houses from time to time. He is known to have visited Lindisfarne, and he stayed for a short while with his friend Egbert, Archbishop of York. He also probably visited King Ceolwulf of Northumbria, a ruler of considerable learning, who resigned his crown three years after Bede's death and became a monk at Lindisfarne. The story that Bede visited Rome at the invitation of Pope Sergius is very unlikely, and rests on a statement by William of Malmesbury which has never been satisfactorily explained.

In the year 735 Bede fell ill, and the day drew near that he had so often described in his account of others as their 'heavenly birthday'. We are fortunate in possessing a touching eyewitness account of his last days in a letter written by Cuthbert, one of Bede's scholars and later Abbot of Wearmouth and Jarrow, to his friend and contemporary Cuthwin. I have no hesitation in quoting this moving account in full.

'To his fellow teacher Cuthwin, most beloved in Christ, from his school-friend Cuthbert. Health for ever in God.

'I was delighted to receive your little gift, and was pleased to read your devout and learned letter in which I learned that, as I had greatly hoped, you are diligently offering Masses and holy prayers for our father and master Bede, whom God loved so well. Out of love for him rather than any confidence in my ability to do so, I am glad to give you a short account of his passing from this world, since I understand that you wish and request this.

'For nearly a fortnight before the Feast of our Lord's Resurrection he was troubled by weakness and breathed with great difficulty, although he suffered little pain. Thenceforward until Ascension Day he remained cheerful and happy, giving thanks to God each hour day and night. He gave daily lessons to us his students, and spent the rest of the day in singing the psalms so far as his strength allowed. He passed the whole night in joyful prayer and thanksgiving to God, except when slumber overcame him; but directly he awoke, he continued to meditate on scriptural themes, and never failed to thank God with hands outstretched. I can truthfully affirm that I have

18

never seen or heard of anyone who gave thanks so unceasingly to the living God as him. O truly blessed man! He used to repeat the saying of the holy Apostle Paul, *It is a fearful thing to fall into the hands of the living God,* and many other sayings from holy scripture, and in this manner he used to arouse our souls by the consideration of our last hour. Being well-versed in our native songs, he described to us the dread departure of the soul from the body by a verse in our own tongue, which translated means: "Before setting forth on that inevitable journey, none is wiser than the man who considers – before his soul departs hence – what good or evil he has done, and what judgement his soul will receive after its passing." To comfort both us and himself, he also used to sing antiphons, one of which is, "O King of glory, Lord of might, Who on this day ascended in triumph above all heavens, do not leave us orphaned, but send to us the Spirit of truth, the promise of the Father. Alleluia." And when he reached the words "do not leave us orphaned", he broke into tears and wept much. An hour later he began to repeat what he had begun and so continued all day, so that we who heard him sorrowed and wept with him. In such grace we passed the days of Lent until the above day, and he remained full of joy, thanking God that he had deserved this weakness. He often quoted, "God scourgeth every son that He receiveth", and Saint Ambrose's saying, "I have not lived so that I am ashamed to live among you, and I do not fear to die for God is gracious." [1]

'During these days, in addition to the daily instruction that he gave us and his recitation of the psalter, he was working to complete two books worthy of mention. For he translated the Gospel of Saint John into our own language for the benefit of the Church of God as far as the words *but what are these among so many.* He also made some extracts from the works of Bishop Isidore (of Seville), saying "I do not wish my sons to read anything untrue, or to labour unprofitably after my death." But on the Tuesday before our Lord's Ascension his breathing became increasingly laboured, and his feet began to swell. Despite this he continued cheerfully to teach and dictate all day, saying from time to time, "Learn quickly. I do not know how long I can continue, for my Lord may call me in a short while." It seemed to us that he might well be aware of the time of his departure, and he spent that night without sleeping, giving

1. Paulinus' *Life of Saint Ambrose,* chap. 45.

thanks to God. When dawn broke on Wednesday, he told us to write diligently what we had begun, and we did this until Terce. After Terce we walked in procession with the relics of the Saints as the customs of the day required, but one of us remained with him, who said, "There is still one chapter missing in the book that you have been dictating; but it seems hard that I should trouble you any further." "It is no trouble," he answered: "Take your pen and sharpen it, and write quickly." And he did so. But at None he said to me, "I have a few articles of value in my casket, such as pepper, linen and incense. Run quickly and fetch the priests of the monastery, so that I may distribute among them the gifts that God has given me." In great distress I did as he bid me. And when they arrived, he spoke to each of them in turn, requesting and reminding them diligently to offer Masses and prayers for him. They readily promised to do so, and all were sad and wept, grieving above all else at his statement that they must not expect to see his face much longer in this world. But they were heartened when he said, "If it be the will of my Maker, the time has come when I shall be freed from the body and return to Him Who created me out of nothing when I had no being. I have had a long life, and the merciful Judge has ordered it graciously. The time of my departure is at hand, and my soul longs to see Christ my King in His beauty." He also told us many other edifying things, and passed his last day happily until evening. Then the same lad, named Wilbert, said again: "Dear master, there is one sentence still unfinished." "Very well," he replied: "write it down." After a short while the lad said, "Now it is finished." "You have spoken truly," he replied: "It is well finished. Now raise my head in your hands, for it would give me great joy to sit facing the holy place where I used to pray, so that I may sit and call on my Father." And thus, on the floor of his cell, he chanted "Glory be to the Father, and to the Son, and to the Holy Spirit" to its ending, and breathed his last.

'We may confidently believe that as he had devoted himself with such ardour to the praises of God here on earth, his soul was borne by the angels to the longed-for joys of Heaven. And all who saw and heard of the death of our father Bede declared that they had never known anyone end his days in such deep devotion and peace. For as you have learned, as long as his soul remained in his body, he said "Glory be to the Father" and other chants to the glory of God, offering unceasing thanks to God with hands outstretched. And although my lack of eloquence renders this present account brief, you should know that many other things could be related of him. However, in due course I hope with God's help to describe all that I have seen and heard more fully.'

Bede passed away on the evening of May the twenty-fifth, 735, after First Vespers of the Feast of the Ascension. He is commemorated in the Church's Calendar on May the twenty-seventh.

Bede's body was first laid to rest in the south porch of his monastery church, but was later translated to a place of honour near the altar. About the year 1020, a Durham monk named Aelred stole his relics and brought them secretly to Durham, where they were placed in the tomb of Saint Cuthbert and became a cherished possession of that church. During the episcopate of Bishop Hugh Puiset they were enshrined in a silver and gold reliquary set on a marble base supported by five pillars in the Galilee, and were carried in procession at great festivals. During the spoliation of the monasteries by Henry VIII the reliquary was seized, but the bones are said to have been secreted in a tomb in the Galilee, where certain remains were discovered when the tomb was examined in 1831. But the principal and lasting memorial of the first of English historians, whom Saint Boniface described as *Candela ecclesiae quam illuxit Spiritus Sanctus* is the inspiration of his holy life and the value of the great work that he bequeathed to posterity.

BEDE AS AN HISTORIAN

The centuries on which Bede concentrates are a crucial and formative period in our island history, during which the future shape and pattern of the English Church and nation were beginning to emerge. Once the shield of Roman protection was withdrawn, the Celtic peoples of Britain were steadily forced to yield ground before the ever increasing pressure of the incoming Angles, Saxons, and Jutes, and were driven westward into the remote and inaccessible regions along the storm-swept Atlantic coast. Even here they enjoyed little security, and were harried by raiding parties of Irish pirates, as Saint Patrick, himself a victim, describes in his *Confessions*. Here in Devon and Cornwall, Wales, Cumberland, and south-west Scotland the Romano-Britons clung desperately to the shreds of their native independence and customs. Many were sustained by the Christian faith, brought to this island centuries before Augustine (A.D. 597) in the more peaceful days when Britain enjoyed the protection and administration of Rome as an integral *Provincia* of the Empire. Rallied by such contrasting leaders as Ambrosius, 'last of the Romans' (I. 16), Saint Germanus (I. 20) and the semi-legendary King Arthur, the Britons won sufficient successes against the Saxons to maintain a constantly menaced independence, but were isolated from the remainder of Christendom by their heathen enemies, for whom they felt nothing but bitterness and contempt. Meanwhile the Picts and Scots in their northern fastnesses remained as hostile to Briton and Saxon as they had to the legions of Rome. Bede traces the gradual conversion of all these mutually antipathetic peoples to the religion of Christ, and illustrates the enriching influence of the Catholic Church, which brought them into contact with the rest of Christendom, and, in so doing, brought to these semi-barbaric peoples the wisdom, art, and civilization of Christian Rome. During these vital centuries we see Columba and Aidan bring the Gospel to the north; Ninian to the Picts; Patrick to the Irish; David and his contemporaries to the Celts of Wales and Cornwall; and Augustine to the newly established Saxon peoples.

In Bede's pages we trace the gradual decay of the Celtic tribal and monastic systems, and their supersession by the highly developed and centralized system of the Roman Church. As Dom Louis Gougaud shows in his *Christianity in Celtic Lands*, the principal difference between the Celtic and Roman system of church administration was that the former was monastic, while the latter was diocesan. In the Celtic churches the highest administrative officer was the Abbot, who might or might not be in episcopal orders, and who, as in the case of the Abbot of Iona, ruled the churches over a considerable *provincia*. A striking example of this is Saint Columba, who never received episcopal consecration, but who exercised a wide and unquestioned authority. The Celtic bishop, as a member of a monastic community, was subject to his abbot, and exercised his spiritual functions at the latter's request and direction (see III. 4). It was the abbot who chose and presented candidates for ordination or consecration to the bishop (IV. 24), and appointed members of the community to their various tasks inside or outside the monastery. The duties of the Celtic bishop, therefore, were wholly spiritual, in contrast to those of the Roman prelate, who gradually acquired or had thrust upon him onerous administrative responsibilities, not only in ecclesiastical but in national and provincial affairs. This Celtic emphasis on the spiritual and apostolic nature of the episcopal office might well be borne in mind in these days when bishops are over-burdened by countless financial and administrative details, and their true function obscured. However, although one can readily appreciate that the free-lance methods of the learned and saintly Celtic missionaries were supremely effective in breaking new ground and winning converts for Christ, they were not such as would develop and administer a growing Christian community of nation-wide extent. None will deny the holiness of the wandering Celtic saints or their appeal to the imagination, but they were bound to give place to the more regular, stable, and disciplined ways of life introduced and practised by the monks of Saint Benedict. And while much was lost as Celtic Christianity and culture declined, even more was gained. For although the leaders of the British Church rejected Augustine's claim to jurisdiction and refused their co-operation in evangelizing the pagan Saxons, contacts between the Roman and Celtic Churches increased as time went on. Mutual appreciation began to heal the wounds of suspicion and controversy, and a common belief in Christ gradually drew together the peoples of Britain into the English nation.

A decisive step towards this national and spiritual unity was taken in A.D. 664 at the Council of Whitby (IV. 25), described by R. H. Hodgkin in his *History of the Anglo-Saxons* as 'one of the great turning-points in the history of the race. ... The Synod turned the scales, and decided that the English should take their religion and their civilization from the Roman world rather than from what Wilfrid called "one remote corner of the most remote island." ' From that day the Celtic cause was doomed to gradual extinction. These bonds of national unity were to be greatly tempered and strengthened in the fiery trials of the Danish invasions that began sixty years after Bede's death, when under the devoted leadership of Alfred, noblest of England's kings, one may fairly say that the spirit of England was born. This unification of many races into one people is the imperishable memorial of this great king, who said: 'I have always striven to live worthily, and at my death to leave to those who follow me a worthy memorial of my deeds.' And in Bede we see how Christian leaders and scholars such as Aidan, Cuthbert, and Augustine became the pastors and counsellors of king and peasant alike, laying the foundations of that close alliance between the power spiritual and the power temporal which was to bring such strength and stability to the English nation in centuries to come.

It is almost certain that the first (partial) translation of Bede's *History* from Latin into the vernacular was made by King Alfred himself, who, despite his countless pressing problems and responsibilities, made time for this task in order to inform and inspire his English subjects. This high tribute is evidence that the *History* quickly established itself as a unique and authoritative record of our national history. Even during his lifetime Bede's reputation for learning extended far into Europe, and for generations after his death his *Commentaries*, *Martyrology*, and other works were recognized as standard works of reference in the West. That a new translation of his *History* is published in the Penguin Classics today testifies that the work which he compiled with such skill and labour over twelve centuries ago still retains its value and freshness for readers of this age.

There should be few in these islands to whom the name of Bede is unknown, but there are perhaps many who do not realize the greatness of our debt to him. Nevertheless, were it not for the rich fund of information that he gathered and sifted with such care, our knowledge of the vital and stirring centuries that he describes would be scanty, while a treasury of tales loved by every English child would have been lost for ever. So any readers who take up this book for the first time can rest assured that they will not find it a dreary chronicle of events and dates; on the contrary, a rich living tapestry will unfold before them, and they will discover a source of interest and enjoyment that may well be lifelong, and stimulate them to learn more about the storied past on which our present and future is built. Such is the interest of the subject-matter and the vividness of Bede's characteristic style that the scenes and folk of long ago live again. We are transported back into the fens and forests, highlands and islands of Celtic Britain and Saxon England, and we feel strangely 'at home'. These are our own people and our own land, and with a little imagination and historical sense we have little difficulty in picturing the contemporary scene, or in appreciating the viewpoint, plans, and problems of the kings, saints, and lesser folk whom Bede describes so well. We can understand Augustine's sense of inadequacy when summoned from his quiet Roman cloister and directed to the tremendous task of converting the heathen Saxons about whom he had heard such grim rumours (I. 23). We can visualize the tense scene as the heathen high-priest Coifi rides out before King Edwin and his thanes to defy his gods and defile their temple (II. 13). We can stand beside the gallant King Oswald at Heavenfield as he sets up a great oaken cross with his own hands, and summons his army to prayer before engaging the heathen hordes in desperate battle (III. 2). Above all, we cannot but be impressed and deeply moved by the selfless Christ-like lives of the northern Celtic saints – Columba, Cuthbert, and Aidan – and their disciples. Men of great personal gifts and radiant faith, they fearlessly carried the Gospel alone among alien peoples, gladly accepting lifelong 'exile for Christ' as his apostles. Redoubtable travellers by sea and land, able scholars, scribes, and craftsmen, the loveliness of their hard and holy lives has won the admiration and captured the imagination of all succeeding centuries. When we read Bede's account of such men and their doings, we realize ever more clearly that the past is not dead and done with, but a force to be reckoned with, silently moulding the present and the future.

As already mentioned, Bede's *History* belongs to his latter years, when he had already won a wide reputation by his many other works, a list of which he appends to the closing chapter of the *History*. But it is by the latter that he is best known today, and by which he has richly earned the title of 'Father of English History'. For Bede was not content to compile a bare chronicle of events and dates, or to restrict himself to hagiography as his predecessors had done. He set himself to examine all available records, to secure verbal or written accounts from reliable living authorities, to record local traditions and stories, to interpret significant events, and, in short, to compile as complete and continuous a history of the English Church and people as lay within his power. He was the first to conceive or attempt such a formidable project, and posterity acknowledges his pioneer work as a remarkably successful achievement.

In order to accomplish his purpose, Bede sets out his *History* in five convenient periods or 'books'. In the first Book, after a preliminary geographical survey of Britain drawn entirely from earlier authorities such as Pliny, Orosius, and Gildas, and a brief account of the Roman occupation, Bede proceeds to tell the story of Christian-

ity in Britain up to the period immediately preceding the death of
its great apostle Gregory the Great. The second Book continues the
story from his death up to the death of King Edwin and the overthrow of the Northumbrian kingdom by the pagan chieftain Penda.
The third Book recounts the Church's struggle against heathenism
in the North, and the planting of the Faith among the Mercians and
East Saxons. The fourth Book records the appointment of Theodore
the Greek to the Archbishopric of Canterbury and his reform and
reorganization of the English Church; the lives of Cuthbert and
Wilfrid; and the progress of the Church in the south-eastern provinces. The fifth Book carries on the story from the time of Bishop
John of Beverley up to the date of the work's completion in A.D.
731.

BEDE'S TREATMENT OF MATERIAL

As he mentions in his Preface, Bede was encouraged to undertake
the writing of a history by 'the learned and reverend Abbot Albinus', who succeeded Archbishop Theodore's colleague Hadrian as
abbot of the monastery of Saint Peter and Saint Paul at Canterbury
in the year A.D. 709. Abbot Albinus was a close and valued friend of
Bede, who addresses him elsewhere as his 'best and most beloved
father in Christ', and who received great assistance from the latter's
researches into the history of the Church in Kent and the adjoining
provinces. Bede's Preface affords concise information on his sources,
and testifies to his careful treatment of all material, whether written
or verbal. He tells how Nothelm, 'a devout priest of the Church in
London' (later Archbishop of Canterbury, A.D. 735-40), had made
a journey to Rome and obtained permission from Pope Gregory II
to examine the papal archives, and to make copies of all letters relevant to the mission of Augustine and the subsequent progress of the
Church in England. Doubtless a considerable number of documents
were also available at Canterbury. Bede also mentions that he had
sought and obtained assistance from various provincial bishops. He
mentions in particular Bishop Daniel of the West Saxons, who had
provided information about that province and the Isle of Wight;
Abbot Esius, who gave facts about East Anglia; and the monks of
Lastingham, who did the same for Mercia. And while Bede is naturally best acquainted with events in his own Northumbria, he is careful to supplement and check his facts by recourse to 'innumerable

26

witnesses', such as his friend Bishop Acca and the monks of Lindisfarne, to whom he submitted the draft of his *Life of Saint Cuthbert* for their comment and approval.

Bede's industry and scholarship are generally acknowledged, but his most significant achievement lies in his inspired ability to select and integrate the vast mass of facts and traditions that he had gathered into a single framework. He doubtless rejected much material as unreliable or irrelevant, but all that he retained he welded together into a coherent and eminently readable unity. Even a modern historian, with the advantage of greatly superior facilities and assisted by the researches of many generations of experts, faces a formidable task when compiling a history covering several centuries. And when we consider Bede's limited facilities and resources, it is clear that his achievement is unique. For although Bede's monastery at Jarrow possessed a library, it would seem insignificant by modern standards, and while it contained theological works of the Greek and Latin Fathers, there was little material useful for Bede's purpose except Gildas' *History* and a number of individual *Lives,* such as Constantius' *Life of Saint Germanus* and Possidius' *Life of Saint Augustine.* Furthermore, in addition to the slowness and uncertainty of communications, the physical conditions under which the writers of that day had to work were extremely inconvenient and austere during the long northern winters. Writing to Lullus, Archbishop of Mainz, not long after Bede's death, Abbot Cuthbert of Wearmouth apologizes for the delay in sending copies of Bede's works for which the Archbishop had asked, and explains that the hands of the scribes had been so numbed by the bitter winter weather that they had been forced to discontinue their work for considerable periods. And it is easy to visualize the ageing Bede himself, wrapped in a sheepskin cloak, busily working away under such conditions with a pile of documents on his desk, and rising from time to time to beat his frozen limbs into restored circulation. But it is noteworthy that despite the many difficulties under which it was written, Bede's *History* contains relatively few errors, and modern research has confirmed the accuracy of most of his statements. In his Preface Bede himself concedes that there may be unintentional inaccuracies in his pages, and begs the reader not to blame him too severely since, 'as the laws of history demand, I have laboured honestly to transmit whatever I could learn from common report for the instruction of posterity.' And although he is remarkably accurate and well informed on events in his own north country where he is able to check facts and interrogate responsible persons, he is naturally on less sure ground when dealing with happenings in far distant provinces. Nevertheless he makes every attempt to verify facts and present them in an orderly sequence, and to give us an accurate insight into the beliefs, customs, and everyday life of the times.

Like all writers, Bede is influenced by the circumstances and outlook of his own day, and some of his personal convictions are clearly indicated in his interpretation of events. The modern reader may find it difficult to envisage the intensity of feeling aroused by such matters as the paschal controversy, or he may consider Bede unduly prejudiced when he describes the Britons as *perfida gens* – a faithless race – because of their refusal to admit Augustine's jurisdiction (II. 2). In such matters Bede reflects the viewpoint of his race and generation as we of our own, but he is free from all pettiness and personal rancour, and never stoops to misrepresent the actions of those whose convictions he cannot share. For instance, although a convinced upholder of Roman customs as against Celtic, he records the lives and holiness of the Celtic saints with unstinted admiration, and writes of the Roman and Celtic leaders with equal justice and appreciation. An eloquent tribute to these noble qualities in Bede was paid by Bishop Hensley Henson of Durham in 1935 on the twelve hundredth anniversary of the former's death: 'The more closely Bede's career is studied, the more amazing it appears. In him two streams of spiritual influence seemed to meet and blend – the evangelistic passion of the Celtic missionaries, and the disciplined devotion of the Benedictine monks. He was near enough to the original conversion to have personal links with those who had companied with the missionaries from Iona, and to feel the thrill of their triumphant enthusiasm: and yet he was remote enough to have grown up in another atmosphere, and to have been shaped by the system which disallowed and replaced theirs. He was too near not to know their merits; too generous not to recognize them; too religious not to revere their sanctity; too wise not to perceive their defects. So he stood at the point of a new departure – a Benedictine monk in the yet living tradition of Celtic piety, an English student in the rich treasury of Celtic learning, a disciple of Rome inspired by the intellectual passion of Ireland.'

Introduction

The Miraculous Element in Bede's History

The age of Bede was an age of faith. Almighty God was acknowledged as the Source of all life; the world was God's world, and Christians were God's people. The workings of God were recognized in everyday life, and any unusual or striking events, whether storms and comets, victories and recoveries of health, were regarded as signs of his direct intervention in human affairs. God heard and answered prayer, and the holiness of his saints enabled them to draw upon the hidden powers of the spiritual world in order to work wonders and miracles in his Name. The veil separating the seen from the unseen world was not impenetrable, and mortal man might at times have converse with angels and with saints departed. It would therefore be very strange if we found no miracles and wonders among the events and traditions recorded by Bede. But while the modern reader will subject these stories to closer scrutiny than Bede's earlier readers, there is no need to question his sincerity or to assume that he uncritically accepted them all as of equal accuracy. It should be remembered that Bede not only records historical events, but also preserves the stories and legends current in his day. In this way he gives us some account of what people thought and believed, which is a most valuable contribution to our knowledge of the times. He records nothing that he has not subjected to careful consideration, whether it be a description of events or the telling of a popular tale. At the same time, he has a deep respect for tradition and long-established beliefs, and he reproduces current tales and legends of wonder-working relics if he thinks them interesting or edifying to his readers. In this respect Bede is more careful and less credulous than many later mediaeval writers.

Lest the inclusion of miracles may cause any reader to jump to the unjustified conclusion that all Bede's statements are suspect, let us see briefly how he deals with his sources in this respect. Firstly, these sources are of greatly varying historical value. Some material – such as the legend of Saint Alban – Bede has taken direct from an early manuscript of unknown authorship. Other miracle-stories are based on current traditional stories. Others were reported to Bede by those who claimed to have personal acquaintance either with the saint performing the miracle or with the persons benefiting from it.

Secondly, Bede does not write as an eyewitness of everything that he records, but simply gives an account of what is reliably said to have happened, whether miraculous or otherwise. And it is note-worthy that when describing events or persons of which he had direct personal knowledge, as in his *Lives of the Abbots*, Bede does not record any miracles, although in the preface to his poem on Saint Cuthbert he claims to have been healed by that Saint, saying: 'Fresh miracles occur daily through his relics ... one of which took place in my own case, when I was cured [of an impediment?] in my tongue while I was writing in praise of his miracles.' On the other hand, when recording the miracles of such saints as Oswald and Chad, he mentions the source of his information, while in the pro-logue to his *Life of Saint Cuthbert* he expressly states that he has made a careful investigation into the events described and submitted his draft to the monks of Lindisfarne for their comment and approval. So Bede can be acquitted of carelessness or undue credulity.

When we examine the miracles themselves, we find that some may be discounted as plagiarisms of Gospel miracles, and originally introduced in order to emphasize the similarity between the life of Christ and that of his saintly follower. Others are clearly pious for-geries woven into the life of an historic person such as Saint Alban (I. 7) to impress the pagans with the superiority of the Christian saints over the old heathen gods. Others may spring from perfervid imagination or from coincidence. Others, again, may be due to causes that would not be regarded as miraculous today. But even when ruthless pruning has greatly reduced their number, there re-mains an indissoluble core that cannot be explained by any known natural means, and attributable solely to the supernatural power of God displayed in and through His saints. And this is as it should be. For a true miracle (and who may doubt that such occur?) is not due to the supersession or inversion of the natural laws of the universe ordained by the Creator, but to the operation of cosmic laws as yet unrealized by man, activated by non-material forces whose potency is amply demonstrated in the Gospels.

In his valuable work *Psychology, Religion, and Healing*, Dr Leslie Weatherhead defines a miracle as 'a law-abiding event by which God accomplishes His redemptive purposes through the release of energies which belong to a plane of being higher than any with which we are normally familiar'. And what we term a miracle, whether occurring in the second century or the twentieth, may take place as a result of the interaction of many forces and factors such as faith in God, the influence of mind over matter, and the power of suggestion. In a miracle a combination of spiritual and mental forces acts upon the material, and modern medicine and psychology are only beginning to recognize the potency of those forces today. God is not bound or restricted in the means by which he manifests his power or answers *the prayer of faith*, and the well-attested miracles that occur today should be a salutary reminder to our materialistic generation that greater things are effected by prayer and faith than we can ever know or comprehend. It is an indication of the temper of the age in which we live that some who profess and call themselves Christians have so little faith in the reality of God's power and mercy that they regard an unmistakable answer to prayer as something unlooked for and extraordinary, almost indecent. It was otherwise among the Christians of Bede's day.

THE PRESENT TRANSLATION

I have been moved to undertake this task by the realization that increasing numbers of people in all walks of life are finding interest and pleasure in historical matters. This is evident in the widespread reading of historical works, biographies, novels, and articles, and in the popular appeal of historical pageants and films, as well as in the interest taken in historical buildings and sites both of regional and national significance. This is largely due to the fortunate circumstance that England has several contemporary historians of the first rank, whose work has shown that historical studies can be of absorbing interest and significance not only to the expert, but to ordinary folk as well. But the foundation of all modern English historical writing was well laid long ago by the Father of English History, and the reading of his unique work will prove a valuable groundwork and prelude to anyone who wishes to read and appreciate history today.

The present translation is based on the annotated Latin text of Bede's works prepared by Charles Plummer, and first published by the Clarendon Press. My purpose is to offer an accurate and readable version in modern English, and with this in mind I have restricted notes to the minimum. Where these are necessary to eluci-

date a statement, the word or passage is marked by an asterisk, and
the note can be found under its page number at the end of the book.
Place names are normally left in their original form, but where the
ancient name is not readily recognizable, its modern form is placed
as a footnote. In conclusion, I would like to acknowledge my in-
debtedness to Dr E. V. Rieu, C.B.E., Editor of the Penguin Classics,
for much patience and wise guidance during the preparation of this
work.

LEO SHERLEY-PRICE

PREFACE

¶ *To the Most Glorious King Ceolwulf*
Bede the Priest and Servant
of Christ

SOME while ago, at Your Majesty's request, I gladly sent
you the history of the Church in England which I had
recently completed, in order that you might read it and give
it your approval. I now send it once again to be transcribed,
so that Your Majesty may consider it at greater leisure. I
warmly welcome the diligent zeal and sincerity with which
you study the words of Holy Scripture, and your eager desire
to know something of the doings and sayings of great men
of the past, and of our own nation in particular. For if history
records good things of good men, the thoughtful hearer is
encouraged to imitate what is good: or if it records evil of
wicked men, the good, religious listener or reader is encouraged to avoid all that is sinful and perverse, and to follow
what he knows to be good and pleasing to God. Your
Majesty is well aware of this; and since you feel so deeply responsible for the general good of those over whom divine
Providence has set you, you wish that this history may be
better known both to yourself and to your people.

But in order to avoid any doubts as to the accuracy of what
I have written in the minds of yourself or of any who may
listen to or read this history, allow me briefly to state the
authorities upon whom I chiefly depend.

My principal authority and adviser in this work has been
the most reverend Abbot Albinus,* an eminent scholar educated in the church of Canterbury by Archbishop Theodore

and Abbot Hadrian, both of them respected and learned men. He carefully transmitted to me verbally or in writing through Nothelm, a priest of the church of London, anything he considered worthy of mention that had been done by disciples of the blessed Pope Gregory in the province of Canterbury or the surrounding regions. Such facts he ascertained either from records or from long established traditions. Nothelm himself later visited Rome, and obtained permission from the present Pope Gregory (II) to examine the archives of the holy Roman Church. He found there letters of Pope Gregory (I) and other Popes, and when he returned, the reverend father Albinus advised him to bring them to me for inclusion in this history. So from the period at which this volume begins until the time when the English nation received the Faith of Christ, I have drawn extensively on earlier writers. But from that time until the present, I owe much of my information about what was done in the See of Canterbury by the disciples of Pope Gregory and their successors, and under what kings events occurred, to the remarkable industry of Abbot Albinus made known to me through Nothelm. They also provided some of my information about the bishops and kings under whom the provinces of the East and West Saxons, the East Angles, and the Northumbrians received the grace of the Gospel. Indeed, it was due to the persuasion of Albinus that I was encouraged to begin this work. Also the most reverend Bishop Daniel of the West Saxons sent to me in writing certain facts about the history of the Church in his province, in the adjoining province of the South Saxons, and in the Island of Vectis.[1] I am indebted to the brethren of Lastingham monastery for their careful account of the conversion of the province of Mercia to Christ by the holy priests Cedd and Ceadda, their founders; of how the province of the East Saxons rejected and recovered the Faith; and of how their holy fathers lived and died. In addition, I have traced the progress of the Church in the province of the East Angles, partly

1. The Isle of Wight.

from old traditions, and partly from the account given by the most reverend Abbot Esi. The growth of the Christian Faith and succession of bishops in the province of Lindsey I have learned either from the letters of the most reverend Bishop Cynebert, or by word of mouth from other reliable persons. But with regard to events in the various districts of the province of Northumbria, from the time that it received the Faith of Christ up to the present day, I am not dependent on any one author, but on countless faithful witnesses who either know or remember the facts, apart from what I know myself. In this connexion, it should be noted that whatever I have written concerning our most holy father and Bishop Cuthbert, whether in this book or in my separate account of his life and doings, I have in part taken and accurately copied from a Life already compiled by the brethren of the Church of Lindisfarne; and I have carefully added to this whatever I could learn from the reliable accounts of those who knew him. Should the reader discover any inaccuracies in what I have written, I humbly beg that he will not impute them to me, because, as the laws of history require, I have laboured honestly to transmit whatever I could ascertain from common report for the instruction of posterity.

I earnestly request all who may hear or read this history of our nation to ask God's mercy on my many failings of mind and body. And in return for the diligent toil that I have bestowed on the recording of memorable events in the various provinces and places of greater note, I beg that their inhabitants may grant me the favour of frequent mention in their devout prayers.

BRITAIN
during the Anglo-Saxon settlement
Miles 0 ▭▭▭ 50

R. Tweed
Lindisfarne
BERNICIA
Bebbanburh
NORTHUMBRIA
Galloway
Hagulstad
Jarrow
Whitherne
Wearmouth
St Bega
Dunholm
R. Tees
Richmond
Strenaeshalh (Whitby)
DEIRA
STRATHCLYDE
Catterick
(Ripon) Hripum
Isle
Eoforwic
of Man
(York)
Beverley
(Leeds) Loidis
R. Aire
R. Derwent
LINDISSE
Lincoln
Bangor
St Asaph
Southwell
Partney
N. WALES
Lichfield
EAST
Oswaldstre
R. Severn
Croyland
Northwic
(Norwich)
MERCIA
Oundle
ANGLIA
Coventry
Grantabridge
Elig (Ely)
(Cambridge)
R. Avon
Colchester
St Davids
Tewkesbury
Evesham
EAST SAXONS
S. WALES
Gloucester
St Albans
Heortford
Harwich
Llandaff
Oxnaford
Dorchester
Hrofesceaster
Chippenham
LONDON
(Rochester)
Bathancester
Tilbury
KENT
(Glastonbury) *Glaestingbyrig*
Sarum
Wintanceaster
Cantwaraburh
Dofre
WESSEX
SOUTH SAXONS
Crediton
Sherborne
Hamptun
Ciceaceaster
Hastings
(Southampton)
Bodmin
Exeter
Dorchester
Selsey
St Germans
Isle
Portus Rhutupiae
Cornwealas
of Wight
(Richborough)

BOOK ONE

CHAPTER 1: *The situation of Britain and Ireland: their earliest inhabitants**

BRITAIN, formerly known as Albion, is an island in the ocean, facing between north and west, and lying at a considerable distance from the coasts of Germany, Gaul, and Spain, which together form the greater part of Europe. It extends 800 miles northwards, and is 200 in breadth, except where a number of promontories stretch further, the coast-line round which extends to 3675 miles. To the south lies Belgic Gaul, from the nearest shore of which travellers can see the city known as Rutubi Portus, which the English have corrupted to Reptacestir.[1] The distance from there across the sea to Gessoriacum,[2] the nearest coast of the Morini, is fifty miles or, as some write it, 450 furlongs. On the opposite side of Britain, which lies open to the boundless ocean, lie the isles of the Orcades.[3] Britain is rich in grain and timber; it has good pasturage for cattle and draught animals, and vines are cultivated in various localities. There are many land and sea birds of various species, and it is well known for its plentiful springs and rivers abounding in fish. There are salmon and eel fisheries, while seals, dolphins, and sometimes whales are caught. There are also many varieties of shell-fish, such as mussels, in which are often found excellent pearls of several colours, red, purple, violet, and green, but mainly white. Cockles are abundant, and a beautiful scarlet dye is extracted from them which remains unfaded by sunshine or rain; indeed, the older the cloth, the more beautiful its colour. The country has both salt and hot springs, and the waters flowing

1. Richborough.   2. Boulogne.   3. The Orkneys.

from them provide hot baths, in which the people bathe separately according to age and sex. As Saint Basil says: 'Water receives its heat when it flows across certain metals, and becomes hot, and even scalding.' The land has rich veins of many metals, including copper, iron, lead, and silver. There is also much black jet of fine quality, which sparkles in firelight: when burned, it drives away snakes, and, like amber, when it is warmed by friction, it clings to whatever is applied to it. In old times, the country had twenty-eight noble cities, and innumerable castles, all of which were guarded by walls, towers, and barred gates.

Since Britain lies far north toward the pole, the nights are short in summer, and at midnight it is hard to tell whether the evening twilight still lingers or whether dawn is approaching; for in these northern latitudes the sun does not remain long below the horizon at night. Consequently both summer days and winter nights are long, and when the sun withdraws southwards, the winter nights last eighteen hours. In Armenia, Macedonia, and Italy, and other countries of that latitude, the longest day lasts only fifteen hours and the shortest nine.

At the present time there are in Britain, in harmony with the five books of the divine law, five languages and four nations – English, British, Scots,* and Picts. Each of these have their own language, but all are united in their study of God's truth by the fifth – Latin – which has become a common medium through the study of the scriptures. The original inhabitants of the island were the Britons, from whom it takes its name, and who, according to tradition, crossed into Britain from Armorica,[1] and occupied the southern parts. When they had spread northwards and possessed the greater part of the island, it is said that some Picts from Scythia[2] put to sea in a few longships, and were driven by storms around the coasts of Britain, arriving at length on the north coast of Ireland. Here they found the nation of the Scots, from whom they asked permission to settle, but their request was refused.

1. Brittany.   2. Scandinavia.

Ireland is the largest island after Britain, and lies to the west.
It is shorter than Britain to the north, but extends far beyond
it to the south towards the northern coasts of Spain, although
a wide sea separates them. These Pictish seafarers, as I have
said, asked for a grant of land to make a settlement. The
Scots replied that there was not room for them both, but
said: 'We can give you good advice. There is another island
not far to the east, which we often see in the distance on clear
days. Go and settle there if you wish; should you meet resistance, we will come to your help.' So the Picts crossed into
Britain, and began to settle in the north of the island, since
the Britons were in possession of the south. Having no
women with them, these Picts asked wives of the Scots, who
consented on condition that, when any dispute arose, they
should choose a king from the female royal line rather than
the male. This custom continues among the Picts to this day.
As time went on, Britain received a third nation, that of the
Scots, who migrated from Ireland under their chieftain
Reuda, and by a combination of force and treaty, obtained
from the Picts the settlements that they still hold. From the
name of this chieftain, they are still known as Dalreudians,
for in their tongue *dal* means a division.

Ireland is broader than Britain, and its mild and healthy
climate is superior. Snow rarely lies longer than three days,
so that there is no need to store hay in summer for winter use,
or to build stables for beasts. There are no reptiles, and no
snake can exist there; for although often brought over from
Britain, as soon as the ship nears land, they breathe its scented
air, and die. In fact, almost everything in this isle enjoys im-
munity to poison, and I have heard that folk suffering from
snake-bite have drunk water in which scrapings from the
eaves of books from Ireland had been steeped, and that this
remedy checked the spreading poison and reduced the swelling. The island abounds in milk and honey, and there is no
lack of vines, fish, and birds, while deer and goats are widely
hunted. It is the original home of the Scots, who, as already

mentioned, later migrated and joined the Britons and Picts
in Britain. There is a very extensive arm of the sea,[1] which
originally formed the boundary between the Britons and the
Picts. This runs inland from the west for a great distance as
far as the strongly fortified British city of Alcuith.[2] It was to
the northern shores of this firth that the Scots came and
established their new homeland.

CHAPTER 2: *On Caius Julius Caesar, the first Roman to
reach Britain*

BRITAIN remained unknown and unvisited by the
Romans until the time of Caius Julius Caesar, who
became Consul with Lucius Bibulus 693 years after the
founding of Rome, and sixty years before the birth of our
Lord. During a campaign against the Germans and Gauls,
whose common boundary was the Rhine, he entered the
province of the Morini, from which is the nearest and quick-
est crossing into Britain. Here he assembled about eighty
transports and galleys, and crossed into Britain, where his
forces were reduced in a fierce battle; meanwhile his fleet,
caught in a violent gale, suffered considerable loss, and many
troops and nearly all his horses were drowned. So he returned
to Gaul, dispersed his legions to winter quarters, and gave
orders for the construction of 600 vessels of both types. With
these he made a second attempt on Britain in the spring; but
while he was advancing against the enemy with large forces,
the fleet lying at anchor was struck by a storm, and the ships
were either dashed against each other, or driven ashore and
destroyed. Forty ships were wrecked, and the remainder were
only repaired with great difficulty. At the first encounter,
Caesar's cavalry suffered a defeat at the hands of the Britons,
and the Tribune Labienus was killed. In a second battle,
which involved considerable risk, he put the Britons to flight.

1. Firth of Clyde.   2. Dumbarton.

His next objective was the Thames, where a vast host of the
enemy under Cassobelaunus was holding the far bank, and
had constructed a defence system of sharpened stakes which
ran along the bank, and under water across the ford. Traces
of these stakes can still be seen; cased in lead and thick as a
man's thigh, they stand fixed and immovable in the river-
bed. But they were noticed and avoided by the Romans, and
the barbarians, unable to resist the charge of the legions, hid
themselves in the forests and harassed the Romans by frequent fierce sorties. Meanwhile the strong city of Trinovan-
tum and its commander Androgius surrendered to Caesar
and gave him forty hostages. Following its example, several
other cities came to terms with the Romans, and acting on
their information, Caesar, after a severe struggle, captured
the stronghold of Cassobelaunus, which was sited between
two swamps, flanked by forests, and well provisioned. After
this, Caesar left Britain for Gaul, but no sooner had he sent
his legions into winter quarters than he was suddenly troubled
and distracted by sudden wars and revolts on all sides.

CHAPTER 3: *Claudius, the second Roman to reach Britain,
annexes the Isles of Orkney to the Roman Empire: under
his direction Vespasian subdues the Isle of Wight*

IN the 798th year after the founding of Rome, Claudius,
fourth successor to Augustus, wishing to prove himself a
benefactor to the State, applied himself to war and conquest
on a grand scale, and undertook an expedition against Britain
which had been roused to revolt by the Roman refusal to
give up certain deserters. Claudius was the only Roman,
either before or since Julius Caesar, who had dared to land on
the island; yet, within a few days, he received the surrender of
the greater part of the island. He also annexed to the Empire
the Isles of Orkney,* which lie in the ocean beyond Britain;
and returning to Rome only six months after his departure,

41

he granted his son the title of Britannicus. He brought this campaign to a close in the fourth year of his reign, and in the forty-sixth year after the birth of our Lord. This was the year in which a very serious famine occurred in Syria, which is mentioned in the Acts of the Apostles as having been foretold by the prophet Agabus. Vespasian, who was to succeed Nero as Emperor, was sent by the same Claudius, and brought the Isle of Wight under Roman rule. This island lies off the south coast of Britain, and is about thirty miles in length from east to west, and twelve from north to south. Six miles of sea separate it from the mainland at its eastern end, but only three at the west. When Nero succeeded Claudius as Emperor, he attempted no military expeditions, and in consequence, apart from other damage to the Roman State, he nearly lost Britain, for during his reign two most noble towns were taken and destroyed.

CHAPTER 4: *Lucius, a British king, writes to Pope Eleutherius and asks to be made a Christian*

IN the year of our Lord's Incarnation 156, Marcus Antoninus Verus, fourteenth after Augustus, became co-Emperor with his brother Aurelius Commodus. During their reign, and while the holy Eleutherius ruled the Roman Church, Lucius, a British king, sent him a letter, asking to be made a Christian. This pious request was quickly granted, and the Britons held the Faith which they received in all its purity and fullness until the time of the Emperor Diocletian.

CHAPTER 5: *Severus divides Roman Britain from the rest by an earthwork*

IN the year of our Lord 189, Severus, an African born at Leptis in the province of Tripolitania, became seventeenth Emperor after Augustus and ruled seventeen years. Harsh by nature, he was engaged in almost constant warfare, and ruled the State boldly, but with great difficulty. He was victorious in the grave civil wars that troubled his reign, but was compelled to come to Britain by the desertion of nearly all the tribes allied to Rome. After many critical and hard-fought battles, he decided to separate that portion of the island under his control from the remaining unconquered peoples, and he did this not with a wall, as some imagine, but with an earthwork. For a wall is built of stone, but an earthwork, such as protects a camp from enemy attack, is constructed with sods cut from the earth and raised high above ground level, fronted by the ditch from which the sods were cut, and surmounted by a strong palisade of logs. Severus built a rampart and ditch of this type from sea to sea, and fortified it by a series of towers. After this he was taken ill and died in Eboracum,[1] leaving two sons, Bassianus and Geta. The latter was subsequently condemned to death as an enemy of the State, but Bassianus became Emperor, with the cognomen of Antoninus.

CHAPTER 6: *The reign of Diocletian: his persecution of the Christian Church*

IN the year of our Lord 286, Diocletian, a nominee of the army, became the thirty-third successor to Augustus. He ruled twenty years, and chose Maximian, known as Herculius, as his co-Emperor. During their reign, Carausius, a man of humble birth but a capable and experienced soldier, was appointed to protect the sea-coasts which were then being ravaged by Franks and Saxons. But he put his own interests before those of the Republic, and suspicion arose that he was deliberately permitting the enemy to raid the frontiers, and that any loot that he recovered from the pirates was not restored to its rightful owners, but retained for his own

1. York.

advantage. Maximian ordered his execution, but Carausius assumed imperial power and seized Britain, which he won and held with great daring. He lost his life through the betrayal of his colleague Allectus, who then held the island for ten years, after which he was defeated by Asclepiodotus, Prefect of the Praetorian Guard, who thus restored Britain to the Empire.

Meanwhile Diocletian in the East and Herculius in the West ordered all churches to be destroyed, and all Christians to be hunted out and killed. This was the tenth persecution since Nero, and was more protracted and horrible than all that had preceded it. It was carried out without any respite for ten years, with the burning of churches, the outlawing of innocent people, and the slaughter of martyrs. But at length the glory of these martyrs' devoted loyalty to God was to light all Britain.

CHAPTER 7: *The martyrdom of Saint Alban and his companions, who shed their life-blood for Christ at this time* [A.D. 301]

IN this persecution suffered Saint Alban, of whom the priest Fortunatus in his *Praise of Virgins*, in which he mentions all the blessed martyrs who came to God from every part of the world, says:

> In fertile Britain's land
> Was noble Alban born.

When these unbelieving Emperors were issuing savage edicts against all Christians, Alban, as yet a pagan, gave shelter to a Christian priest fleeing from his pursuers. And when he observed this man's unbroken activity of prayer and vigil, he was suddenly touched by the grace of God, and began to follow the priest's example of faith and devotion. Gradually instructed by his teaching of salvation, Alban renounced the darkness of idolatry, and sincerely accepted Christ. But when the priest had lived in his house some days, word came to the ears of the evil ruler that Christ's holy confessor, whose time of martyrdom had not yet come, lay hidden in Alban's house. Accordingly he gave orders to his soldiers to make a thorough search, and when they arrived at the martyr's house, holy Alban, wearing the priest's long cloak, at once surrendered himself in the place of his guest and teacher, and was led bound before the judge.

When Alban was brought in, the judge happened to be standing before an altar, offering sacrifice to devils. Seeing Alban, he was furious that he had put himself in such hazard by surrendering himself to the soldiers in place of his guest, and ordered him to be dragged before the idols where he stood. 'Since you have chosen to conceal a sacrilegious rebel,' he said, 'rather than surrender him to my soldiers to pay the well-deserved penalty for his blasphemy against our gods, you shall undergo all the tortures due to him if you dare to abandon the practice of our religion.' But Saint Alban, who had confessed himself a Christian to the enemies of the Faith, was unmoved by these threats, and armed with spiritual strength, openly refused to obey this order. 'What is your family and race?' demanded the judge. 'How does my family concern you?' replied Alban; 'if you wish to know the truth about my religion, know that I am a Christian, and am bound by the laws of Christ.' 'I demand to know your name,' insisted the judge, 'tell me at once.' 'My parents named me Alban,' he answered, 'and I worship and adore the living and true God, who created all things.' The judge was very angry, and said: 'If you want to enjoy eternal life, sacrifice at once to the great gods.' Alban replied: 'You are offering these sacrifices to devils, who cannot help their suppliants, nor answer their prayers and vows. On the contrary, whosoever offers sacrifice to idols is doomed to the pains of hell.'

Incensed at this reply, the judge ordered God's holy confessor Alban to be flogged by the executioners, hoping to shake his constancy of heart by torture, since threats had no effect. But, for Christ's sake, he bore the most horrible torments patiently and gladly, and when the judge saw that no torture could break him or make him renounce the worship of Christ, he ordered Alban's immediate decapitation. Led out to execution, the saint came to a river which flowed swiftly between the wall of the town and the arena where he was to die. There he saw a great crowd of men and women of all ages and conditions, who were doubtless moved by God's will to attend the death of his blessed confessor and martyr. This crowd had collected in such numbers that he could hardly have crossed that evening, and so many people had come out from the city that the judge was left unattended. Saint Alban, who ardently desired a speedy martyrdom, approached the river, and as he raised his eyes to heaven in prayer, the river ran dry in its bed and left him a way to cross. When the appointed executioner saw this, he was so moved in spirit that he hurried to meet Alban at the place of execution, and throwing down his sword, fell at his feet, begging to die with the martyr if he could not die in his place.

While this man changed from a persecutor to a companion in the true Faith, and other executioners hesitated to pick up his sword from the ground, the most reverend confessor of God ascended the hill about five hundred paces from this spot, accompanied by the crowd. This hill, whose sides were not steep or rough, rose gently from a plain, and was covered with many kinds of flowers, its beauty providing a worthy place to be hallowed by a martyr's blood. As he reached the summit, holy Alban asked God to give him water, and at once a living stream bubbled up at his feet – a sign to all present that it was at the martyr's prayer that the river also had dried in its course. For it was not likely that the martyr who had dried up the waters of the river should lack water on a hill-top unless he willed it so. But the river, having performed its due service, gave proof of its obedience, and

returned to its natural course. Here, then, the gallant martyr
met his death, and received the crown of life which God has
promised to those who love him. But the man whose impious
hands delivered the death-blow was not permitted to boast
of his deed, for as the martyr's head fell, his eyes dropped out
onto the ground.

The soldier who had been moved by divine intuition to
refuse to slay God's confessor was beheaded at the same time
as Alban. And although he had not received the purification
of Baptism, he was certainly cleansed by the shedding of his
own blood, and rendered fit to enter the kingdom of heaven.
Astonished by these many strange miracles, the judge called
a halt to the persecution, and whereas he had formerly fought
to crush devotion to Christ, he now began to honour the
death of his saints.

Saint Alban suffered on the twenty-second day of June
near the city of Verulamium, which the English now call
Verlamacestir or Vaeclingacaestir. When the peace of Christian times was restored, a beautiful church worthy of his
martyrdom was built, where sick folk are healed and frequent
miracles take place to this day.

In the same persecution suffered Aaron and Julius, citizens
of the City of Legions,[1] and many others of both sexes
throughout the land. After enduring many horrible physical
tortures, death brought an end to the sufferings, and their
souls entered the joys of the heavenly City.

CHAPTER 8: *The Church in Britain enjoys peace from the
end of this persecution until the time of the Arian heresy*

WHEN this storm of persecution came to an end, faithful Christians, who during times of danger had taken
refuge in woods, deserted places, and caves, came into the
open, and rebuilt the ruined churches. Everywhere the Faith

1. Possibly Caerleon-on-Usk.

advanced victoriously; the shrines of the martyrs were built and endowed, the festivals of the Church were observed, and its rites performed reverently and sincerely. The Christian Church in Britain remained in peace until the time of the Arian heresy.* This dangerous error, spreading over the whole world, at length crossed the sea and infected even this remote island; and having once obtained a hold, many other pestilential errors at once poured into this island, whose people are ready to listen to anything novel, and never hold firmly to anything.

At this time, Constantius, a man of exceptional kindness and courtesy, who had governed Gaul and Spain during the lifetime of Diocletian, died in Britain. His son Constantine, the child of Helena his concubine, succeeded him as ruler of Gaul. Eutropius writes that Constantine, proclaimed Emperor in Britain, succeeded to his father's domains. In his time, the Arian heresy sprang up, and although it was exposed and condemned at the Council of Nicaea, the deadly poison of its false teaching nevertheless infected not only the continental churches, but even those of these islands.

CHAPTER 9: *During the reign of Gratian, Maximus is created Emperor in Britain, and returns to Gaul with a large army*

IN the year of our Lord 377, Gratian, fortieth successor to Augustus, ruled as Emperor for six years from the death of Valens; he had already reigned as co-Emperor with his uncle Valens and his brother Valentinian. Finding the affairs of the State in grave disorder and approaching disaster, he chose the Spaniard Theodosius to restore the Empire in its need, investing him with the royal purple at Sirmium, and creating him Emperor of Thrace and the East.

At this juncture, however, Maximus, an able and energetic man, well fitted to be Emperor had not ambition led him to

break his oath of allegiance, was elected Emperor by the
army in Britain almost against his will, and he crossed into
Gaul at its head. Here he treacherously killed the Emperor
Gratian, who had been dumbfounded at his sudden attack,
and was attempting to escape into Italy. His brother the
Emperor Valentinian was driven out of Italy, and took refuge
in the east, where Theodosius received him with fatherly
affection. Within a short time, however, he regained the
Empire, and trapping the tyrant Maximus in Aquileia, he
captured him and put him to death.

CHAPTER 10: *During the reign of Arcadius, the Briton
Pelagius presumptuously belittles the grace of God*

IN the year of our Lord 394, Arcadius, son of Theodosius,
forty-third successor to Augustus, became joint-Emperor
with his brother Honorius, and ruled for thirteen years. In
his time, the Briton Pelagius* spread far and wide his noxious
and abominable teaching that man had no need of God's
grace, and in this he was supported by Julius of Campania, a
bishop who resented his own recent deposition. Saint Augustine and other orthodox fathers quoted many thousand Catholic authorities against them, but they refused to abandon
their folly; on the contrary, their obstinacy was hardened by
contradiction, and they refused to return to the true faith.
Prosper the rhetorician has aptly expressed this in heroic
verse:

> Against the great Augustine see him crawl,
>   This wretched scribbler with his pen of gall!
> In what black caverns was this serpent bred
>   That from the dirt presumes to rear its head?
> Either the coasts of Britain saw his birth,
>   Or else his heart pours its own venom forth.

CHAPTER 11: *During the reign of Honorius, Gratian and Constantine set up as Dictators in Britain: the former is killed shortly afterwards in Britain, and the latter in Gaul*

In the year 407, Honorius, the younger son of Theodosius, was Emperor, and forty-fourth successor to Augustus. This was two years before the invasion of Rome by Alaric, King of the Goths, on which occasion the nations of the Alani, Suevi, Vandals, and many others defeated the Franks, crossed the Rhine, and devastated all Gaul. At this juncture, Gratianus Municeps set himself up as a Dictator and was killed; and in his place Constantine, a common trooper of no merit, was chosen Emperor solely on account of his name. Once he had obtained power, he crossed into Gaul, where he was hood-winked into many worthless treaties by the barbarians, and caused great harm to the commonwealth. At the orders of Honorius, Count Constantius entered Gaul with an army, besieged him in the city of Arles, captured him, and put him to death. His son Constans, a monk whom he had created Caesar, was also put to death by Count Gerontius in Vienne.

Rome fell to the Goths in the 1164th year after its foundation, and Roman rule came to an end in Britain almost 470 years after the landing of Caius Julius Caesar. The Romans had occupied the country south of the earthwork which, as I have said, Severus built across the island, as the cities, temples, bridges, and paved roads bear witness to this day: they also held nominal jurisdiction over the more remote parts of Britain and the islands beyond it.

CHAPTER 12: *The Britons, harassed by the Scots and Picts, seek help from the Romans, who come and build a second wall across the island. Notwithstanding, these enemies again break in and reduce the Britons to worse straits*

HENCEFORWARD, all Britain south of the wall, which had been hurriedly stripped of all troops and military equipment and robbed of the flower of its young men, who had been led away by rash tyrants and were never to return, lay wholly exposed to attack, since its people were untrained in the science of war. Consequently for many years Britain suffered attacks from two savage alien races, the Scots from the west, and the Picts from the north. I term these races alien, not because they came from overseas, but because their lands lay far away from those of the Britons: for two sea estuaries lay between, one of which runs broad and deep into the country from the sea to the east, and the other from the west, although they do not meet. On the centre of the eastern estuary stands the city of Giudi,[1] while on the right bank of the western stands the city of Alcuith,[2] which in their language means 'the rock Cluith', as it stands near a river of that name.

When these tribes invaded them, the Britons sent messengers to Rome with moving appeals for help, promising perpetual submission if only the Romans would drive out their enemies. An armed Legion was quickly dispatched to the island, where it engaged the enemy, inflicted heavy losses on them, and drove the survivors out of their allies' territory. Having done this, the Romans advised them to construct a protective wall across the island from sea to sea in order to keep their foes at bay. The victorious Legion then returned home. The islanders raised this wall as they had been instructed, but having no engineers capable of so great an undertaking, they built it of earth and not of stone, so that it was of small value. However, they raised it for many miles

1. Inchkeith.   2. Dumbarton.

between the two above-mentioned estuaries, hoping that where the sea provided no protection, they might use the rampart to preserve their borders from hostile attack. The remains of this extensive earthwork can be clearly seen to this day. It begins about two miles west of the monastery of Abercurnig[1] at a place which the Picts call Peanfahel, and the English Penneltun, and runs westward to the vicinity of the city of Alcluith. But as soon as the old enemies of the Britons learned that the Roman forces had left, they made a seaborne invasion, breaking in and destroying wholesale, slaughtering right and left as men cut ripe corn. The Britons therefore sent more envoys to Rome with pitiful appeals for help, without which their unhappy land would be utterly ravaged, and the name of a once illustrious Roman province be brought into disgrace and obliterated by barbarous tribes, who year by year were carrying off their plunder unchecked. Once more a Legion was dispatched, which arrived unexpectedly in autumn and inflicted heavy casualties on the invaders, forcing all who survived to escape by sea.

The Romans, however, now informed the Britons that they could no longer undertake such troublesome expeditions for their defence, and urged them to take up arms in their own part, pointing out that it was solely their lack of spirit which gave their enemies an advantage over them. And in order to assist these allies whom circumstances forced them to abandon, they built a strong wall of stone directly from sea to sea between the towns that had been built as strong-points, and not far from the earthwork of Severus. This famous and remarkable wall was built from public and private resources, with the Britons lending assistance. It is eight feet in breadth, and twelve in height; and, as can be seen, ran straight from east to west. When the wall was completed, the Romans gave firm advice to the dispirited Britons, together with instructions on the manufacture of weapons. In addition, they built towers at intervals overlooking the

1. Abercorn.

south coast where their ships lay, because the raids of the barbarians were most likely in this quarter. Then they bade farewell to their allies, and never returned.

On the departure of the Romans, the Picts and Scots, learning that they would not return, were quick to attack, and becoming bolder than ever, occupied all the northern and outer part of the island up to the wall. Here a dispirited British garrison stationed on the fortifications pined in terror night and day, while from beyond the wall the enemy constantly harassed them with hooked weapons, dragging the cowardly defenders down from their wall, and dashing them to the ground. At length the Britons abandoned their cities and wall and fled in disorder. Pursued by their foes, the slaughter was more ghastly than ever before, and the wretched citizens were torn in pieces by their enemies, as lambs are torn by wild beasts. They were driven from their homes, and sought to save themselves from starvation by robbery and violence against one another, their own internal anarchy adding to the miseries caused by others, until there was no food left in the whole land except whatever could be obtained by hunting.

CHAPTER 13: *During the reign of Theodosius the Younger, Palladius is sent to the Christians among the Scots. The Britons make an unsuccessful appeal to the Consul Aetius* [A.D. 446]

IN the year of our Lord 423, Theodosius the Younger, next after Honorius and forty-fifth successor to Augustus, ruled the Empire for twenty-six years. In the eighth year of his reign, the Roman Pontiff Celestine sent Palladius* to the Scots who believed in Christ to be their first bishop. In the twenty-third year of his reign, Aetius, an illustrious patrician, became Consul for the third time together with Symmachus. To him the wretched remnant of the Britons sent a

letter, which commences: 'To Aetius, thrice Consul, come
the groans of the Britons', and in the course of the letter they
describe their calamities: 'The barbarians drive us into the
sea, and the sea drives us back to the barbarians. Between
these, two deadly alternatives confront us, drowning or
slaughter.' But even this plea could not obtain help, for at the
time Aetius was already engaged in two serious wars with
Blaedla and Attila, the kings of the Huns. And although
Blaedla had been assassinated the previous year through the
treachery of his brother Attila, the latter remained so dangerous an enemy to the State that he devastated nearly all Europe,
invading and destroying cities and strongholds alike. During
this period there was a famine at Constantinople, followed
closely by a plague, and much of the walls of that city and
fifty-seven towers fell into ruin. Many other cities fell into
disrepair, and the polluting stench of rotting corpses spread
disease among men and beasts alike.

CHAPTER 14: *The Britons, made desperate by famine, drive
the Barbarians out of their land. There soon follows an
abundance of corn, luxury, plague, and doom on the
nation*

MEANWHILE famine which left a lasting memory of its
horrors to posterity distressed the Britons more and
more. Many were compelled to surrender to the invaders;
others, trusting in God's help where no human hand could
save them, continued their resistance. Making frequent sallies
from the mountains, caves, and forests, they began at length
to inflict severe losses on the enemy who had plundered their
country for so many years. These shameless pirates then returned home to Ireland, intending to return after a short
interval; but the Picts meanwhile remained inactive in the
northern parts of the island, save for occasional raids and
forays to plunder the Britons.

When the depredations of its enemies had ceased, the land enjoyed an abundance of corn unknown in former years, but with plenty came an increase in luxury, followed by every kind of crime, especially cruelty, hatred of truth, and love of falsehood. If anyone happened to be more kindly or truthful than his neighbours, he was hated and ill-treated as though he were an enemy of Britain. And not only the pagans were guilty of these things, but even the Lord's flock and their pastors. Giving themselves up to drunkenness, hatred, quarrels, and violence, they threw off the gentle yoke of Christ. Suddenly a terrible plague struck this corrupt people, and in a short while destroyed so large a number that the living could scarcely bury the dead. But not even the fear of their own death or the death of their friends was sufficient to recall the survivors from the spiritual death to which their crimes had doomed them. Not long afterwards, an even more terrible retribution was to overtake this wicked nation, for they consulted how they might obtain help to repel the frequent fierce attacks of their northern neighbours, and all agreed with the advice of their king, Vortigern, to call on the assistance of the Saxon peoples across the sea. This decision, as its evil results were to show, seems to have been ordained by God as a punishment on their wickedness.

CHAPTER 15: *The Angles are invited into Britain. At first they repel the enemy, but soon come to terms with them, and turn their weapons against their own allies*

IN the year of our Lord 449, Martian became Emperor with Valentinian and forty-sixth successor to Augustus, ruling for seven years. In his time the Angles or Saxons came to Britain at the invitation of King Vortigern in three longships, and were granted lands in the eastern part of the island on condition that they protected the country: nevertheless, their real intention was to attack it. At first they engaged the enemy advancing from the north, and having defeated them, sent back news of their success to their homeland, adding that the country was fertile and the Britons cowardly. Whereupon a larger fleet quickly came over with a great body of warriors, which, when joined to the original forces, constituted an invincible army. These also received grants of land and money from the Britons, on condition that they maintained the peace and security of the island against all enemies.

These new-comers were from the three most formidable races of Germany, the Saxons, Angles, and Jutes. From the Jutes are descended the people of Kent and the Isle of Wight, and those in the province of Wessex opposite the Isle of Wight are called Jutes to this day. From the Saxons – that is, the country now known as Old Saxony – came the East, South, and West Saxons. And from the Angles – that is, the country known as Angulus, which lies between the provinces of the Jutes and Saxons, and remains unpopulated to this day – are descended the East and Middle Angles, the Mercians, all the Northumbrian peoples (that is, those peoples living north of the river Humber), and other English peoples. Their first chieftains are said to have been Hengist and Horsa. The latter was subsequently killed in battle against the Britons, and was buried in east Kent, where a monument bearing his name still stands. They were the sons of Victgilsus, whose father was Vecta, son of Woden, from whose stock sprang the royal house of many provinces. It was not long before such hordes of these alien peoples crowded into the island that the natives who had invited them began to live in terror, for the Angles suddenly made an alliance with the Picts whom they had recently repelled, and prepared to turn their arms against their allies. They began by demanding a greater supply of provisions; then, seeking to provoke a quarrel, threatened that unless larger supplies were forthcoming, they would terminate their treaty and ravage the whole island. Nor were they slow to carry out their threats. n short, the fires kindled by the pagans proved to be God's just punishment on the sins of the nation, just as the fires once kindled by the Chaldeans destroyed the walls and palaces of Jerusalem. For, as the just Judge ordained, these heathen conquerors devastated the surrounding cities and countryside, extended the conflagration from the eastern to the western shores without opposition, and established a stranglehold over nearly all the doomed island. Public and private buildings were razed; priests were slain at the altar; bishops and people alike, regardless of rank, were destroyed with fire and sword, and none remained to bury those who had suffered a cruel death. A few wretched survivors captured in the hills were butchered wholesale, and others, desperate with hunger, came out and surrendered to the enemy for food, although they were doomed to lifelong slavery even if they escaped instant massacre. Some fled overseas in their misery; others, clinging to their homeland, eked out a wretched and fearful existence among the mountains, forests, and crags, ever on the alert for danger.

CHAPTER 16: *Under the leadership of Ambrosius, a Roman, the Britons win their first victory against the Angles* [*c.* A.D. 493]

WHEN the victorious Angles had scattered and destroyed the native peoples and returned to their own dwellings, the Britons slowly began to take heart and recover their strength, emerging from the dens where they had hidden themselves, and joining in prayer that God might help them to avoid complete extermination. Their leader at this time was Ambrosius Aurelius, a modest man of Roman origin, who was the sole survivor of the catastrophe in which his royal parents had perished. Under his leadership the Britons took up arms, challenged their conquerors to battle, and with God's help inflicted a defeat on them. Thenceforward victory swung first to one side, and then to the other, until the battle of Badon Hill, when the Britons made a considerable slaughter of the invaders. This took place about forty-four years after their arrival in Britain: but I shall deal with this later.

CHAPTER 17: *Bishop Germanus sails to Britain with Lupus: with God's help he quells a storm at sea and refutes the Pelagians* [A.D. 429]

A FEW years prior to their arrival, the Pelagian heresy introduced by Agricola, son of Severianus a Pelagian prelate, had seriously infected the faith of the British Church. But although the British rejected this perverse teaching, so blasphemous against the grace of Christ, they were unable to refute its plausible arguments by controversial methods, and wisely decided to ask help from the bishops of Gaul in this spiritual conflict. The latter summoned a great synod, and consulted together whom to send to support the Faith. Their unanimous choice fell upon the apostolic bishops Germanus of Auxerre and Lupus of Troyes, whom they appointed to visit the Britons, and to confirm their belief in God's grace. The two bishops readily accepted the commands and decisions of Holy Church, and put to sea. They had safely sailed half-way on their voyage from Gaul with a favourable wind when they were suddenly subjected to the hostile anger of devils, who were furious that such men as they should dare to recall the Britons to the Faith. They raised violent storms and turned day into night with black clouds. The sails were torn to shreds by the gale, the skill of the sailors was defeated, and the safety of the ship depended on prayer rather than on seamanship. Germanus their leader and bishop, spent and exhausted, had fallen asleep, when the storm reached a fresh pitch of violence, and seemed about to overwhelm the vessel in the roaring waves. At this juncture, Lupus and his companions roused their leader, and begged him to oppose the fury of the elements. More resolute than they in the face of imminent disaster, he called upon Christ, and cast holy water on the waves in the Name of the Sacred Trinity, encouraging his companions, and directing them all to join him in prayer. God heard their cry and their adversaries were put to flight; the wind veered round to help them on their course, and after a swift and peaceful passage, they arrived safely at their destination. Here great crowds gathered from all quarters to greet the bishops, whose arrival had been fore-told even by the predictions of their opponents. For when the evil spirits had disclosed their fears, and the bishops had expelled them from the persons of those whom they had possessed, they revealed the origin of the storms and perils they had raised, and acknowledged themselves overcome by the merits and power of the saints.

Meanwhile, the island of Britain was rapidly influenced by the reasoning, preaching, and virtues of these apostolic bishops, and the word of God was preached daily not only in the churches, but in streets and fields, so that Catholics everywhere were strengthened, and heretics corrected. They won the honour and authority of apostles by their holy wit-ness, obedience by their learning, and virtue by their merits. So the majority of the people readily accepted their teaching, while the authors of false doctrines made themselves scarce, grieving like evil spirits over the people who were snatched from their grasp. At length, after due deliberation, they dared to challenge the saints, and appeared with rich ornaments and magnificent robes, supported by crowds of flattering fol-lowers. For they preferred to hazard a trial of strength, rather than submit in shameful silence before the people whom they had subverted, lest they should appear to admit defeat. An immense gathering had assembled there with their wives and children to watch and judge, but the contestants were greatly dissimilar in bearing. On one side stood the bishops, upheld by holiness and faith in Christ; on the other stood the Pela-gians, full of presumption and pride. The holy bishops gave their adversaries the privilege of speaking first, which they did at great length and with vain arguments. The venerable bishops then eloquently expounded the true teaching of the Apostles and evangelists, confirming their own words by the word of God, and supporting their principal statements by quotation from the scriptures. The conceit of the Pelagians was pricked, their lies exposed, and unable to defend any of their arguments, they admitted their errors. The people, who were acting as their judges, were hardly restrained from violence, and greeted their overthrow with acclamation.

CHAPTER 18: *Germanus gives sight to the blind daughter of a tribune. He takes some relics from the tomb of Saint Alban, and deposits relics of the Apostles and other Martyrs*

IMMEDIATELY after this, a man who held the status of a tribune came forward with his wife, and asked the bishops to cure his blind daughter, a child of ten. They directed him to take her to their opponents, but the latter, smitten by guilty consciences, joined their entreaties to those of the girl's parents, and begged the bishops to heal her. Seeing their opponents yield, they offered a short prayer; then Germanus called on the Trinity, and taking into his hands a casket containing relics of the saints that hung around his neck, he applied it to the girl's eyes in the sight of them all. To the joy of the parents and the amazement of the crowd, the child's sight was immediately restored. Thenceforward all erroneous arguments were expunged from the minds of the people, who eagerly accepted the teaching of the bishops.

Once this abominable heresy had been put down, its authors refuted, and the people established in the pure faith of Christ, the bishops paid a visit to the tomb of the blessed martyr Alban to return thanks to God through him. Germanus, who had with him relics of all the Apostles and several martyrs, first offered prayer, and then directed the tomb to be opened, so that he could deposit these precious gifts within it. For he thought it fitting that as the equal merits of the saints had won them a place in heaven, so their relics should be gathered together from different lands into a common resting-place. And when he had reverently deposited these relics, Germanus took away with him a portion of earth from the place where the blessed martyr's blood had been shed. This earth appeared to have retained the martyr's blood and reddened the martyr's shrine, where his persecutors had grown pale with fear. As a result of these events, a great number of people were converted to our Lord.

CHAPTER 19: *Germanus is detained by illness. He puts out a fire among houses by his prayer, and is healed of his sickness by a vision*

WHILE they were returning from this place, the everwatchful Devil contrived that Germanus should fall and break a leg, not knowing that, like blessed Job, his merits would be enhanced by bodily affliction. While he was thus detained by illness, fire broke out in a cottage near his lodging, and after destroying the adjoining dwellings which were thatched with reeds, it was carried by the wind to the cottage where he lay. The people ran to pick up the bishop and carry him to a place of safety, but, full of trust in God, he reproved them and would not allow them to do so. In despair, the people ran off to fight the fire, but to afford clearer evidence of God's power, whatever the crowd endeavoured to save was destroyed. Meanwhile the flames leaped over the house where the saint lay disabled and helpless, but although they raged all around it, the place that sheltered him stood untouched amid a sea of fire. The crowd was overjoyed at the miracle, and praised God for this proof of his power, while innumerable poor folk kept vigil outside his cottage day and night hoping for healing of soul or body.

It is impossible to relate all that Christ effected through his
servant, and what wonders the sick saint performed. And
while he refused any treatment for his own illness, he saw
beside him one night a being in shining robes, who seemed
to reach out his hand and raise him up, ordering him to stand
on his feet. From that moment his pain ceased, his former
health was restored, and when dawn came, he continued on
his journey undaunted.

CHAPTER 20: *The two bishops obtain God's help in battle,
and return home* [A.D. 429]

MEANWHILE the Saxons and Picts joined forces and made
war on the Britons, whom necessity had compelled to
arm; and since the latter feared that their strength was un-
equal to the challenge, they called on the saintly bishops for
help. They came at once as they had promised, and put such
heart into the timid people that their presence was worth a
large army. Under these apostolic leaders, Christ himself
commanded in the camp. It also happened that the holy
season of Lent was beginning, and was so reverently kept
under the bishops' direction that the people came each day
for instruction, and flocked to receive the grace of Baptism.
Most of the army sought Holy Baptism, and in readiness for
the Feast of our Lord's Resurrection, a church was constructed of interlaced boughs and set up in that armed camp
as though it were a city. Strong in faith, and fresh from the
waters of Baptism, the army advanced; and whereas they
had formerly despaired of human strength, all now trusted
in the power of God. But the strength and disposition of the
British forces was well known to the enemy, who, anticipat-
ing an easy victory over an ill-trained army, advanced
rapidly, closely observed by the British scouts.

After the Feast of Easter, the greater part of the British
forces were newly baptized, and as they were preparing to

arm and continue the struggle, Germanus promised to direct
the battle in person. He picked out the most active men, and
having surveyed the surrounding country, observed a valley
among the hills lying in the direction from which he expected
the enemy to approach. Here he stationed the untried forces
under his own orders, and gave instructions that directly the
main body of their remorseless enemies came within sight of
those whom he had placed in ambush, they were to join him
in a mighty shout when he raised the standard. The enemy
advanced confidently, expecting to take the Britons un-
awares; whereupon the bishops three times shouted, 'Alleluia!' The whole army joined in this shout, until the surrounding hills echoed with the sound. The enemy column
panicked, thinking that the very rocks and sky were falling
on them, and were so terrified that they could not run fast
enough. Throwing away their weapons in headlong flight,
they were well content to escape naked, while many in their
hasty flight were drowned in a river which they tried to
cross. So the British army saw its defeats avenged, and became an inactive spectator of the victory granted to it. The
scattered spoils were collected, and the Christian forces rejoiced in the triumph of heaven. So the bishops overcame the
enemy without bloodshed, winning a victory by faith and
not by force.

Having restored peace to the island, and overcome all its
enemies, both material and spiritual, the bishops prepared to
return home. Their own merits and the prayers of the blessed
martyr Alban obtained them a peaceful voyage, and they
sailed gladly home to their own welcoming people.

CHAPTER 21: *The Pelagian heresy revives, and Germanus returns to Britain with Severus. He heals a lame youth, and after denouncing or converting the heretics, restores the British Church to the Catholic Faith* [A.D. 447]

AFTER no great interval, news came from Britain that certain people were again promulgating the Pelagian heresy. Once again all the clergy requested blessed Germanus to defend God's cause as before. Accordingly he took ship and made a peaceful crossing to Britain with a favouring wind, taking with him a man of great holiness named Severus. The latter had been a disciple of the most blessed father Lupus, Bishop of Troyes; he subsequently became Bishop of Treves, and preached the Word in western Germany.

Meanwhile evil spirits throughout the land had been obliged to foretell Germanus' coming, so that a local chieftain named Elafius hurried to meet the saints before receiving any definite news. He brought with him his son, who although in the flower of his youth, was crippled by a painful disease of the leg, whose muscles had so contracted that the limb was entirely useless. Accompanying Elafius was a great crowd of people from his province. On the arrival of the bishops, they were met by the ignorant folk, to whom they spoke and gave their blessing. And having assured themselves that the people as a whole remained loyal to the Faith as they had left them, and that the error was restricted to a minority, they sought out its adherents and rebuked them. Elafius then threw himself at the bishops' feet, and presented to them his son, the sight of whose infirmity proclaimed his need louder than words. All were moved to pity at the spectacle, especially the bishops, who earnestly prayed God to show mercy. Blessed Germanus then asked the youth to sit down, and drawing out the leg wasted with disease, he passed his healing hand over the afflicted area, and at his touch health swiftly returned. The withered limb filled, the muscles regained

their power, and in the presence of them all, the lad was
restored healed to his parents. The people were amazed at
this miracle, and the Catholic Faith was firmly implanted in
all their hearts. Germanus then warned them to live better,
and to shun all error. And the false teachers, who by common
consent had been condemned to banishment, were brought
before the bishops to be taken to the Continent, so that the
country might be rid of them, and they themselves brought
to recognize their error. Henceforward, the Faith was maintained uncorrupted in Britain for a long time.

Having settled all these matters, the blessed bishops returned home as successfully as they had come.

Germanus subsequently visited Ravenna to obtain peace
for the people of Armorica.[1] There he was received with
honour by the Emperor Valentinian and his mother Placidia,
and while still in this city he departed to Christ. His body
was carried back with a splendid escort to his own city and
many signs of his holiness were shown. Not long afterwards,
in the fifth year of Marcian's reign, Valentinian was murdered
by supporters of the patrician Aetius whom he had executed,
and with him fell the Empire of the West.

CHAPTER 22: *The Britons enjoy a respite from foreign invasions, but exhaust themselves in civil wars and plunge
into serious crimes*

MEANWHILE Britain enjoyed a rest from foreign,
though not from civil wars. Amid the wreckage of
deserted cities destroyed by the enemy, the natives who had
survived the enemy now attacked each other. So long as
there remained any kings, priests, nobles, and private indi-
viduals who remembered the former disasters, these used
their influence to restrain such evils. But when they died,
there grew up a generation who knew nothing of these

1. Brittany.

things, and had experienced only the present peaceful order. Then were all restraints of truth and justice so utterly abandoned that no trace of them remained, and very few of the people even recalled their existence. Among other unspeakable crimes, recorded with sorrow by their own historian Gildas, they added this – that they never preached the Faith to the Saxons who dwelt among them. But God in his goodness did not utterly abandon the people whom he had chosen, for he remembered them, and sent this nation more worthy preachers of truth to bring them to the Faith.

CHAPTER 23: *The holy Pope Gregory sends Augustine and other monks to preach to the English nation, and encourages them in a letter to persevere in their mission* [A.D. 596]

IN the year of our Lord 582, Maurice, fifty-fourth successor to Augustus, became Emperor, and ruled for twenty-one years. In the tenth year of his reign, Gregory, an eminent scholar and administrator, was elected Pontiff of the apostolic Roman see, and ruled it for thirteen years, six months, and ten days. In the fourteenth year of this Emperor, and about the one hundred and fiftieth year after the coming of the English to Britain, Gregory was inspired by God to send his servant Augustine with several other God-fearing monks to preach the word of God to the English nation. Having undertaken this task at the Pope's command and progressed a short distance on their journey, they became afraid, and began to consider returning home. For they were appalled at the idea of going to a barbarous, fierce, and pagan nation, of whose very language they were ignorant. They unanimously agreed that this was the safest course, and sent back Augustine – who was to be consecrated bishop in the event of their being received by the English – so that he might humbly request the holy Gregory to recall them from so dangerous, arduous, and uncertain a journey. In reply, the Pope wrote them a letter of encouragement, urging them to proceed on their mission to preach God's word, and to trust themselves to his aid. This letter ran as follows:

'GREGORY, Servant of the servants of God, to the servants of God. My very dear sons, it is better never to undertake any high enterprise than to abandon it when once begun. So with the help of God you must carry out this holy task which you have begun. Be constant and zealous in carrying out this enterprise which, under God's guidance, you have undertaken: and be assured that the greater the labour, the greater will be the glory of your eternal reward. When Augustine your leader returns, whom We have appointed your abbot, obey him humbly in all things, remembering that whatever he directs you to do will always be to the good of your souls. May Almighty God protect you with His grace, and grant me to see the result of your labours in our heavenly home. And although my office prevents me from working at your side, yet because I long to do so, I hope to share in your joyful reward. God keep you safe, my dearest sons.

'Dated the twenty-third of July, in the fourteenth year of the reign of our most devout lord Maurice Tiberius Augustus, and the thirteenth year after the Consulship of our said Lord. The fourteenth indiction.'

CHAPTER 24: *Pope Gregory writes commending them to the Bishop of Arles*

THE venerable Pontiff also wrote to Etherius, Archbishop of Arles, asking him to offer a kindly welcome to Augustine on his journey to Britain. This letter reads:

'To his most reverend and holy brother and fellow-bishop Etherius: Gregory, servant of the servants of God.

'Religious men should require no commendation to priests who exhibit the love that is pleasing to God, but since a suitable opportunity to write has arisen, We have written this letter to you, our brother, to certify that its bearer, God's servant Augustine and his companions, of whose zeal we are assured, has been directed by us to proceed to save souls with the help of God. We therefore request Your Lordship to assist them with pastoral care, and to make early provision for their needs. And in order that you may assist them the more readily, we have particularly directed Augustine to give you full information about his mission, being sure that when you are acquainted with this, you will supply all their needs for the love of God. We also commend to your love the priest Candidus, our common son in Christ, whom we have transferred to a small patrimony in our church. God keep you safely, most reverend brother.

'Dated the twenty-third day of July, in the fourteenth year of the reign of our most devout lord Maurice Tiberius Augustus, and the thirteenth year after his Consulship. The fourteenth indiction.'*

CHAPTER 25: *Augustine reaches Britain, and first preaches in the Isle of Thanet before King Ethelbert, who grants permission to preach in Kent* [A.D. 597]

REASSURED by the encouragement of the blessed father Gregory, Augustine and his fellow-servants of Christ resumed their work in the word of God, and arrived in Britain. The King of Kent at this time was the powerful King Ethelbert, whose domains extended northwards to the river Humber, which forms the boundary between the north and south Angles. To the east of Kent lies the large island of Thanet, which by English reckoning is six hundred hides* in extent; it is separated from the mainland by a waterway about three furlongs broad called the Wantsum, which joins the sea at either end, and is fordable only in two places. It was here that God's servant Augustine landed with companions, who are said to have been forty in number. At the direction of blessed Pope Gregory, they had brought interpreters from among the Franks, and they sent these to Ethelbert, saying that they came from Rome bearing very glad news, which infallibly assured all who would receive it of eternal joy in heaven, and an everlasting kingdom with the living and true God. On receiving this message, the king ordered them to remain in the island where they had landed, and gave directions that they were to be provided with all necessaries until he should decide what action to take. For he had already heard of the Christian religion, having a Christian wife of the Frankish royal house named Bertha, whom he had received from her parents on condition that she should have freedom to hold and practise her faith unhindered with Bishop Liudhard whom they had sent as her chaplain.

After some days, the king came to the island, and sitting down in the open air, summoned Augustine and his companions to an audience. But he took precautions that they should not approach him in a house, for he held an ancient superstition that if they were practisers of magical arts, they might have opportunity to deceive and master him. But the monks were endowed with power from God, not from the Devil, and approached the king carrying a silver cross as their standard, and the likeness of our Lord and Saviour painted on a board. First of all they offered prayer to God, singing a litany for the eternal salvation both of themselves and of those for whose sake they had come. And when, at the king's command, Augustine had sat down and preached the word of life to the king and his court, the king said: 'Your words and promises are fair indeed, but they are new and strange to us, and I cannot accept them and abandon the age-old beliefs of the whole English nation. But since you have travelled far, and I can see that you are sincere in your desire to instruct us in what you believe to be true and excellent, we will not harm you. We will receive you hospitably, and take care to supply you with all that you need; nor will we forbid you to

preach and win any people you can to your religion.' The
king then granted them a dwelling in the city of Canterbury,
which was the chief city of all his realm, and in accordance
with his promise, he allowed them provisions and did not
withdraw their freedom to preach. Tradition says that as
they approached the city, bearing the holy cross and the likeness of our great King and Lord Jesus Christ as was their
custom, they sang in unison this litany: 'We pray Thee, O
Lord, in all Thy mercy, that Thy wrath and anger may be
turned away from this city and from Thy holy house, for we
are sinners. Alleluia.'

CHAPTER 26: *The life and doctrine of the primitive Church
are followed in Kent: Augustine establishes his episcopal
see in the king's city*

As soon as they had occupied the house given to them
they began to emulate the life of the apostles and the
primitive Church. They were constantly at prayer; they
fasted and kept vigils; they preached the word of life to
whomsoever they could. They regarded worldly things as of
little importance, and accepted only necessary food from
those they taught. They practised what they preached, and
were willing to endure any hardship, and even to die for the
Faith which they proclaimed. A number of heathen, admir-
ing the simplicity of their holy lives and the comfort of their
heavenly message, believed and were baptized. On the east
side of the city stood an old church, built in honour of Saint
Martin during the Roman occupation of Britain, where the
Christian queen went to pray. Here they first assembled to
sing the psalms, to pray, to say Mass, to preach, and to baptize, until the king's own conversion to the Faith enabled
them to preach openly, and to build and restore churches
everywhere.

At length the king and others, edified by the pure lives of

these holy men and their gracious promises, the truth of which they confirmed by many miracles, believed and were baptized. Thenceforward great numbers gathered each day to hear the word of God, forsaking their heathen rites, and entering the unity of Christ's holy Church as believers. While the king was pleased at their faith and conversion, he would not compel anyone to accept Christianity, for he had learned from his instructors and guides to salvation that the service of Christ must be accepted freely and not under compulsion; nevertheless, he showed greater favour to believers, because they were fellow-citizens of the kingdom of heaven. And it was not long before he granted his teachers a property of their own in his capital of Canterbury, and gave them possessions of various kinds to supply their wants.

CHAPTER 27: *Augustine is consecrated bishop: he sends to inform Pope Gregory what has been achieved, and receives replies to his questions*

MEANWHILE God's servant Augustine visited Arles, and in accordance with the holy father Gregory's directions, was consecrated archbishop of the English nation by Etherius, archbishop of that city. On his return to Britain, he sent the priest Laurentius and the monk Peter to Rome to inform the blessed Pope Gregory that the English had accepted the Faith of Christ, and that he himself had been consecrated bishop. At the same time, he sought advice on certain current problems. The Pope answered his enquiries without delay, and I have thought it proper to record these replies in my history.

I. The first question of Augustine, Bishop of the Church of Canterbury: What is to be the relationship between the bishop and his clergy? And how are the offerings made by the faithful at the altar to be apportioned? And what are the functions of a bishop in his church?

Gregory, Pope of the City of Rome, replies: Holy
Scripture, with which you are certainly well acquainted,
offers us guidance in this matter, and in particular the letters
of blessed Paul to Timothy, in which he carefully instructs
him on a bishop's duties in the house of God. But it is the
custom of the Apostolic See to instruct all newly consecrated
bishops that all money received is to be allocated under four
heads: one for the bishop and his household, for hospitality
and other commitments; another for the clergy; a third for
the poor; and a fourth for the maintenance of churches. In
your case, my brother, being subject to monastic Rule, you
may not live apart from your clergy of the English Church,
which by God's help has lately been brought to the Faith.
You are therefore to follow the way of life practised by our
forefathers of the primitive Church, who regarded no property as personal, but shared all things in common. If there
are any clerics* who have not received Sacred Orders and
who do not wish to remain single, let them marry and receive
their stipends separately; for it is written by the fathers whom
we have mentioned, that 'division is to be made to each
according to his need.' So give consideration to the provision
of their stipends, and see that they observe the Church's discipline and live orderly, attend to the singing of the Psalter,
and by God's help preserve themselves in thought, word, and
deed from everything unbecoming to their office. But for
those who live as a Community there should be no need for
us to mention allocating portions, exercising hospitality, and
showing mercy. Everything that can be spared is to be
devoted to holy and religious purposes, as the Lord and
Master of all bids; 'Give alms of such things as you have; and
behold, all things are clean unto you.'

II. Augustine's second question: Since we hold the same
Faith, why do customs vary in different Churches? Why, for
instance, does the method of saying Mass differ in the holy
Roman Church and in the Churches of Gaul?

Pope Gregory's reply: My brother, you are familiar with

the usage of the Roman Church, in which you were brought up. But if you have found customs, whether in the Roman, Gallican, or any other Churches that may be more acceptable to God, I wish you to make a careful selection of them, and teach the Church of the English, which is still young in the Faith, whatever you can profitably learn from the various Churches. For things should not be loved for the sake of places, but places for the sake of good things. Therefore select from each of the Churches whatever things are devout, religious, and right; and when you have arranged them into a unified rite, let the minds of the English grow accustomed to it.

III. Augustine's third question: What punishment should be awarded to those who rob churches?

Pope Gregory's reply: The punishment must depend on the circumstances of the offender. For some commit theft although they have means of subsistence, and others out of poverty. Some, therefore, should be punished by fines, others by beating; some severely, and others more leniently. But when the punishment has to be severe, let it be administered in charity, not in anger; for the purpose of such correction is to save the wicked from hell-fire. We must maintain discipline among the faithful as good fathers among their children, whom they punish for wrongdoing, and yet make them their heirs, while they preserve their possessions for the benefit of those whom they appear to treat harshly. So charity must always be our motive and indicate the means of correction, so that we may do nothing unreasonable. You may add that thieves are to restore whatever they have taken from churches, but God forbid that the Church should make a profit from any worldly goods she may lose, or seek any gain from these empty things.

IV. Augustine's fourth question: Is it permissible for two brothers to marry two sisters, providing there be no blood ties between the families?

Pope Gregory's reply: This is quite permissible. There is nothing in holy Scripture that seems to forbid it.

V. Augustine's fifth question: To what degree may the faithful marry with their kindred? And is it lawful for a man to marry his step-mother or relative?

Pope Gregory's reply: Roman civil law permits first-cousins to marry. But experience shows that such unions do not result in children, and sacred law forbids a man '*to uncover the nakedness of his kindred.*' Necessity therefore forbids a closer marriage than that between the third or fourth generation, while the second generation, as we have said, should wholly abstain from marriage. But to wed one's step-mother is a grave sin, for the Law says: '*You shall not uncover the nakedness of your father.*' Now the son cannot uncover the nakedness of his father; but since it says, '*They shall be one flesh*', whosoever presumes to wed his step-mother, who was one flesh with his father, thereby commits this offence. It is also forbidden to marry a sister-in-law, since by a former union she had become one with his own brother: it was for denouncing this sin that John the Baptist was beheaded and met his holy martyrdom. For John was not ordered to deny Christ, but was in fact put to death as a confessor of Christ. For since our Lord Jesus Christ said: '*I am the Truth*', John shed his blood for Christ in that he gave his life for the truth.

But since there are many among the English who, while they were still heathen, seem to have contracted these unlawful marriages, when they accept the Faith they are to be instructed that this is a grave offence, and that they must abstain from it. Warn them of the terrible judgement of God lest their bodily desires incur the pains of eternal punishment. Nevertheless, they are not on that account to be deprived of the Communion of the Body and Blood of Christ, lest they appear to be punished for sins committed unknowingly before they received the purification of Baptism. For in these days the Church has to correct some things strictly, and allow others already established by custom; others have to be tolerated for a while, in the hope that forbearance may sometimes eradicate an evil of which she disapproves. But all who come to the Faith are to be warned against doing these things, and should any subsequently be guilty of them, they are to be forbidden to receive the Communion of the Body and Blood of our Lord. For while these offences may to some extent be condoned in those who acted in ignorance, they must be severely punished in those who presume to sin knowingly.

VI. Augustine's sixth question: If a long journey is involved, so that bishops cannot easily assemble, is it permissible for a bishop to be consecrated without other bishops being present?

Pope Gregory's reply: In the case of the Church in England where as yet you are the only bishop, you cannot do otherwise than consecrate a bishop without other bishops being present. But when bishops from Gaul pay a visit, they can be present as witnesses to the consecration. It is our wish, brother, that the consecration of a bishop be arranged at a time when other bishops are not far distant, so that other pastors whose presence is desirable may be readily summoned. Therefore, when in due time bishops are appointed in various places at no great distance from one another, no consecration is to take place except in the presence of three or four bishops. For in spiritual matters we may often with advantage follow the customs of the world, and arrange these things carefully and wisely. When a wedding is celebrated, married folk are invited, so that those who are already married may share the joy of the new couple. So, at this spiritual consecration, when a man is joined to God in the sacred ministry, why should not those be invited who will take pleasure in the elevation of the new bishop, or offer their prayers to God for his protection?

VII. Augustine's seventh question: What are to be our relations with the bishops of Gaul and Britain?

Pope Gregory's reply: We give you no authority over the bishops of Gaul, for since ancient times the Bishop of Arles has received the *pallium** from my predecessors, and his authority is to be in no way infringed. If, therefore, you have

occasion to cross over into the province of Gaul, you are to
consult with the Bishop of Arles how to correct any faults
among the bishops; and should he be remiss in administering
discipline, inspire him with your own zeal. We have already
written to him, requesting him to offer you every assistance
whenever you visit Gaul, and to ensure that his bishops observe no customs contrary to the laws of God our Maker.
Although we give you no authority over the bishops of
Gaul, you should nevertheless advise, encourage and show
them a good example. Recall the minds of any wrong-doers
to the pursuit of holiness, for it is written in the Law: '*When
you pass through the harvest-field of another man, you may
pluck some ears with your hand, but you may not reap it with
a sickle.*' Similarly, you may not use the sickle of authority
in the field entrusted to another man, but use your good
influence to separate the Lord's wheat from their sins, and by
your teaching and persuasion bring them into the body of the
Church. But no official action is to be taken without the authority of the Bishop of Arles, so that the long-established insti-
tutions of our fathers may not fall into disuse. All the bishops
of Britain, however, we commit to your charge. Use your
authority to instruct the unlearned, to encourage the weak,
and correct the obstinate.

VIII. Augustine's eighth question: May an expectant
mother be baptized? How soon after childbirth may she
enter church? And how soon after birth may a child be baptized if in danger of death? How soon after child-birth may
a husband have relations with his wife? And may a woman
properly enter church at certain periods? And may she receive
Communion at these times? And may a man enter church
after relations with his wife before he has washed? Or receive
the sacred mystery of Communion? These uncouth English
people require guidance on all these matters.

Pope Gregory's reply: I have no doubt, my brother, that
questions such as these have arisen, and I think I have already
answered you: but doubtless you desire my support for your

statements and rulings. Why should not an expectant mother be baptized? – it is no offence in the sight of Almighty God to bear children. For when our first parents sinned in the Garden, they justly forfeited God's gift of immortality. But although God deprived man of immortality for his sin, he did not destroy the human race on that account, but of his merciful goodness left man his ability to continue the race. On what grounds, then, can God's free gift to man be excluded from the grace of Holy Baptism? For it would be foolish to suppose that his gift of grace is contrary to the sacred mystery by which all guilt is washed away.

As you are aware, the Old Testament lays down the interval that must elapse after childbirth before a woman may enter church; that is, for a male child thirty-three days and for a female, sixty-six. But this is to be understood as an allegory, for were a woman to enter church and return thanks in the very hour of her delivery, she would do nothing wrong. The fault lies in the bodily desires, not in the pain of childbirth; the desire is in the bodily union, the pain is in the birth, so that Eve, the mother of us all, was told: '*In sorrow shalt thou bring forth children.*' If, then, we forbid a woman who is delivered of a child to enter church, we make this penalty into a sin. There is no obstacle to the Baptism either of a woman who has been delivered, or who is expecting a child, even if it is administered to her in the very hour of her delivery, or to the child at the hour of its birth, providing that there be danger of death. For as the grace of this sacred mystery is to be duly offered to the living and conscious, so also is it to be administered without delay to the dying; for if we wait to offer them this mystery of redemption, the person to be redeemed may well depart this life unbaptized.

Until a child is weaned, a man should not approach his wife. For a bad custom has arisen among married people that women disdain to suckle their own children, and hand them over to other women to nurse. This custom seems to have arisen solely through incontinency, for when women are

unwilling to be continent, they refuse to suckle their children.
So those who observe this bad custom of giving their children
to others to nurse must not approach their husbands until the
time of their purification has elapsed. For even apart from
childbirth, women are forbidden to do so during their
monthly courses, and the Old Law prescribed death for
any man who approached a woman during this time. But a
woman should not be forbidden to enter church during these
times, for the workings of nature cannot be considered culp-
able, and it is not just that she should be refused admittance,
since her condition is beyond her control. We know that the
woman who suffered an issue of blood, humbly approaching
behind our Lord, touched the hem of his robe, and was at
once healed of her sickness. If, therefore, this woman was
right to touch our Lord's robe, why may not one who suffers
nature's courses be permitted to enter the church of God?
And if it is objected that the woman in the Gospels was compelled by disease while these latter are bound by custom, then
remember, my brother, that everything that we suffer in this
mortal body through the infirmity of its nature is justly ordained by God since the Fall of man. For hunger, thirst, heat,
cold, and weariness originate in this infirmity of our nature;
and our search for food against hunger, drink against thirst,
coolness against heat, clothing against cold, and rest against
weariness is only our attempt to obtain some remedy in our
weakness. So if it was a laudable presumption in the woman
who, in her disease, touched our Lord's robe, why may not
the same concession be granted to all women who endure
the weakness of nature?

A woman, therefore, should not be forbidden to receive
the mystery of Communion at these times. If any out of
a deep sense of reverence do not presume to do so, this is
commendable; but if they do so, they do nothing wrong.
Sincere people often acknowledge their faults even when
there is no actual fault, because a blameless action may often
spring from a fault. For instance, eating is no fault, but being

hungry originates in Adam's sin; similarly, the monthly courses of women are no fault, because nature causes them. But the corruption of our nature is apparent even when we have no deliberate intention to do evil, and this corruption springs from sin; so may we recognize the judgement that our sin has brought on us. But let the man who deliberately commits sin bear the unwelcome punishment of his wrongdoing. So, when women after due consideration do not presume to approach the Sacrament of the Body and Blood of the Lord during their courses, they are to be commended. But if they are moved by devout love of this holy mystery to receive it as pious custom requires, they are not to be discouraged. For while the Old Testament makes outward observances important, the New Testament does not regard these things so highly as the inward disposition, which is the sole true criterion. For instance, the Law forbade the eating of many things as unclean, but in the Gospel our Lord says: '*That which enters the mouth does not defile a man, but that which issues from his mouth.*' He also said: '*Out of the mouth proceed evil thoughts.*' Here Almighty God clearly shows us that evil actions spring from evil thoughts. Similarly, Saint Paul says: '*To the pure all things are pure, but to those who are corrupt and unbelieving, nothing is pure.*' And later, he indicates the cause of this corruption, adding: '*For even their mind and conscience are corrupt.*' If, therefore, no food is unclean to one of a pure mind, how can a woman who endures the laws of nature with a pure mind be considered impure?

It is not fitting that a man who has approached his wife should enter church before he has washed, nor is he to enter at once, though washed. The ancient Law prescribed that a man in such cases should wash, and forbade him to enter a holy place before sunset. But this may be understood spiritually, for when a man's mind is attracted to those pleasures by lawless desire, he should not regard himself as fitted to join in Christian worship until these heated desires cool in the mind, and he has ceased to labour under wrongful passions.

And although various nations have differing views on this matter and observe different customs, it was always the ancient Roman usage for such a man to seek purification, and out of reverence to refrain awhile from entering a holy place. In making this observation, we do not condemn marriage itself, but since lawful intercourse must be accompanied by bodily pleasure, it is fitting to refrain from entering a holy place, since desire itself is not blameless. For even David, who said: '*Behold, I was conceived in iniquity, and in sin my mother brought me forth*', was not himself born of any illicit union, but in lawful wedlock. But knowing himself to have been conceived in iniquity, he grieved that he had been born in sin, as surely as the branches of a tree draws up moisture through its roots. In saying this, he does not term the union of married people iniquity, but the pleasures of such union. For there are many things that are lawful and legitimate, and yet in the doing of them we are to some extent contaminated. For example, we often correct our faults under stress of anger and thereby disturb our peace of mind; and though we are right to do so, it is not good that we should lose our peace of mind in the process. He who said: '*My eye was disquieted by anger*' had been roused by the crimes of evil men, and because only a quiet mind can rest in the light of contemplation, he was perforce withdrawn and prevented from contemplating heavenly things so long as he was distracted by the wicked doings of men. So while anger against evil is commendable, it is harmful to a man because he regards his anger as a symptom of some guilt. Lawful intercourse should be for the procreation of offspring, and not for mere pleasure; to obtain children, and not to satisfy lust. But if any man is not moved by a desire for pleasure, but only by a desire for children, he is to be left to his own judgement either as to entering church, or to receiving the Communion of the Body and Blood of our Lord; for we have no right to debar one who does not yield to the fires of temptation. But when lust takes the place of desire for children, the pair have cause for regret; and although the holy teachings give them permission, yet this carries a warning with it. For when the Apostle Paul said: '*Whoever cannot contain, let him marry*', he at once added, '*This I say by way of permission, not as a command.*' This concession makes it lawful, yet not good; so when he spoke of permission, he indicated that it was not good.

It should be carefully considered that when God was about to speak to the people on Mount Sinai, he first ordered them to abstain from women. And if such a degree of bodily purity was required in those who were to hear the word of God when he spoke to men through a subject creature, how much the more should women preserve themselves in purity of body when about to receive the Body of Almighty God himself, lest they be overwhelmed by the very greatness of this ineffable mystery? For this reason the priest instructed David that, if his men were clean in this respect, they might be given the shewbread which would have been entirely forbidden had not David first certified that they were clean. Similarly the man who has cleansed himself is allowed to approach the mystery of Holy Communion, and may enter church in accordance with this decision.

IX. Augustine's ninth question: May a man receive communion after an illusion in sleep; or, if a priest, may he celebrate the holy mysteries?

Pope Gregory's reply: The Testament of the Old Law, as I have already mentioned, speaks of such a man as unclean and does not permit him to enter church until evening and after purification. But this is to be understood spiritually in another sense; for although he is under a delusion and tempted to impurity only in a dream, he is nevertheless defiled by mental pictures, and must therefore wash himself and purge his sinful thoughts by penitence. And unless the urge of temptation dies earlier, he should regard himself as unclean until evening. But we should carefully examine the origin of such illusions in the mind of a sleeper, for sometimes they arise from over-eating, sometimes from excess or lack of bodily strength, and sometimes from impure thoughts. When such illusion occurs through excess or lack of bodily vigour, it should cause no distress, and it is unfortunate if the mind of one who was unconscious of its happening should suffer as a result. But when a greedy appetite runs riot and overloads the stomach, the mind is to blame, although not to the extent that a man must be forbidden to receive the holy mystery, or to say mass when a feast-day requires it, or when necessity demands that he administer the sacrament in the absence of another priest. But if there are others who can perform this ministry, then this illusion caused by greed need not debar a man from receiving the holy mystery unless the mind of the sleeper has been excited by impure thoughts; but I think that humility should move him to refrain from offering the holy mysteries under these circumstances. But there are others who are not mentally disturbed by impure thoughts, although subject to these illusions. This shows that the mind is not innocent even in its own judgement, for although it remembers nothing that occurs during sleep, yet it does remember its greedy appetites. But if the sleeper's illusion springs from ignoble thoughts when awake, his guilt stands clear in his mind and he recognizes the source of his sin, because he has unconsciously revealed whatever has been in his conscious thoughts. But the question is whether an evil thought merely occurs to a man, or whether he proceeds to take pleasure in it, or, worse still, to assent to it. For all sin occurs in three ways, that is, by suggestion, pleasure, and consent. Suggestion comes through the devil, pleasure through the body, and consent through the will. The Serpent suggested the first sin, and Eve, as flesh, took physical pleasure in it, while Adam, as spirit, consented; but only the subtlest mind can discern between suggestion and pleasure, and between pleasure and consent. For when the Evil Spirit suggests a sin, no sin is committed unless the mind takes pleasure in it; but when the body begins to take pleasure, then sin is born; and if deliberate consent is given, sin is complete. The origin of sin, therefore, is in suggestion, its growth in pleasure, and its completion in consent. It often happens, however, that what the Evil Spirit whispers to the mind and the flesh anticipates with pleasure, the soul rejects. And although the body cannot experience pleasure without the mind, yet the mind, in contending against the desires of the body, is to some extent unwillingly chained to them, having to oppose them for conscience sake, and strongly regretting its bondage to bodily desires. It was for this reason that Paul, that great soldier in God's army, confessed with sorrow: '*I see another law in my body warring against the law of the mind, and bringing me into captivity to the law of sin, which indwells my body.*' Now if he was a captive, he fought but little; yet he did fight. So he was both captive and also fighting with the law of the mind, to which the law of the body is opposed. And if he fought thus, he was no captive. So one may say that a man is both captive and free; free through the law of right which he loves, and captive through the law of bodily pleasure, of which he is an unwilling victim.

CHAPTER 28: *Pope Gregory writes to the Bishop of Arles, asking him to help Augustine in his work for God* [A.D. 601]

SUCH were the blessed Pope Gregory's replies to the questions of the most reverend Bishop Augustine. The Pope also wrote a letter to the Bishop of Arles which was delivered to Vergilius, successor to Etherius. This ran as follows:

'To our most reverend and holy brother Vergilius, our fellow-bishop: Gregory, servant of the servants of God.

'It is well established that brethren who visit us on their own initiative should be warmly welcomed, since most visitors are invited out of affection. Therefore if our mutual brother Bishop Augustine happens to visit you, I beg you to receive him with proper affection and kindness, so that he may be encouraged by your goodwill, and that others may learn how brotherly love is to be cultivated. And since it often happens that an independent observer sees what needs correction more clearly than the man on the spot, I ask that should he bring to your notice any wrong-doing among clergy or others, you make careful enquiry into these matters with his help. In this way you will show yourself strict and alert against all abuses that offend God and incur His displeasure, so that the guilty may be corrected, the innocent vindicated, and others mend their ways. God keep you safe, most reverend brother.

'Dated the twenty-second day of June, in the nineteenth year of our most devout Lord and Emperor Maurice Tiberius Augustus, and the eighteenth year after his Consulship. The fourth indiction.

CHAPTER 29: *Gregory sends Augustine the Pallium, a letter, and several clergy* [A.D. 601]

HEARING from Bishop Augustine that he had a rich harvest but few to help him gather it, Pope Gregory sent with his envoys several colleagues and clergy, of whom the principal and most outstanding were Mellitus, Justus, Paulinus, and Rufinianus. They brought with them everything necessary for the worship and service of the Church, including sacred vessels, altar coverings, church ornaments, vestments for priests and ministers, relics of the holy Apostles and martyrs, and many books. Gregory also sent a letter to Augustine, informing that he had dispatched the *pallium* to him, and giving him directions on the appointment of bishops in Britain. This letter runs as follows:

'To our most reverend and holy brother and fellow-bishop Augustine: Gregory, servant of the servants of God.

'While Almighty God alone can grant His servants the ineffable joys of the kingdom of heaven, it is proper that we should reward them with earthly honours, and encourage them by such recognition to devote themselves to their spiritual labours with redoubled zeal. And since the new Church of the English has now, through the goodness of God and your own efforts, been brought to the grace of God, we grant you the privilege of wearing the *pallium* in that Church whenever you perform the solemnities of the Mass. You are to consecrate twelve bishops in different places, who will be subject to your jurisdiction: the bishop of the city of London will thenceforward be consecrated by his own synod, and will receive the honour of the *pallium* from this apostolic See which, by divine decree, we at present occupy. We wish you also to send a bishop of your own choice to the city of York, and if that city and province accepts the word of God, this bishop is to consecrate twelve other bishops, and hold the dignity of Metropolitan. If we live to see this, we intend to grant him the *pallium* also, but he is to remain subject to Your Lordship's authority. After your death, however, he is to preside over the bishops whom he has consecrated and to be wholly independent of the Bishop of London. Thenceforward, seniority of consecration is to determine whether the Bishop of London or York takes precedence; but they are to consult one another and take united action in all matters concerning the Faith of Christ, and take and execute all decisions in agreement.

'You, my brother, are to exercise authority in the Name of our Lord and God Jesus Christ both over those bishops whom you shall consecrate, and any who shall be consecrated by the Bishop of York, and also over all the British bishops. Let Your Grace's words and example show them a pattern of right belief and holy life, so that they may execute their office in right belief and practice, and, when God wills, attain the kingdom of heaven. God keep you safe, most reverend brother.

'Dated the twenty-second of June, in the nineteenth year of our most devout Lord and Emperor Maurice Tiberius

Augustus, and the nineteenth after his Consulship. The fourth indiction.'

CHAPTER 30: *A copy of the letter sent by Pope Gregory to Abbot Mellitus on his departure for Britain* [A.D. 601]

WHEN these messengers had left, the holy father Gregory sent after them letters worthy of our notice, which show most clearly his unwearying interest in the salvation of our nation. The letters runs as follows:

'To our well loved son Abbot Mellitus: Gregory, servant of the servants of God.

'Since the departure of yourself and your companions, we have been somewhat anxious, because we have received no news of the success of your journey. Therefore, when by God's help you reach our most reverend brother, Bishop Augustine, we wish you to inform him that we have been giving careful thought to the affairs of the English, and have come to the conclusion that the temples of the idols in that country should on no account be destroyed. He is to destroy the idols, but the temples themselves are to be aspersed with holy water, altars set up, and relics enclosed in them.* For if these temples are well built, they are to be purified from devil-worship, and dedicated to the service of the true God. In this way, we hope that the people, seeing that its temples are not destroyed, may abandon idolatry and resort to these places as before, and may come to know and adore the true God. And since they have a custom of sacrificing many oxen to devils, let some other solemnity be substituted in its place, such as a day of Dedication or the Festivals of the holy martys whose relics are enshrined there. On such occasions they might well construct shelters of boughs for themselves around the churches that were once temples, and celebrate the solemnity with devout feasting. They are no longer to sacrifice beasts to the Devil, but they may kill them for food

to the praise of God, and give thanks to the Giver of all gifts
for His bounty. If the people are allowed some worldly
pleasures in this way, they will more readily come to desire
the joys of the spirit. For it is certainly impossible to eradicate
all errors from obstinate minds at one stroke, and whoever
wishes to climb to a mountain top climbs gradually step by
step, and not in one leap. It was in this way that God revealed
Himself to the Israelite people in Egypt, permitting the sacrifices formerly offered to the Devil to be offered thenceforward to Himself instead. So He bade them sacrifice beasts to
Him, so that, once they became enlightened, they might
abandon a wrong conception of sacrifice, and adopt the right.
For, while they were to continue to offer beasts as before,
they were to offer them to God instead of to idols, thus trans-
forming the idea of sacrifice. Of your kindness, you are to
inform our brother Augustine of this policy, so that he may
consider how he may best implement it on the spot. God
keep you safe, my very dear son.

'Dated the seventeenth of June, in the nineteenth year of
the reign of our most devout Lord and Emperor Maurice
Tiberius Augustus, and the eighteenth after his Consulship.
The fourth indiction.'

CHAPTER 31: *Pope Gregory writes to Augustine, warning
not to boast of his achievements* [A.D. 601]

AT the same time, hearing that Augustine had performed
miracles, Pope Gregory sent him a letter in which he
warned him not to fall into the peril of pride on this account.
He wrote:

'My very dear brother, I hear that Almighty God has done
great things through you because of your love for the nation
which He has chosen. Therefore let your joy be tempered
with awe at God's heavenly gifts, and thank Him that the
souls of the English are being drawn to inward grace

through outward miracles. At the same time, beware lest the frail mind becomes proud because of these wonderful events, for when it receives public recognition, it is liable to fall into senseless conceit. We should remember how the disciples returned from their preaching full of joy, and said to their heavenly Master: '*Lord, in Thy Name even the devils obey us*'; but He at once told them: '*Your true cause for joy is not this, but that your names are written in heaven.*' For when the disciples rejoiced at these miracles, they were thinking of their transitory personal joy; but Christ recalled them from personal to universal, and from transitory to eternal joy, saying: '*Rejoice in this, that your names are written in heaven.*' For God's chosen do not all work miracles, yet the names of all are written in heaven. For those who are disciples of the truth should rejoice only in that good thing which they share with all men, and which they shall enjoy for ever.

'Finally, dearest brother, always strictly examine your inner dispositions in all the outward actions which by God's help you perform. Clearly understand your own character, and how much grace is in this nation for whose conversion God has given you the power to work miracles. And if you remember that you have ever offended our Creator by word or action, let the memory of your sin crush any temptation to pride that may arise in your heart. And bear in mind that whatever powers to perform miracles you have received or shall receive from God are entrusted to you solely for the salvation of your people.'

CHAPTER 32: *Pope Gregory sends letters and gifts to King Ethelbert*

POPE GREGORY also sent a letter to King Ethelbert with several gifts, wishing to bestow earthly honours on this king whose exertions and zeal had brought him to knowledge of heavenly glory. A copy of this letter follows.

'To our excellent son, the most glorious King Ethelbert, King of the English: the Bishop Gregory.

'Almighty God raises good men to govern nations, in order that through them He may bestow the gifts of His mercy on all whom they rule. We know that this is so in the case of the English nation, over whom you reign so gloriously, so that by means of the good gifts that God grants to you, He may bless your people as well. Therefore, my illustrious son, zealously foster the grace that God has given you, and work to extend the Christian Faith among the people committed to your charge. Make their conversion your first concern; abolish the worship of idols, and destroy their shrines; raise the moral standards of your subjects by your own innocence of life, encouraging, warning, persuading, correcting, and showing them an example by your good deeds. God will most surely grant you His rewards in heaven if you faithfully proclaim His Name and truth upon earth; and He whose honour you seek and uphold among your peoples will make your own name glorious to posterity.

'The devout Emperor Constantine in this way turned the Roman State from its ignorant worship of idols by his own submission to our mighty Lord and God Jesus Christ, and with his subjects accepted Him with all his heart. The result is that his glorious reputation has excelled that of all his predecessors, and he has outshone them in good works as greatly as in reputation. Now, therefore, let Your Majesty do your utmost to bring to your subject princes and peoples the knowledge of the One God, Father, Son, and Holy Spirit, so that your own merit and repute may excel that of all the former kings of your nation. And when your subjects are thus absolved from their sins, you will stand with greater confidence before the judgement seat of God.

'Our most reverend brother Bishop Augustine has been trained under monastic Rule, has a complete knowledge of holy scripture, and, by the grace of God, is a man of holy life.

Therefore I beg you to consider his advice with care and
follow it exactly; for if you listen to him when he speaks in
God's name, his prayers for you will be the sooner answered.
But if you ignore his advice – which God forbid – and disregard him when he speaks in God's name, how will God
answer his prayers on your behalf? Work sincerely and
whole-heartedly with him in fervent faith, and support him
in all his work, so that you may receive a place in the kingdom of Christ, Whose Faith you profess and uphold in your
own realm.

'We would also have Your Majesty know what we have
learned from the words of Almighty God in holy Scripture,
that the end of this present world and the eternal kingdom of
the Saints is approaching.* When the end of the world is
near, unprecedented things will occur – portents in the sky,
terrors from heaven, unseasonable tempests, wars, famines,
plagues, and widespread earthquakes – all of which things
will not happen during our own lifetimes, but will ensue in
due course. Therefore if any such things occur in your own
country, do not be anxious, for these portents of the end are
sent to warn us to consider the welfare of our souls and
remember our last end, so that when our Judge comes, He
may find us prepared by good lives. I have mentioned these
matters in this short letter, my illustrious son, in the hope
that as the Christian Faith grows more strong in your kingdom, our correspondence with you may become more frequent, and we shall be pleased to write further when we
receive the glad news of the complete conversion of your
people.

'I have sent some small presents, which will not appear
without value since they are accompanied by the blessing of
the blessed Apostle Peter. May Almighty God continue to
perfect you in His grace, prolong your life for many years,
and after this life receive you among the citizens of our
heavenly home. May the grace of heaven preserve Your
Majesty in safety.

'Dated the twenty-second day of June, in the nineteenth year of our most devout lord and Emperor Maurice Tiberius Augustus, and the eighteenth after his Consulship. The fourth indiction.'

CHAPTER 33: *Augustine repairs the Church of Our Saviour and builds the monastery of Saint Peter the Apostle. A note on Peter, its first Abbot* [A.D. 602]

HAVING been granted permission to establish his episcopal see in the royal capital, as already recorded, Augustine proceeded with the king's approval to repair a church which he was informed had been built long ago by Roman Christians. This he hallowed in the Name of our Saviour, God, and Lord Jesus Christ,* and established a dwelling for himself and his successors nearby. He also built a monastery a short distance to the east of the city, where at his suggestion, King Ethelbert founded a church dedicated to the blessed Apostles Peter and Paul, enriching it with many gifts. It was here that the bodies of Augustine and all the Archbishops of Canterbury, and of the Kings of Kent were to rest. This church was not consecrated by Augustine himself, however, but by Laurentius his successor.

The first abbot of this monastery was the priest Peter, who was sent on an embassy to Gaul, and was drowned at sea in a bay called Amfleat,[1] where the local inhabitants buried him without honour. But as evidence of his holy life, Almighty God caused a heavenly light to appear over his grave every night, until the local people saw it, and realising that a holy man lay buried there, they made enquiries as to whose the body might be. Then they took up the body, and interred it in a church in the city of Boulogne with the honours due to so great a man.

1. Ambleteuse.

ABOUT this time, Ethelfrid, a very powerful and ambitious king, ruled the kingdom of Northumbria. He ravaged the Britons more cruelly than all other English leaders, so that he might well be compared to Saul the King of Israel, except that he was ignorant of true religion. He overran a greater area than any other kings or chiefs, exterminating or enslaving the inhabitants, extorting tribute, and annexing their lands for the English. One might fairly apply to him the words of the patriarch Jacob's blessing of his son: '*Benjamin shall ravage like a wolf; in the morning he shall devour the prey, and at night he shall divide the spoils.*'

Alarmed at his advance, Aidan, King of those Scots who lived in Britain, came against him with a large and strong army, but was defeated by Ethelfrid's smaller forces and put to flight, losing almost his entire army at a famous place known as Degsastan, that is, Degsa's Stone. In this battle, Ethelfrid's brother Theobald and all his men were killed, Ethelfrid brought this campaign to a close in the year of our Lord 603, the eleventh of his reign, which lasted twenty-four years. It was also the first year of the reign of Phocas, who then occupied the throne of the Roman Empire. From that day until the present, no king of the Scots has dared to invade Britain to make war on the English.

BOOK TWO

CHAPTER I: *On the death of Pope Gregory*

IN the year of our Lord 605, having ruled the apostolic Roman Church most illustriously for thirteen years, six months, and ten days, the blessed Pope Gregory died and was taken up to his eternal home in heaven. And it is fitting that he should receive special mention in this history, since it was through his zeal that our English nation was brought from the bondage of Satan to the Faith of Christ, and we may rightly term him our own apostle. For during his pontificate, while he exercised supreme authority over all the churches of Christendom that had already long since been converted, he transformed our still idolatrous nation into a church of Christ. So we may rightly describe him as our own apostle, for while others may not regard him in this light, he was certainly an apostle to our own nation, and we are *the seal of his apostleship in the Lord*.

Gregory was Roman-born, son of Gordian, and came of a noble and devout family. Felix, once bishop of the same apostolic see, a man of high distinction in the Church of Christ, was one of his ancestors, and Gregory maintained this family tradition by the nobility and devotion of his religious life. By God's grace, he employed his recognized worldly position solely to win the glory of eternal honour, for he soon retired from secular life and sought admission to a monastery. There he entered upon a life of such perfection in grace that in later years he used to recall with tears how his mind was set on high things, soaring above all that is transitory, and how he was able to devote himself entirely to the spiritual life. Remaining in the body, he could yet transcend

its limitations in contemplation, and looked forward to
death, which most men regard as a punishment, as the gate-
way to life and reward of his labours. He used to mention
this, not in order to call attention to his increase in virtue, but
lamenting the loss of virtue sustained in his spiritual life
through his pastoral responsibilities. One day, in conversation with his deacon Peter, Gregory described his former
spiritual state, then sadly continued: 'My pastoral responsibilities now compel me to have dealings with worldly men,
and when I recall my former peace, it seems that my mind is
bespattered with the mire of daily affairs. For when I am
wearied by attention to the worldly affairs of numberless
people and wish to meditate on spiritual things, I seem to approach them with unmistakably lessened powers. So when
I compare what I now endure with what I have lost, and
when I weigh that loss, my burden seems greater than ever.'

Holy Gregory spoke in this way from deep humility, yet
we cannot help but feel that he lost none of his monastic perfection through his pastoral cares, and gained greater merit
by his labours for the conversion of souls than in his former
peaceful life, especially since, even when he became Pope, he
ordered his house as a monastery. When he was first summoned from his monastery, ordained to the ministry of the
altar, and sent to Constantinople as representative of the
apostolic see, he never abandoned his spiritual exercises,
although compelled to mix with people of the Imperial
court. For some of his fellow-monks were so devoted to him
that they accompanied him to the Imperial city, and he began
to maintain a regular religious observance with them. In this
way, as he records, their example proved an anchor-cable
that held him fast to the peaceful shore of prayer while he
was tossed on the restless waves of worldly affairs, and his
studies in their company enabled him to refresh a mind distracted by earthly concerns. He was not only strengthened
against the temptations of the world by their fellowship, but
inspired to ever greater spiritual activity.

When these companions urged him to write a mystical commentary on the often obscure book of Job, he could not refuse a task imposed on him by brotherly affection, which would be of help to many people. So he first gave a clear exposition of its literal meaning in thirty-five sections, and followed by showing how the book refers to Christ and the sacraments of the Church, and in what sense it applies to all the faithful. He began this work when Papal representative in the Imperial city, and completed it in Rome after he became Pope. It was during his stay in Constantinople that Gregory, a mighty champion of Catholic truth, suppressed at its birth a new heresy about our state at the resurrection. For Eutyches, bishop of that city, taught that our bodies will then be impalpable, more intangible than wind and air: but when Gregory heard this, he quoted the example of our Lord's Resurrection, and showed logically how this opinion was utterly opposed to the orthodox belief. For the Catholic belief is that the body is transfigured in the glory of immortality and refined by the operation of spiritual power, but remains palpable by reason of its nature. This is exemplified in our Lord's risen body, of which he said: '*Touch Me, and see, for a spirit has not flesh and bones as you see Me have.*' In defence of the Faith, our venerable father Gregory contested this rising heresy so effectively that, with the help of the devout Emperor Tiberius Constantine, it was entirely suppressed, and no one has since been found to revive it.

Gregory also wrote a notable book, *The Pastoral Office*, in which he describes in clear terms the qualities essential in those who rule the Church, showing how they should live; how they should carefully instruct all their people; and how they should always bear in mind their own frailty. He also compiled forty *Homilies* on the Gospel, which he divided into two volumes. He wrote four books of *Dialogues*, in which at the request of his deacon Peter, he included the lives of the saints of Italy to serve as patterns of holy life for posterity. So whereas in his *Commentaries* he showed what virtues are necessary, in describing the miracles of the saints he made clear the potency of those virtues. In twenty-two homilies he also revealed the profound teaching latent in the early and latter parts of the prophet Ezekiel, which had hitherto remained very obscure. Further, he compiled a book of answers in reply to the questions of Saint Augustine, first bishop of the English nation, which I have already mentioned and quoted in full in this history. In conjunction with the bishops of Italy he also compiled the short *Synodical Book*, which deals with the administration of the Church. He also wrote a large number of personal letters. The extent of his writings is a source of amazement when one considers that throughout his youth he was often in agony from gastric pain, and frequently troubled by a slow fever. But in all these afflictions he reflected that holy scripture says: '*The Lord scourgeth every son that He receiveth*', and the greater his worldly sufferings, the greater his assurance of eternal joy.

Much might be said of his imperishable genius, which was unimpaired even by the most severe physical afflictions; for while other popes devoted themselves to building churches and enriching them with costly ornaments, Gregory's sole concern was to save souls. He regularly gave whatever money he had to relieve the poor, in order that '*his righteousness might remain for ever, and his horn be exalted with honour.*' Like Job, he might justly claim, '*When the ear heard me, then it blessed me; and when the eye saw me, it gave witness to me, because I delivered the poor that cried, and the fatherless, and him that had none to help him. The blessing of him that was ready to perish came upon me, and I caused the widow's heart to sing for joy. I put on righteousness, and it clothed me; my judgement was as a robe and diadem. I was the eye to the blind, and feet was I to the lame. I was father to the poor; and the cause which I knew not, I searched out. And I broke the jaws of the wicked, and plucked the spoil from his teeth.*' And again, '*I have not withheld the poor from their desire, nor caused the eye of the widow to fall; nor have I eaten my portion myself alone, and the fatherless hath not eaten*

*thereof. For in my youth compassion grew up with me, and from my
mother's womb it came forth with me.'* In addition to his deeds of
kindness and justice, we should remember with gratitude
how Gregory saved our nation from the grasp of the ancient
Enemy by the preachers whom he sent us, and brought it
into the abiding liberty of God. He was full of joy at its conversion and salvation, as he mentions in his Commentary on
Job: 'The Britons, who formerly knew only their own barbaric tongue, have long since begun to cry the Hebrew *Alleluia* to the praise of God. The once restless sea now lies quiet
before the feet of His saints, and its ungovernable rages, which
no earthly princes could tame by the sword, are now quelled at
the simple word of His priests in the fear of God. Heathen
nations who never trembled before armed hosts now accept
and obey the teachings of the humble. For now that the
grace of the knowledge of God has enlightened them and
they see His heavenly truths and mighty wonders, the fear of
God restrains them from their former wickedness, and they
desire with all their hearts to win the prize of eternal life.'
Gregory also tells how the holy Augustine and his companions guided the English nation to knowledge of the truth
both by their preaching and their miracles.

Among many other matters, blessed Pope Gregory decreed
that Mass should be said over the tombs of the holy Apostles
Peter and Paul in their churches. He also introduced into the
Canon of the Mass three excellent and valuable petitions:
*Order our days in Thy peace, preserve us from eternal damnation,
and number us in the flock of Thine elect, Through Christ our
Lord.*

Gregory ruled the Church during the reigns of the Emperors Maurice and Phocas, and in the second year of the latter's
reign he passed from this life and entered the true life of
heaven. His body was laid to rest on March the fourth in the
church of Saint Peter the Apostle before the sacristy, whence
he will one day rise in glory with other shepherds of Holy
Church. On his tomb was inscribed this epitaph:

Receive, O earth, the body that you gave,
Till God's lifegiving power destroy the grave.
His heaven-bound soul no deadly power, no strife
Can harm, whose death is but the gate of life.
The tomb of this high Pontiff, now at rest,
Recalls his life and deeds for ever blest.
He fed the hungry, and he clothed the chill,
And by his message saved their souls from ill.
Whate'er he taught, he first fulfilled in deed,
And proved a pattern in his people's need.
To Christ he led the Angles, and by grace
To Faith and Church he added a new race.
O holy pastor, all your work and prayer
To God you offered with a shepherd's care.
High place in heaven is your just reward,
In triumph and in joy before the Lord.

I must here relate a story which shows Gregory's deep desire for the salvation of our nation. We are told that one day some merchants who had recently arrived in Rome displayed their many wares in the crowded market-place. Among other merchandise Gregory saw some boys exposed for sale. These had fair complexions, fine-cut features, and fair hair. Looking at them with interest, he enquired what country and race they came from. 'They come from Britain,' he was told, 'where all the people have this appearance.' He then asked whether the people were Christians, or whether they were still ignorant heathens. 'They are pagans,' he was informed. 'Alas!' said Gregory with a heartfelt sigh: 'how sad that such handsome folk are still in the grasp of the Author of darkness, and that faces of such beauty conceal minds ignorant of God's grace! What is the name of this race?' 'They are called Angles,' he was told. 'That is appropriate,' he said, 'for they have angelic faces, and it is right that they should become fellow-heirs with the angels in heaven. And what is the name of their Province?' 'Deira,' was the answer. 'Good. They shall indeed be *de ira* – saved

from wrath – and called to the mercy of Christ. And what is
the name of their king?' he asked. 'Aella', he was told. 'Then
must *Alleluia* be sung to the praise of God our Creator in
their land,' said Gregory, making play on the name.

Approaching the Pope of the apostolic Roman see—for
he was not yet Pope himself – Gregory begged him to send
preachers of the word to the English people in Britain to convert them to Christ, and declared his own eagerness to
attempt the task should the Pope see fit to direct it. But this
permission was not forthcoming, for although the Pope himself was willing, the citizens of Rome would not allow
Gregory to go so far away from the city. But directly
Gregory succeeded to the Papacy himself, he put in hand this
long cherished project and sent other missionaries in his
place, assisting their work by his own prayers and encouragement. And I have thought it fitting to include this traditional
story in the history of our Church.

CHAPTER 2: *Augustine urges the British bishops to cement
Catholic unity, and performs a miracle in their presence.
Retribution follows their refusal* [A.D. 603]

MEANWHILE, with the aid of King Ethelbert, Augustine summoned the bishops and doctors of the nearest
British province* to a conference at a place still known to the
English as Augustine's Oak, which lies on the border between the Hwiccas and the West Saxons. He began by urging
them to establish brotherly relations with him in Catholic
unity, and to join with him in God's work of preaching the
Gospel to the heathen.

Now the Britons did not keep Easter at the correct time,
but between the fourteenth and twentieth days of the moon
– a calculation depending on a cycle of eighty-four years.
Furthermore, certain other of their customs were at variance
with the universal practice of the Church. But despite pro-

tracted discussions, neither the prayers, advice, or censures of
Augustine and his companions could obtain the compliance
of the Britons, who stubbornly preferred their own customs
to those in universal use among Christian Churches. Augustine then brought this lengthy and fruitless conference to a
close, saying: 'Let us ask our Lord, *who makes men to be of one
mind* in His Father's house, to grant us a sign from heaven and
show us which tradition is to be followed, and by what
means we are to enter His kingdom. Bring in some sick person, and let the beliefs and practice of those who can heal him
be accepted as pleasing to God and binding upon us all.' On
the reluctant agreement of his opponents, a blind Englishman was led in and presented to the British priests, from
whose ministry he obtained no healing or benefit. At this
critical juncture, Augustine then knelt in prayer to the Father
of our Lord Jesus Christ, imploring that the man's lost sight
might be restored and prove the means of bringing the light
of spiritual grace to the minds of countless believers. Immediately the blind man's sight was restored, and all acknowledged Augustine as the true herald of the light of Christ.
The Britons admitted that his teaching was true and right,
but said again that they could not abandon their ancient customs without the consent and approval of their own people,
and therefore asked that a second and fuller conference might
be held.

This was arranged, and seven British bishops and many
very learned men are said to have attended, who came mainly
from their most famous monastery which the English call
Bancornaburg,[1] then ruled by Abbot Dinoot. Those summoned to this council first visited a wise and prudent hermit,
and enquired of him whether they should abandon their own
traditions at Augustine's demand. He answered: 'If he is a
man of God, follow him.' 'But how can we be sure of this?'
they asked. 'Our Lord says, *Take My yoke upon you and learn
of Me, for I am meek and lowly of heart,*' he replied. 'Therefore

1. Bangor.

if Augustine is meek and lowly of heart, it shows that he
bears the yoke of Christ himself, and offers it to you. But if
he is haughty and unbending, then he is not of God, and you
should not listen to him.' Then they asked, 'But how can we
know this?' 'Arrange that he arrives first at the place
appointed for the conference,' answered the hermit. 'If he
rises courteously as you approach, rest assured that he is the
servant of Christ and do as he asks. But if he ignores you and
does not rise, then, since you are in the majority, do not com-
ply with his demands.'

The British bishops carried out his suggestion, and it
happened that Augustine remained seated in his chair. Seeing
this, they became angry, accusing him of pride and contra-
dicting all that he said. Augustine then declared: 'Your customs conflict with those of the universal Church in many
respects; nevertheless, if you will agree with me on three
points, I am ready to countenance all your other customs,
although they are contrary to our own. These points are: to
keep Easter at the correct time;* to administer the Sacrament
of Baptism by which we are reborn to God according to the
rites of the holy, Roman, and apostolic Church; and to join
with us in preaching the word of God to the English.' But
the bishops refused these things, nor would they recognize
Augustine as their archbishop, arguing that if he would not
rise to greet them in the first instance, he would have little
regard for them once they submitted to his authority. In
reply, Augustine is said to have threatened that if they refused
to unite with their fellow-Christians, they would be attacked
by their enemies the English; and if they refused to preach
the Faith of Christ to them, they would eventually be punished by meeting death at their hands. And, as though by
divine judgement, all these things happened as Augustine
foretold.

Some while after this, the powerful king Ethelfrid, whom
I have already mentioned, raised a great army at the City of
Legions – which the English call Legacestir, but which the

Britons more correctly name Carlegion – and made a great
slaughter of the faithless Britons. Before battle was joined,
he noticed that their priests were assembled in a safer place to
pray for their soldiers, and he enquired who they were and
what they were doing. Most of these priests came from the
monastery of Bangor, where there are said to have been so
many monks that although it was divided into seven sections,
each under its own abbot, none of these sections contained
less than three hundred monks, all of whom supported themselves by manual work. Most of these monks, who had kept
a three-day fast, gathered to pray at the battle, and were
guarded from the heathen enemy by a certain Brocmail. As
soon as King Ethelfrid was informed of their purpose, he
said: 'If they pray to their God against me, they are fighting
against us even if they do not bear arms.' He therefore
directed his first attack against them, and then destroyed the
rest of the British forces, although his own army suffered
heavy casualties. About twelve hundred monks perished in
this battle, and only fifty escaped by flight, while Brocmail
and his men took to their heels at the first assault, leaving
those whom he should have protected unarmed and helpless.
Thus, long after his death, was fulfilled Bishop Augustine's
prophecy that the faithless Britons, who had rejected the
offer of eternal salvation, would incur the punishment of
temporal destruction.

CHAPTER 3: *Augustine consecrates Mellitus and Justus as
bishops: his own death* [A.D. 604]

IN the year of our Lord 604, Augustine, Archbishop of
Britain, consecrated two bishops, Mellitus and Justus.
Mellitus was appointed to preach in the province of the East
Saxons, which is separated from Kent by the river Thames,
and bounded on the east by the sea. Its capital is the city of
London, which stands on th banks of the Thames, and is a

trading centre for many nations who visit it by land and sea. At this time Sabert, Ethelbert's nephew through his sister Ricula, ruled the province under the suzerainty of Ethelbert, who governed all the English peoples as far north as the Humber. When this province had received the Faith through the preaching of Mellitus, King Ethelbert built a church dedicated to the holy Apostle Paul in the city of London, which he appointed as the episcopal see of Mellitus and his successors. Augustine also consecrated Justus as bishop of a Kentish city which the English call Rofaecestir[1] after an early chieftain named Rof. This lies nearly twenty-four miles west of Canterbury, and a church in honour of Saint Andrew the Apostle was built here by King Ethelbert, who made many gifts to the bishops of both these churches as well as to Canterbury; he later added lands and property for the maintenance of the bishop's household.

When our father Augustine, the beloved of God, died, his body was laid to rest at the entrance to the church of the holy Apostles Peter and Paul, since the church was not yet completed or consecrated. But as soon as it was dedicated, his body was brought inside and buried in the north porch with great honour. This was to be the last resting-place of all succeeding archbishops except Theodore and Berctwald, whose bodies lie inside the church, no space remaining in the porch. Almost in the centre of the church stands an altar dedicated in honour of blessed Pope Gregory, at which a priest says solemn mass in their memory each Saturday. On the tomb of Augustine is inscribed this epitaph:

'Here rests the Lord Augustine, first Archbishop of Canterbury, sent here by blessed Gregory, Bishop of the City of Rome, who with God's help and supported by miracles guided King Ethelbert and his people from the worship of idols to the Faith of Christ. He ended his days in peace, and died on the twenty-sixth day of May in the above King's reign.'

1. Rochester.

CHAPTER 4: *Laurentius and his fellow-bishops urge the Scots to maintain the unity of the Church, particularly in the observance of Easter: Mellitus visits Rome* [A.D. 605]

AUGUSTINE was succeeded in the archbishopric by Laurentius, whom he had nominated during his own lifetime, for he feared that even a short interval without a pastor might cause a setback to the newly established Church. In so doing, he followed the precedent set by the Church's first Pastor, blessed Peter, Prince of the Apostles, who, having established the Church in Rome, is said to have consecrated Clement as his assistant and successor. On receiving the dignity of archbishop, Laurentius gave constant encouragement and a holy example to his flock, working tirelessly to perfect the edifice of the Church whose foundations had been so nobly laid. Nor was his interest limited to the Church newly established among the English, for he sought also to extend his pastoral care to the original inhabitants of Britain, and to the Scots of Ireland adjacent to this island of Britain. For having learned that in their own country the life and customs of the Scots and of the Britons were unorthodox – particularly in the observance of Easter, which they did not keep at the right time, but between the fourteenth and twentieth days of the moon – he wrote a letter jointly with his fellow-bishops, urging them to join with him in maintaining the unity, peace, and Catholic customs of the Christian Church established throughout the world. This letter commences:

'To our dear brothers the lord bishops and abbots throughout Scotland: from Laurentius, Mellitus, and Justus, servants of the servants of God.

'When, in accordance with its custom, the apostolic see sent us to the western lands to preach the Gospel to the heathen peoples, we came to this island of Britain. Until we realized the true situation, we had a high regard for the devotion of the Britons and Scots, believing that they followed

the customs of the universal Church; but on further acquaintance with the Britons, we imagined that the Scots must be
better. We have now, however, learned through Bishop
Dagan on his visit to this island, and through Abbot Columbanus in Gaul, that the Scots are no different to the Britons
in their behaviour. For when Bishop Dagan visited us, he not
only refused to eat with us, but even to take his meal in the
same house as ourselves.'

Laurentius and his fellow-bishops also wrote a dignified
letter to the British bishops, in which he tried to bring them
into Catholic unity, but the present state of affairs shows how
little he succeeded.

At this time Mellitus, Bishop of London, visited Rome to
acquaint the Pope with the progress of the Church in England. This most reverend Pope had summoned a council of
the bishops of Italy in order to draw up regulations for monastic life and discipline, and he invited Mellitus to sit with
them at this council, which took place on the twenty-seventh
of February 610 in the thirteenth year of the Emperor Phocas.
The presence of Mellitus enabled him to ratify all the regular
decisions of the council, and to convey them to the English
Church for its acceptance and promulgation on his return to
Britain. He also brought back letters from the Pope both to
God's beloved Archbishop Laurentius and his clergy, and to
King Ethelbert and his people. This Pope was Boniface,
fourth Bishop of Rome after Gregory, who persuaded the
Emperor Phocas to give the Christian Church the Roman
temple anciently known as the *Pantheon*, in which stood
images of all the gods. After solemn purification, Boniface
consecrated it as the Church of the Holy Mother of God and
all Christian Martyrs; and once its horde of devils had been
cast out, it became a memorial to the Company of Saints.

IN the year of our Lord 616 – the twenty-first year after Augustine and his companions were dispatched to preach to the English nation – King Ethelbert of Kent died after a glorious reign of fifty-six years, and entered the eternal joys of the kingdom of heaven. He was the third English king to become High-King (Bretwalda) of all the provinces south of the river Humber, but he was the first to enter the kingdom of heaven. The first king to hold this position was Aella, King of the South Saxons; the second was Caelin, King of the West Saxons, known to his people as Ceaulin; the third, as I have mentioned, was Ethelbert; the fourth was Redwald, King of the East Angles, who during the lifetime of Ethelbert was his vassal. The fifth was Edwin, King of Northumbria, that is, the province north of the Humber, who was a powerful king, and ruled all the peoples of Britain, both Angles and Britons, with the exception of Kent. He also brought under English rule the British Mevanian Isles,[1] which lie between Ireland and Britain. The sixth High-King was Oswald, the most Christian King of Northumbria, who maintained the same frontiers; the seventh was his brother Oswiu, who for a while held the same territory, and later conquered and made tributary the Picts and Scots in the northern parts of Britain. But I shall speak of these kings later.

King Ethelbert died on the twenty-fourth of February, twenty-one years after embracing the Faith, and was buried in Saint Martin's Porch in the Church of the blessed Apostles Peter and Paul, where Bertha his queen also rests. Among the many benefits that his wisdom conferred on the nation, he introduced, with the consent of his counsellors, a code of law framed on the Roman pattern, which was written in English, and remains in force to this day. The first of his laws is

1. Man and Anglesey.

designed to protect the Church he embraced, and decrees that satisfaction must be made by any person who steals property from the Church, the bishop, or other clergy.

Ethelbert was son of Irminric, son of Octa, and after his grandfather Orric, surnamed Oisc, the kings of Kent are commonly known as Oiscings. The father of Orric was Hengist, who first came to Britain with his son Orric at the invitation of Vortigern, as I have already related.

The death of Ethelbert and the accession of his son Eadbald proved to be a severe setback to the recently established Church, for not only did he reject the Faith of Christ, but he was also guilty of such fornication as the Apostle Paul mentions as being unheard of even among the heathen, in that he took his father's (second) wife as his own. His immorality was an incentive to those who, either out of fear or favour to the king his father, had submitted to the discipline of faith and chastity, to revert to their former uncleanness. However, this apostate king did not escape God's punishment and correction, for he was subject to frequent fits of insanity and possessed by an evil spirit.

The death of the Christian King Sabert of the East Saxons aggravated the situation, for he left three sons, all pagans, to inherit his realms. These were quick to profess idolatry, which they had pretended to abandon during the lifetime of their father, and encouraged their people to return to the old gods. It is told that when they saw Bishop Mellitus offering solemn Mass in church, they said with barbarous presumption: 'Why do you not offer us the white bread which you used to give to our father Saba (for so they used to call him), while you continue to give it to the people in church?' The Bishop answered, 'If you will be washed in the waters of salvation as your father was, you may receive it; but so long as you reject the Faith of Christ, you are quite unfit to receive the Bread of Life.' They retorted: 'We refuse to be baptized, and see no need of it, but we insist on receiving this bread.' The Bishop then carefully and repeatedly explained that this was forbidden, and that no one was admitted to receive the most holy Communion without the cleansing of Baptism. At this they were very angry, and said: 'If you will not oblige us in so trifling a matter, you shall no longer remain in our kingdom.' And they drove him into exile, and ordered all his followers to leave their borders.

After his expulsion, Mellitus came to Kent to consult with his fellow-bishops Laurentius and Justus on the best course of action, and they decided that it would be better for all of them to return to their own country and serve God in freedom, rather than to remain impotently among heathen who had rejected the Faith. Mellitus and Justus left first and settled in Gaul to await the outcome of events. But the kings who had driven out the herald of truth did not long remain unpunished for their devil-worship, for they and their army fell in battle against the West Saxons. Nevertheless, the fate of these wicked kings did not cause their people to abandon their evil practices, or to return to the simple faith and love to be found in Christ alone.

CHAPTER 6: *Laurentius is reproved by Saint Peter, and converts King Eadbald to Christ. Mellitus and Justus are recalled* [A.D. 616]

SHORTLY before Laurentius was to follow Mellitus and Justus from Britain, he ordered his bed to be placed one night in the Church of the blessed Apostles Peter and Paul, and after long and fervent prayers for the sadly afflicted Church, he lay down and fell asleep. In the middle of the night, blessed Peter, Prince of the Apostles, appeared to him, and demanded to know why he intended to abandon the flock entrusted to his care, and asked to what shepherds he would commit Christ's sheep left among the wolves when he fled. 'Have you forgotten my example?' asked Peter. 'For the sake of the little ones whom Christ entrusted to me as

proof of His love, I suffered chains, blows, imprisonment,
and pain. Finally, I endured the death of crucifixion at the
hands of unbelievers and enemies of Christ, so that at last I
might be crowned with Him.' Deeply moved by the words
and scourging of blessed Peter, Christ's servant Laurentius
sought audience with the king early next morning, and re-
moving his garment, showed him the marks of the lash. The
king was astounded, and enquired who had dared to scourge
so eminent a man; and when he learned that it was for his
own salvation that the archbishop had suffered so severely at
the hands of Christ's own Apostle, he was greatly alarmed.
He renounced his idolatry, gave up his unlawful wife,
accepted the Christian Faith, and was baptized, henceforward
promoting the welfare of the Church with every means at
his disposal.

The king also sent to Gaul and recalled Mellitus and Justus,
giving them free permission to return and set their churches
in order: so, after three years of exile, they returned. Justus
came back to his own city of Rochester, but the people of
London preferred their own idolatrous priests, and refused
to accept Mellitus as bishop. And since the king's authority
in the realm was not so effective as that of his father, he was
powerless to restore the bishop to his see against the refusal
and resistance of the pagans. After his conversion, however,
he and his people were zealous to observe the teachings of our
Lord, and in the monastery of the most blessed Prince of the
Apostles he built a church to the Holy Mother of God, which
was consecrated by Archbishop Mellitus.

CHAPTER 7: *The prayers of Bishop Mellitus put out a fire
in his city* [A.D. 619]

O N the second day of February in the same king's reign,
the blessed Archbishop Laurentius passed to the kingdom of heaven, and was buried in the monastery church of

the holy Apostle Peter next to his predecessor. Mellitus, Bishop of London, became the third Archbishop of Canterbury after Augustine, while Justus, who was still living, ruled the Church of Rochester. These bishops guided the English Church with great care and energy, and received letters of encouragement from Boniface, Bishop of the apostolic Roman see, who succeeded Deusdedit in the year of our Lord 619. And although Mellitus became crippled with the gout, his sound and ardent mind overcame his troublesome infirmity, ever reaching out to God in love and devotion. Noble by birth, he was even nobler in mind.

I record one among many instances of his virtue. One day the city of Canterbury was set on fire through carelessness, and the spreading flames threatened to destroy it. Water failed to extinguish the fire, and already a considerable area of the city was destroyed. As the raging flames were sweeping rapidly onwards, the bishop, trusting in the help of God where man's skill had failed, ordered himself to be carried into the path of its advance. In the place where the flames were fiercest stood the Church of the Four Crowned Martyrs,* and hither the bishop was borne by his attendants, where by his prayers this infirm man averted the danger which all the efforts of strong men had been powerless to check. For the southerly wind, which had been spreading the conflagration throughout the city, suddenly veered to the north, sparing the places that lay in its path: then it dropped altogether, so that the fires burned out and died. Thus Mellitus, the man of God, afire with love for him, was enabled not only to preserve himself and his people from spiritual powers of evil by his constant prayers and teaching, but also to protect them from bodily harm.

Having ruled the Church five years, Mellitus departed to the heavenly kingdom in the reign of King Eadbald, and was laid to rest with his predecessors in the monastery church of the holy Apostle Peter on the twenty-fourth day of April, in the year of our Lord 624.

J USTUS, Bishop of Rochester, at once succeeded Mellitus as archbishop. He consecrated Romanus as Bishop of Rochester in his place, having received authority to consecrate bishops from Pope Boniface, successor to Pope Deusdedit. This letter of authority runs as follows:

'BONIFACE, to his well beloved brother Justus. The contents of your letter and the success granted to your work are double evidence of your devotion and diligence in spreading the Gospel of Christ. Almighty God has not been unmindful of the honour due to His Name, or of the reward due to your labours, for He has faithfully promised the preachers of the Gospel, "*Lo, I am with you always, even to the end of the world.*" This promise He has of His mercy especially fulfilled in your own ministry, opening the hearts of the nations to receive the mystery of the Gospel through your preaching. For He has crowned the wonderful progress of your good work with His blessing, and has granted a plentiful increase to the faithful employment of the talents entrusted to you, which will set your seal on many generations to come. This is the just reward of the constancy with which you have held to your appointed mission, while with commendable patience you await the redemption of this nation, so that it may profit through the merits of those who work for its salvation: for our Lord Himself has said, "*He who perseveres to the end shall be saved.*" Your own patient hope and courageous endurance will cleanse the hearts of the heathen from the inherent poison of superstition, and obtain mercy for them from their Saviour. We learn, furthermore, from the letters of our son King Ethelwald, how your profound knowledge of God's holy word has guided him to a real conversion and acceptance of the true Faith. We firmly trust in God's patience and mercy, and are confident that your preaching and ministry will effect a complete conversion of his own

people and also of their neighbours. In this way, as the
Scripture says, will you receive the reward of a task well done
from the Lord and Giver of all good things, and all nations
who have received the mysteries of the Christian Faith will
proclaim: "*Their sound is gone out into all the earth, and their
words unto the ends of the world.*"

'Moved by your devotion, my brother, we are sending
you by the bearer of this letter the *pallium*, which we grant
you the privilege of wearing when you celebrate the Holy
Mysteries. We also grant you authority, under the guiding
mercy of our Lord, to consecrate bishops as occasion may
require, in order that the Gospel of Christ may be diffused
more widely among nations as yet unconverted. We are confident that you will worthily maintain this dignity granted
you by the favour of the Apostolic See, as an emblem of
which you have received this highest of honours to wear on
your shoulders. And, as you implore God's mercy, endeavour
so to live and labour that when you stand before the judgement seat of God, you may display this honour which we
grant you not only unstained, but enhanced by the witness
of all the souls which you have won.

God keep you in safety, my dearest brother.'

CHAPTER 9: *The reign of King Edwin: Paulinus comes to
preach the Gospel to him, and first administers the Sacrament of Baptism to his daughter and others* [A.D. 625]

A T this time, the people of Northumbria under Edwin
their king received the Faith through the ministry of
Paulinus, whom I have already mentioned. As a sign of God's
favour on his acceptance of the Faith, King Edwin received
wide additions to his realm, and brought under his sway
all the territories inhabited by the Britons, an achievement
unmatched by any previous English king. He also brought
the Isles of Anglesey and Man under English rule: of these,

the southern island is the largest and most fertile, and by English reckoning, supports a population of nine hundred and sixty families, while the other island supports over three hundred.

The Northumbrian people's acceptance of the Faith of Christ came about through their king's alliance with the kings of Kent, and his marriage to Ethelberga, known as Tata, a daughter of King Ethelbert. Edwin sent an embassy of nobles to her brother Eadbald to request her hand in marriage, but received the reply that it was not permissible for a Christian maiden to be given in marriage to a heathen husband, lest the Christian Faith and Sacraments be profaned by her association with a king who was wholly ignorant of the worship of the true God. When Edwin's messengers returned with this reply, he gave an assurance that he would place no obstacles in the way of the Christian Faith, and would afford complete freedom to Ethelberga and her attendants, both men and women, priests and servants, to live and worship in accordance with Christian belief and practice. He also stated himself willing to accept the religion of Christ if, on examination, his advisers decided that it appeared more holy and acceptable to God than their own.

On this understanding, the maiden was betrothed and sent to Edwin, and in accordance with the agreement, Paulinus, a man beloved of God, was consecrated bishop, so that he could accompany the princess as her chaplain, and by daily Mass and instruction preserve her and her companions from corruption by their constant association with the heathen.

Paulinus was consecrated bishop by Archbishop Justus on July 21st, 625, and came to Edwin with the princess as her spiritual counsellor in the marriage. But he was further determined to bring the nation to which he was sent to the knowledge of the Christian truth, and to fulfil the Apostle's saying, '*to espouse her to one husband, that he might present her as a chaste virgin to Christ.*' Therefore, directly he entered the province he began to toil unceasingly with God's help not only to maintain the faith of his companions unimpaired, but if possible to bring some of the heathen to grace and faith by his teaching. But although he laboured long, yet as the Apostle says, '*the god of this world blinded the minds of the unbelievers, lest the light of the glorious Gospel of Christ should shine upon them.*'

During the following year, an assassin named Eumer was sent into the province by Cuichelm, King of the West Saxons, in order to rob Edwin both of his kingdom and his life. This vile creature employed a double-edged, poisoned dagger, to ensure that if the wound itself were not mortal, the poison would complete its work. On Easter Day Eumer arrived at the king's country-seat by the Derwent, and was admitted into his presence on the pretext of delivering a message from his master. And while he was artfully delivering his pretended message, he suddenly rose, and drawing the dagger from beneath his clothes, attacked the king. Swift to see the king's peril, Lilla, his counsellor and best friend, having no shield to protect the king, interposed his own body to receive the blow; but even so, it was delivered with such force that it wounded the king through the body of his knight. The assassin was immediately attacked on all sides, but killed yet another of the king's men named Forthere in the ensuing struggle.

On the same holy night of Easter Day, the queen was delivered of a daughter, to be named Eanfled, and as the king thanked his gods in the presence of Bishop Paulinus for the birth of his daughter, the bishop gave thanks to Christ, and told the king that it was Christ who had given the queen a safe and painless delivery in response to his prayers. The king was greatly pleased at his words, and promised that if God would grant him life and victory over the king his enemy who had sent the assassin, he would renounce his idols and serve Christ, and as a pledge that he would keep his word, he gave his infant daughter to Paulinus to be consecrated to Christ. Accordingly, on the Feast of Pentecost this infant, together with twelve others of her family, was the first of the Northumbrians to receive Baptism.

When the king had recovered from the assassin's wound, he summoned his forces, marched against the West Saxons, and in the ensuing campaign either slew or forced to surrender all those who had plotted his murder. Returning home victorious, the king would not receive the Sacrament of Christian Baptism at once or without due consideration, although he had already abandoned idol-worship when he promised that he would serve Christ. But he wished, firstly, to receive a full course of instruction in the Faith from the venerable Paulinus, and to discuss his proper course with his chief counsellors, on whose wisdom he placed great reliance. For the king was by nature a wise and prudent man, and often sat alone in silence for long periods, turning over in his mind what he should do, and which religion he should follow.

CHAPTER 10: *Pope Boniface writes to the king, urging him to accept the Faith*

ABOUT this time, the king received a letter from Boniface, Bishop of the apostolic Roman see, urging him to accept the Faith. Here follows a copy of this letter, sent by the blessed and apostolic Pope Boniface of the Church and City of Rome to the illustrious Edwin, King of the English:

'To the illustrious Edwin, King of the English: Boniface, Bishop, servant of the servants of God.

'The words of man can never express the power of the most high God, abiding in His own greatness, invisible, ineffable, eternal; and no human mind, however perceptive and acute, can understand or define it. Nevertheless, God of His goodness has opened the doors of man's heart to grant him some knowledge of Himself, and has mercifully infused into their minds some measure of knowledge. Accordingly, we

have undertaken to extend our priestly responsibility to disclose to you the fullness of the Christian Faith, in order that
we may bring to your knowledge the Gospel of Christ,
which our Saviour commanded to be preached to all nations,
and may offer you the medicine of salvation.

'The clemency of the Divine Majesty, who by His Word
alone created and established the heavens and the earth, the
sea and all that is in them, has ordained the laws by which
they subsist; and by the counsel of His co-eternal Word in the
unity of the Holy Spirit, He has formed man after His own
image and likeness from the dust of the earth. He has further
granted him a most excellent prerogative, placing him above
all other creatures, in order that he may inherit eternal life by
obedience to His commandments. This God – Father, Son,
and Holy Spirit – the undivided Trinity – is adored and
worshipped by the human race from east to west, which con-
fesses Him by faith to salvation as Creator of all things and
Maker of all men. Of His infinite mercy and for the well-
being of all his creatures, He has been pleased to warm with
His Holy Spirit the frozen hearts of the most distant nations
of the world to knowledge of Himself in a most wonderful
manner.

'We are assured that Your Majesty has heard from your
neighbouring kingdom how our Redeemer in His mercy
has brought light to our excellent son Eadbald and his people.
We therefore trust that Heaven's mercy will grant this wonderful gift to you as it has to him, more especially as we
understand that your gracious Queen and true partner is
already endowed with the gift of eternal life through the
regeneration of Holy Baptism. We affectionately urge Your
Majesties to renounce idol-worship, reject the cunning
flatteries of fortune-tellers, and believe in God the Father
Almighty, and in His Son Jesus Christ, and in the Holy
Spirit. This Faith will free you from Satan's bondage, and
through the sustaining power of the holy and undivided
Trinity you will inherit eternal life.

'The profound guilt of those who perversely cling to pernicious superstition and idolatrous worship is clearly shown in the damnable patterns they adore. Of such the Psalmist says: "*All the gods of the heathen are devils; it is the Lord who made the heavens.*" And again: "*They have eyes, and do not see; they have ears, and do not hear; they have noses, and do not smell; they have hands, and do not feel; they have feet, and do not walk. Therefore those that make them are like them, and so are all who put their trust and confidence in them.*" How can such objects have power to help you, when they are made for you from perishable materials by the labour of your own subjects and servants? Even their inanimate resemblance to human form is due solely to man's craftsmanship. Unless you move them they cannot move, but are like a stone fixed in its place: they are manufactured, but have no intelligence, being utterly insensible, and having no power to hurt or help. We cannot understand how people can be so deluded as to worship as gods objects to which they themselves have given a likeness to human form.

'Accept the sign of the Holy Cross, by which the entire human race has been redeemed, and exorcize from your heart the damnable crafts and devices of the Devil, who jealously opposes all the workings of God's goodness. Overthrow and destroy these material objects that you have made your gods, and the very destruction of these things, which never drew the breath of life and could never receive understanding from their makers, will itself afford you clear evidence of the worthlessness of these objects of your former worship. Consider, you yourselves are nobler than they, for God has given you life, and you owe nothing to their power; for Almighty God has ordered your descent through countless generations from the first man that He created. Therefore accept the knowledge of your Creator, who breathed into your frame the breath of life, and who sent His only Son for your salvation, that He might deliver you from the evil power of the Devil, and grant you the prize of Heaven.

'Accept the message of the Christian teachers, and the Gospel that they proclaim. Believe in God the Father Almighty, and in Jesus Christ His Son, and in the Holy Spirit, the undivided Trinity. Spurn the temptations of the Devil, and reject all the suggestions of our malicious and deceitful enemy. Born again by water and the Holy Spirit, God's generous aid will empower you to abide in the splendour of eternal glory with Him in whom you shall come to believe.

'We impart to you the blessing of your protector, blessed Peter, Prince of the Apostles. With it we send you a garment with a golden ornament, and a robe from Ancyra, asking Your Majesty to accept these gifts with the same goodwill as that with which we send them.'

CHAPTER 11: *The Pope writes to the Queen, urging her to exert her influence to obtain the king's salvation*

THE Pope also wrote to Queen Ethelberga as follows. A copy of the letter of the blessed and apostolic Boniface, Pope of the City of Rome, to Ethelberga, Queen of King Edwin:

'To his illustrious daughter, Queen Ethelberga, from Bishop Boniface, servant of the servants of God.

'In His great providence, our loving Redeemer has offered a saving remedy to the human race, which He has saved from the Devil's enslaving tyranny by the shedding of His own precious Blood. Christ has made His Name known to the nations in various ways, so that they may acknowledge their Creator by accepting the mysteries of the Christian Faith. God in His mercy has revealed this truth to Your Majesty's own mind in your own mystical cleansing and regeneration. We have been greatly encouraged by God's goodness in granting you, through your own conversion, an opportunity to kindle a spark of the true religion in your husband, for in this way He will more swiftly inspire not only the mind of

your illustrious Consort to love of Him, but the minds of
your subjects as well.

'We have been informed by those who came to report the
laudable conversion of our glorious son King Eadbald, that
Your Majesty, who has also received the wonderful sacraments of the Christian Faith, shows a shining example of
good works, pleasing to God. We also know that you carefully shun idol-worship, and the temptations of temples and
fortune-tellers; and that, having given your allegiance to
Christ, you are unshakeably devoted to the love of our
Redeemer, and labour constantly to promote the Christian
Faith. Out of pastoral affection, we particularly enquired
about your illustrious husband, and learned that he still serves
abominable idols, and refuses to listen to the teaching of the
preachers. It has caused us deep grief to hear that your partner
remains a stranger to the knowledge of the most high and
undivided Trinity. Our paternal responsibility moves us to
urge Your Christian Majesty under God's guidance not to
avoid the duty always imposed on us, in order that, with the
assistance and strength of our Lord and Saviour Jesus Christ,
the King also may be added to the Christian fold. Only in
this way will you enjoy the full privileges of marriage in perfect union, for the Scripture says, " *The two shall become one
flesh.*" But how can it be called a true union between you, so
long as he remains alienated from your glorious Faith by the
barrier of dark and lamentable error?

'Let it therefore be your constant prayer that God of His
mercy will bless and enlighten the King, so that you, who are
united in earthly marriage, may after this life remain united
for ever in the bond of faith. My illustrious daughter, persevere in using every effort to soften his heart by teaching him
the laws of God. Help him to understand the excellence of
the mystery which you have accepted and believe, and the
wonderful reward that you have been accounted worthy to
receive in this new birth. Melt the coldness of his heart by
teaching him about the Holy Spirit, so that the warmth of

divine faith may enlighten his mind through your constant encouragement, and remove the chilling and ruinous errors of paganism. If you do this, the witness of the Holy Spirit will most certainly be fulfilled in you, that "*the unbelieving husband shall be saved through the believing wife.*" For you have received our Lord's merciful goodness in order that you may develop and increase the fruits of faith, and the boundless blessings entrusted you by your Redeemer. We shall not cease from constant prayer that God will assist and guide you to accomplish this.

'Having mentioned this matter, as fatherly duty and affection demands, we beg you to inform us, as soon as a suitable messenger is available, what measure of success God's goodness grants you in the conversion of your husband and the people over whom you reign. Good news will greatly relieve our mind, which anxiously awaits the longed-for salvation of you and yours. And when we see the glory of God's redemption spreading ever more widely among you, we shall give glad and heartfelt thanks to God the Giver of all good things, and to blessed Peter, Prince of the Apostles.

'We impart to you the blessing of your protector, the holy Peter, Prince of the Apostles, and we send you a silver mirror, together with a gold and ivory comb, asking Your Majesty to accept them with the same kindly feelings as those with which we send them.'

CHAPTER 12: *King Edwin is moved to accept the Faith by a vision seen during his exile* [A.D. 625]

SUCH was the letter written by Pope Boniface on the salvation of King Edwin and his people. But the principal factor influencing the king to study and accept the truths of salvation was a heavenly vision which God in his mercy had once granted the king when he was an exile at the court of Redwald, King of the Angles. For although Paulinus found

it difficult to bring the king's proud mind to accept the
humility of the way of salvation, or to acknowledge the mystery of the life-giving Cross, he nevertheless continued to
preach the word among the people, and to implore God's
mercy to bring about the conversion of the king and his
nation. It appears that at length the nature of the king's
earlier vision was revealed to Paulinus, and he immediately
urged the king to implement the promise that he had made
at the time of the vision, and which he had undertaken to fulfil should he be delivered out of his troubles and ascend the
throne of the kingdom.

Now the vision was this. When his predecessor was per-
secuting him, Edwin wandered as an unknown fugitive for
many years through many lands and kingdoms, until at
length he came to Redwald, and asked him for protection
against the plots of his powerful enemy. Redwald gave him a
ready welcome, and promised to do everything he asked, but
as soon as Ethelfrid heard that he had arrived in that province,
and that he and his companions were living at the king's
court as his friends, he sent messengers to offer Redwald a
large sum of money to murder him. Obtaining no satisfaction, he sent a second and third time, offering even heavier
bribes, and threatening war if his demand were refused. At
length Redwald, either intimidated by his threats or corrupted by his bribes, agreed to his demand and promised
either to kill Edwin, or to surrender him to Ethelfrid's messengers. This plot was discovered by a loyal friend of Edwin,
who went to his room early one night when he was about to
retire, and calling him out, warned him of the king's wicked
intentions, adding: 'If you are willing, I will act as your guide
out of this province, and take you immediately to some place
where neither Redwald nor Ethelfrid can find you.' Edwin
replied: 'Thank you for your goodwill, but I cannot act as you
suggest. I cannot break the agreement that I have made with
so great a king, who has so far done me no harm, nor showed
any hostility towards me. If I must die, I would rather die by

his hand than by an hand less noble. For what refuge remains
for me, who have already wandered for so many years in
every corner of Britain, trying to escape the hatred of my
enemies?' When his friend had left, Edwin remained, sitting
sadly alone outside the palace, burdened with many gloomy
thoughts, and not knowing what to do, or where to turn.

He had remained a considerable time in silence, grieving
and desperate, when suddenly, at dead of night, he saw a
man approaching whose face and clothes were strange to
him, and whose unexpected arrival caused him considerable
alarm. But the stranger came up and greeted him, asking
why he was sitting sadly on a stone, watchful and alone, at an
hour when everyone else was asleep. Edwin asked what concern it might be of his whether he passed the night indoors or
outside. In reply, the man said: 'Don't think that I am unaware why you are sad and sleepless and why you are keeping
watch alone. I know very well who you are, what your
troubles are, and what coming evils you dread. But tell me
this: what reward will you give the man who can deliver you
from your troubles, and persuade Redwald not to harm you
or betray you to death at the hands of your enemies?' Edwin
answered that he would give any reward in his power in
return for such an outstanding service. Then the other went
on: 'And what if he also promised that you should become
king, defeat your enemies, and enjoy greater power than any
of your predecessors who have ever ruled the English nation?'
Heartened by these enquiries, Edwin readily promised that,
in return for such blessings, he would give ample proofs of
his gratitude. The stranger then asked a third question. 'If the
man who can truthfully foretell such good fortune can also
give you better and wiser guidance for your life and salvation
than anything known to your parents and kinsfolk, will you
promise to obey and follow his salutary advice?' Edwin at
once promised that he would faithfully follow the guidance
of anyone who could save him out of so many troubles and
raise him to a throne. On this assurance, the man who

addressed him laid his right hand on Edwin's head, saying: 'When you receive this sign, remember this occasion and our conversation, and do not delay the fulfilment of your promise.' Hereupon, it is said, he vanished, and Edwin realized that it was not a man but a spirit who had appeared to him.

The young prince was still sitting there alone, greatly heartened by what he had heard, and puzzling over the identity and origin of the being who had talked with him, when his loyal friend approached with a cheerful greeting, and said: 'Get up and come inside. You can now sleep without fear, for the king has had a change of heart. He now intends you no harm, and will keep the promise that he made you. For when he privately told the queen of his intention to deal with you as I warned, she dissuaded him, saying that it was unworthy in a great king to sell his best friend for gold, and worse still to sacrifice his royal honour, the most valuable of all possessions, for love of money.' In brief, the king did as she advised, and not only refused to surrender the exiled prince to the envoys of his enemy, but assisted him to recover his kingdom. As soon as the envoys had left, he raised a great army to make war on Ethelfrid, who met him with a much smaller force – Redwald allowing him no time to summon his full strength – and was killed on the east bank of the river Idle. In this battle Regnhere, son of Redwald, was killed. So Edwin, as his vision had foretold, not only escaped the plots of his enemy, but succeeded to his throne at his death.

While king Edwin hesitated to accept the word of God at Paulinus' preaching, he used to sit alone for hours, deliberating what he should do, and what religion he should follow. On one of these occasions, the man of God came to him, and laying his right hand on his head, enquired whether he remembered this sign. The king trembled, and would have fallen at his feet, but Paulinus raised him, and said in a friendly voice: 'God has helped you to escape from the hands of the enemies whom you feared, and it is through His bounty that you have received the kingdom that you desired. Remember

the third promise that you made, and hesitate no longer.
Accept the Faith and keep the commands of Him who has
delivered you from all your earthly troubles, and raised you
to the glory of an earthly kingdom. If you will henceforward
obey His will, which he reveals to you through me, he will
save you from the everlasting doom of the wicked, and give
you a place in His eternal kingdom in heaven.'

CHAPTER 13: *Edwin holds a council with his chief men about
accepting the Faith of Christ. The high priest destroys his
own altars* [A.D. 627]

WHEN Paulinus had spoken, the king answered that he
was both willing and obliged to accept the Faith
which he taught, but said that he must discuss the matter
with his principal advisers and friends,* so that if they were
in agreement, they might all be cleansed together in Christ
the Fount of Life. Paulinus agreed, and the king kept his
promise. He summoned a council of the wise men, and asked
each in turn his opinion of this new faith and new God being
proclaimed.

Coifi, the High Priest, replied without hesitation: 'Your
Majesty, let us give careful consideration to this new teaching, for I frankly admit that, in my experience, the religion
that we have hitherto professed seems valueless and powerless. None of your subjects has been more devoted to the
service of the gods than myself, yet there are many to whom
you show greater favour, who receive greater honours, and
who are more successful in all their undertakings. Now, if
the gods had any power, they would surely have favoured
myself, who have been more zealous in their service. Therefore, if on examination these new teachings are found to be
better and more effectual, let us not hesitate to accept them.'

Another of the king's chief men signified his agreement
with this prudent argument, and went on to say: 'Your
Majesty, when we compare the present life of man with that

time of which we have no knowledge, it seems to me like the swift flight of a lone sparrow through the banqueting-hall where you sit in the winter months to dine with your thanes and counsellors. Inside there is a comforting fire to warm the room; outside, the wintry storms of snow and rain are raging. This sparrow flies swiftly in through one door of the hall, and out through another. While he is inside, he is safe from the winter storms; but after a few moments of comfort, he vanishes from sight into the darkness whence he came. Similarly, man appears on earth for a little while, but we know nothing of what went before this life, and what follows. Therefore if this new teaching can reveal any more certain knowledge, it seems only right that we should follow it.' The other elders and counsellors of the king, under God's guidance, gave the same advice.

Coifi then added that he wished to hear Paulinus' teaching about God in greater detail; and when, at the king's bidding, this had been given, the High Priest said: 'I have long realized that there is nothing in what we worshipped, for the more diligently I sought after truth in our religion, the less I found. I now publicly confess that this teaching clearly reveals truths that will afford us the blessings of life, salvation, and eternal happiness. Therefore, Your Majesty, I submit that the temples and altars that we have dedicated to no advantage be immediately desecrated and burned.' In short, the king granted blessed Paulinus full permission to preach, renounced idolatry, and professed his acceptance of the Faith of Christ. And when he asked the High Priest who should be the first to profane the altars and shrines of the idols, together with the enclosures that surrounded them, Coifi replied: 'I will do this myself, for now that the true God has granted me knowledge, who more suitably than I can set a public example, and destroy the idols that I worshipped in ignorance?' So he formally renounced his empty superstitions, and asked the king to give him arms and a stallion – for hitherto it had not been lawful for the High Priest to carry arms, or to ride anything but a mare – and, thus equipped, he set out to destroy the idols. Girded with a sword and with a spear in his hand, he mounted the king's stallion and rode up to the idols. When the crowd saw him, they thought he had gone mad, but without hesitation, as soon as he reached the temple, he cast a spear into it and profaned it. Then, full of joy at his knowledge of the worship of the true God, he told his companions to set fire to the temple and its enclosures and destroy them. The site where these idols once stood is still shown, not far east of York, beyond the river Derwent, and is known as Goodmanham. Here it was that the High Priest, inspired by the true God, desecrated and destroyed the altars that he had himself dedicated.

CHAPTER 14: *Edwin and his people accept the Faith, and are baptized by Paulinus* [A.D. 627]

So King Edwin, with all the nobility and a large number of humbler folk, accepted the Faith and were washed in the cleansing waters of Baptism in the eleventh year of his reign, which was the year 627, and about one hundred and eighty years after the first arrival of the English in Britain. The king's Baptism took place at York on Easter Day, the 12th of April, in the church of Saint Peter the Apostle, which the king had built of timber* during the time of his instruction and preparation for Baptism, and in this city he established the see of his teacher and bishop Paulinus. Soon after his Baptism, at Paulinus' suggestion, he gave orders to build on the same site a larger and more noble stone basilica, which was to enclose his earlier little oratory. The foundations were laid, and the walls of a square church began to rise around this little oratory, but before they reached their appointed height, the dastardly assassination of the king left the work to be completed by Oswald his successor. Thenceforward for six years, until the close of Edwin's reign, Paulinus preached the word throughout the country with the king's full consent and approval, and as many as were predestined to eternal life believed and were baptized. Among these were Osfrid and Eadfrid, sons of King Edwin, who were both born to him in exile of Quenberga, daughter of Cearl, King of Mercia.

At a later date, other children of his by Queen Ethelberga were baptized; these included a son, Ethelhun; a daughter, Etheldryth; and another son, Wuscfrea. The two former died soon after their baptism, and were buried in the church at York. Iffi, son of Osfrid, was also baptized, and many others of noble and princely rank. Indeed, so great was the fervour of faith and desire for baptism among the people of Northumbria, that Paulinus is said to have accompanied the king and queen to the royal country-seat at Adgefrin,[1] and remained there thirty-six days constantly occupied in instructing and baptizing. During this period, he did nothing from dawn to dusk but proclaim Christ's saving message to the people, who gathered from all the surrounding villages and countryside; and when he had instructed them, he washed them in the cleansing waters of Baptism in the nearby River Glen.[2] This country-seat was abandoned by the later kings, who built another at a place called Melmin.

These events took place in the provinces of Bernicia and Deira, where Paulinus often stayed with the king and baptized in the River Swale, which flows near the village of Catterick; for hitherto it had not been possible to build any churches or chapels for Baptism in those parts. But a church was built at the royal country-seat of Campodunum;[3] but this, together with all the other buildings, was burned by the pagans who killed King Edwin, and later kings replaced this seat by another in the vicinity of Loidis.[4] The stone altar of this church survived the fire, and is preserved in the monastery that lies in Elmete[5] Wood, and is ruled by the most reverend priest and abbot Thridwulf.

1. Yeavering, in Glendale.   2. The river Bowment.
3. Possibly Doncaster.   4. Leeds.
5. Possibly Barwick in Elmete, West Riding.

S o great was Edwin's zeal for the true Faith that he per-suaded King Eorpwald, son of Redwald, King of the East Angles, to abandon his superstitious idolatry, and accept the Faith and Sacraments of Christ with his whole province. His father Redwald had in fact long before this received Christian Baptism in Kent, but to no good purpose; for on his return home, his wife and certain perverse advisers persuaded him to apostatize from the true Faith. So his last state was worse than the first, for, like the ancient Samaritans, he tried to serve both Christ and the ancient gods, and he had in the same temple an altar for the holy Sacrifice of Christ side by side with an altar on which victims were offered to devils. Aldwulf, king of that province, who lived into our own times, testifies that this temple was still standing in his day, and that he had seen it when a boy. This King Redwald was a man of noble descent but ignoble in his actions: he was son of Tytilus, and grandson of Offa, after whom all kings of the East Angles are called Uffings.

Not long after Eorpwald's acceptance of Christianity, he was killed by a pagan named Richbert, and for three years the province relapsed into heathendom, until Eorpwald's brother Sigbert ascended the throne. Sigbert was a devout Christian and a man of learning, who had been an exile in France during his brother's lifetime, and was there converted to the Christian Faith, so that when he began his reign, he laboured to bring about the conversion of his whole realm. In this enterprise he was nobly assisted by Bishop Felix, who came to Archbishop Honorius from Burgundy, where he had been brought up and ordained, and acquainted him with his desire to preach the word of life to the Angles. Nor did he fail in his purpose, for like a good farmer, he reaped a rich harvest of believers. He delivered the entire province from its age-old wickedness and sorrow, brought it to the Christian

Faith and way of life, and – as his own name signifies – guided it towards eternal happiness. His episcopal see was established at Dunwich, and after ruling the province as its bishop for seventeen years, he ended his days there in peace.

CHAPTER 16: *Paulinus preaches the Word of God in the Province of Lindsey. The reign of King Edwin* [A.D. 628]

PAULINUS also preached the word of God in the province of Lindsey, which lies immediately south of the Humber, and extends to the sea. His first convert was Blecca, Reeve of the city of Lincoln, with all his family. Here he built a beautiful stone church, which today, either through neglect or enemy damage, has lost its roof, although the walls are still standing. And each year miracles of healing occur in this place among those who seek it in faith. When Justus had departed to Christ, it was in this church that Paulinus consecrated Honorius as bishop in his stead, as I will describe in due course.

The priest Deda, abbot of the monastery of Parteney and a most reliable authority, when relating the story of the Faith in this province, told me that one of the oldest inhabitants had described to him how he and many others had been baptized by Paulinus in the presence of King Edwin, and how the ceremony took place at noon in the river Trent, close to the city which the English call Tiovulfingacestir.[1] He described Paulinus as a tall man having a slight stoop, with black hair, an ascetic face, and a venerable and majestic presence. In Paulinus' ministry he was assisted by the deacon James, a man of great energy and repute in Christ's Church, who lived until our own day.

In those parts of Britain under King Edwin's jurisdiction, the proverb still runs that a woman could carry her new-born babe across the island from sea to sea without any fear of harm. And such was the king's concern for the welfare of his

1. Possibly Southwell.

people, that in a number of places where he had noticed
clear springs adjacent to the highway, he ordered posts to
be erected with brass bowls hanging from them, so that
travellers could drink and refresh themselves. And so great
was the people's affection for him, and so great the awe in
which he was held, that no one presumed to use these bowls
for any other purpose. The king's dignity was highly respected throughout his realm, and whether in battle or on a
peaceful progress through city, town, and countryside in the
company of his thanes, the royal standard was always borne
before him. And whenever he passed through the streets on
foot, the standard known to the Romans as a *Tufa*,* and to
the English as a *Tuf*, was also carried in front of him.

CHAPTER 17: *Pope Honorius sends a letter of encouragement
to King Edwin, and the* pallium *to Paulinus* [A.D. 634]

AT this time, Honorius had succeeded Boniface as Bishop
of the apostolic see. Learning that the Northumbrian
people and their king had been converted to the Faith and
confession of Christ by the labours of Paulinus, he sent him
the *pallium*, and with it a letter of encouragement to King
Edwin, urging him with fatherly affection to ensure that his
people maintained and made progress in the true Faith that
they had received. This letter ran as follows:

'To his most excellent son, the most illustrious Edwin,
King of the English, from Bishop Honorius, servant of the
servants of God, Greeting.

'Your sincere Christian character, afire with ardent faith
in the worship of your Creator, has shone out far and wide.
It has been spoken of throughout the world, and has reaped
a rich harvest for your labours. For as a king, you live in harmony with the true teaching which you have received about
God your Maker, in which faith you worship Him, and so
far as human nature allows, serve Him with a sincere and
devout mind. And what more can we offer God than our

perseverance in doing good, our worship and confession of Him as Creator of the human race, and the willing fulfilment of our vows? Accordingly, most noble son, our paternal love rightly moves us to urge you to labour with vigilant mind and constant prayer to preserve yourself wholly in that state of grace to which God in His mercy has called you. He who has deigned to deliver you from all error, and led you to the knowledge of His Name, will thus also prepare a place for you in our heavenly home. Make a regular study of the writings of your teacher Gregory of apostolic memory, and constantly bear in mind the loving teaching which he so gladly gave for the benefit of your souls, so that his prayers may obtain an increase in your kingdom and people, and bring you blameless to Almighty God.

'We are glad to accede to your requests on behalf of your bishops without delay, and in so doing, we pay tribute to the sincerity of your own faith, which has often been most highly praised by the bearers of this letter. Accordingly, we have sent the *pallium* to each of the Metropolitans, Honorius and Paulinus, so that whenever either of them shall be summoned from this world to his Maker, the survivor may have our authority to appoint another bishop in his place. We grant this privilege not only out of regard for you, but also in the realization of the great and wide provinces that separate us, and we are willing to show our recognition of your devotion in all matters, and to accede to your pious wishes.

'May the grace of God preserve Your Majesty in safety.'

CHAPTER 18: *On succeeding Justus in the See of Canterbury, Honorius receives the* pallium *and a letter from Pope Honorius* [A.D. 627]

MEANWHILE, Archbishop Justus was taken up into the heavenly kingdom on November the tenth, and Honorius was elected to the see in his place. He therefore came to Paulinus to be consecrated, and meeting him at Lincoln, was there consecrated fifth successor to Augustine in the See of Canterbury. Pope Honorius sent him the *pallium* and a letter confirming the arrangement already made in his letter to King Edwin: namely, that on the death of either of the Archbishops of Canterbury or York, the survivor was to have authority to appoint a successor in place of the deceased archbishop, which privilege would obviate the necessity of a long sea and land journey to Rome for consecration. I have thought it proper to include the text of the letter in this history.

'HONORIUS, to his well-loved brother Honorius.

'Among the many good gifts which the mercy of our Redeemer has deigned to grant His servants, His generous love is never more evident than when He permits us to display our mutual love in brotherly converse, as it were face to face. For this blessing we constantly give thanks to His Divine Majesty, and earnestly pray that He will confirm your loving labours in preaching the Gospel with constant and lasting results, and that in following the rule of your master and patron the holy Gregory, you may bear much fruit; so, through your ministry, will God bless His Church with ever-increasing strength. The souls already won by you and your predecessors, beginning with the Lord Gregory, will be established and grow ever stronger in faith and good works, and in reverence and love for God. And in due time the promises of our Lord Jesus Christ will be fulfilled in you, and His voice summon you to eternal joy, saying: '*Come to Me, all who labour and are heavy-laden, and I will refresh you.*' And again, "*Well done, good and faithful servant; because you have been faithful over a few things, I will make you ruler over many things. Enter into the joy of your Lord.*" Our constant love urges us to offer you these words of encouragement, dearest brothers, and we shall not fail to grant any privileges that we think likely to benefit your churches.

'In response to your request and that of our son your king,

we hereby, in the name of blessed Peter, Prince of the Apostles, grant that whenever God's mercy shall summon either of you to Himself, the survivor shall have authority to appoint a bishop in his place. As proof of this authority we have sent to each of your Lordships the *pallium* to wear at such a consecration, so that our permission and direction may make it acceptable to God. The great expanses of land and sea that separate us make it necessary for us to grant you this authority, in order that no troubles may arise in your churches, and that the devotion of the people committed to your charge may be greatly deepened. God keep you in safety.

'Given the eleventh day of June, in the twenty-fourth year of the reign of our lord Heraclius Augustus, and the twenty-third after his consulship: and in the twenty-third year of his son Constantine, and the third after his consulship: and in the third year of the most illustrious Caesar Heraclius, his son: the seventh indiction: the year of our Lord 634.'

CHAPTER 19: *Pope Honorius, and later Pope John, write letters to the Scots about Easter and the Pelagian heresy*

[A.D. 634]

POPE HONORIUS also wrote to the Scots whom he learned to be in error about the observance of Easter, as I mentioned earlier. He earnestly warned them not to imagine that their little community, isolated at the uttermost ends of the earth, had a monopoly of wisdom over all the ancient and new churches throughout the world, and he asked them not to keep a different Easter, contrary to the paschal calculations and synodical decrees of all the bishops of the world.

Similarly John (IV), who succeeded Severinus, successor to Honorius, on his election to the pontificate, sent them authoritative and learned letters to correct this error, showing clearly how Easter Day falls between the fifteenth and

twenty-first days of the moon, as was proved at the Council
of Nicaea. In this letter he particularly warned them to beware of and suppress the heresy of Pelagius, which, he
learned, was reviving among them. The letter begins as
follows:

'To our well-beloved and holy Tomianus,* Columbanus,
Cromanus, Dimanus, and Baithanus, bishops: to Cromanus,
Hernianus, Laistranus, Scellanus, and Syenus, priests: to
Saranus and the other Scottish teachers and abbots. Greetings
from Hilarus, Arch-priest and Guardian (during its vacancy)
of the holy Apostolic See: John, (Pope-) elect in the Name
of God: John, First Secretary and Guardian of the holy
Apostolic See: and John, servant of God, Counsellor of the
Apostolic See.

'Certain letters addressed to Pope Severinus, of blessed
memory, remained unanswered at the time of his death.
Therefore lest any pressing matters should remain long un-
considered, we opened them, and learned that certain persons
in your province are attempting to revive a new heresy from
an old one, contrary to the orthodox faith, and that they
ignorantly refuse to observe our Easter on which Christ was
sacrificed, arguing that it should be observed with the
Hebrew Passover on the fourteenth day of the moon.'

From the beginning of this letter it is evident that this
heresy had arisen only in very recent times, and that the error
was restricted to a limited number of persons in the nation.
Having therefore explained the proper calculation of Easter,
they add this on Pelagianism:

'We learn that the pernicious Pelagian heresy has once
again revived among you, and we strongly urge you to expel
the venom of this wicked superstition from your minds. You
cannot be unaware that this detestable heresy has already
been condemned, for not only has it been suppressed these
two hundred years, but lies under our perpetual anathema.
We therefore beg you not to rake up the ashes of controver-
sies long since burned out, for who cannot but condemn the

insolent and impious assertion that man can live without sin of his own free will? In the first place, it is blasphemous folly to say that man is sinless, for no one can be sinless save the one Mediator between God and man, the Man Jesus Christ, who was conceived and born without sin. All other men are born in original sin, and bear unmistakeable evidence of Adam's fall, even when they are innocent of actual sin. For, as the prophet says, "*Behold, I was conceived in iniquity, and in sin did my mother conceive me.*"'

CHAPTER 20: *King Edwin is killed, and Paulinus returns to Kent, where he receives the Bishopric of Rochester* [A.D. 633]

THE glorious reign of Edwin over the English and Britons lasted seventeen years, during the last six of which he laboured for the kingdom of Christ. But the King Cadwalla* rebelled against him, supported by Penda, a warrior of the Mercian royal house, who ruled that nation with varying success for twenty-two years. In a fierce battle at Heathfield[1] on the twelfth of October 633, Edwin was killed, and his entire army destroyed or scattered. Prior to his death in this campaign, Osfrid, a young warrior, one of Edwin's sons, was also killed, while another son, Eadfrid, was compelled to surrender to Penda, who subsequently broke his promise and put him to death during the reign of Oswald.

At this time a terrible slaughter took place among the Northumbrian church and nation, the more horrible because it was carried out by two commanders in particular, one of whom was a pagan, and the other a barbarian more savage than any pagan. For Penda and all his Mercians were idol-worshippers, but Cadwalla, although he professed to call himself a Christian, was utterly barbarous in temperament and behaviour. He was set upon exterminating the entire English race in Britain, and spared neither women nor inno-

1. Hatfield, near Doncaster.

cent children, putting them all to horrible deaths with ruthless savagery, and continuously ravaging the whole country.
He had no respect for the newly established religion of
Christ, and even in our own days the Britons pay no respect
to the faith and religion of the English, and have no more
dealings with them than with the heathen. The head of King
Edwin was carried to York, and subsequently placed in the
church of the blessed Apostle Peter which he had begun to
build, but which his successor Oswald completed. It rested in
the porch dedicated to the holy Pope Gregory, from whose
disciples he had received the word of life.

As a result of this disaster, the affairs of Northumbria were
in such utter disorder that flight offered the sole hope of
safety. Paulinus took Queen Ethelberga, whom he had previously accompanied to the province, and returned by sea to
Kent, where he was most honourably received by Archbishop Honorius and King Eadbald. On his journey he was
escorted by Bassus, a gallant knight of King Edwin, and
brought with him Eanfleda, Edwin's daughter, and Wuscfrea
his son; also Iffi, son of Osfrid his son, whom his mother,
fearing Eadbald and Oswald, later sent over to Gaul to be
brought up by her friend, King Dagobert. The two children,
however, both died in infancy, and were buried in church
with the honour due to royal children and innocents in
Christ. Paulinus also brought away with him many precious
things belonging to King Edwin, among them a great cross
of gold and a golden chalice hallowed for the use of the altar.
These are still preserved and can be seen in the church at
Canterbury.

At this time, the church of Rochester was in great need of
a pastor, since Romanus its bishop, who had been sent by
Archbishop Justus to Pope Honorius as his representative,
had been drowned at sea off Italy. Therefore, at the request of
Archbishop Honorius and King Eadbald, Paulinus assumed
this charge, which he held until he departed to the kingdom
of heaven with the glorious fruit of his labours. He died in

the church, and left there the *pallium* that he had received from the Roman Pontiff.

Paulinus left behind his deacon James to care for the church of York. The latter was a holy churchman who remained a long time in that church, teaching and baptizing, and snatching much prey from the clutches of our old enemy the Devil. The village close to Catterick, where he usually lived, bears his name to this day. James had a wide knowledge of church music, and when peace was at length restored to the province and the number of believers increased, he began to teach many people to sing the music of the Church after the Uses of Rome and Canterbury. At last, old and *full of days* as the Scripture says, he went the way of his fathers.

BOOK THREE

CHAPTER 1: *King Edwin's immediate successors abandon their people's Faith and lose their kingdom: the most Christian King Oswald restores both* [A.D. 633]

AFTER Edwin's death in battle, the kingdom of Deira, to which his family belonged and where he began his reign, devolved upon Osric, son of Edwin's uncle Elfric, who had been baptized into the Christian Faith by Paulinus. But the kingdom of Bernicia – for the kingdom of Northumbria had anciently been divided into these two provinces – fell to Eanfrid, son of Ethelfrid, who claimed descent from the royal family of that province.

During the whole of Edwin's reign the sons of Ethelfrid his predecessor, together with many young nobles who had lived in exile among the Scots or Picts, were instructed in the teachings of the Scottish Church, and received the grace of Baptism. But on the death of their enemy Edwin, they received permission to return to their own land, and Eanfrid, as eldest son, inherited the crown of Bernicia. As soon as they had obtained control of their earthly kingdoms, however, both these kings apostatized from the faith of the kingdom of heaven which they had accepted, and reverted to the corruption and damnation of their former idolatry.

Not long afterwards they were justly punished, and met their death at the hands of the godless Cadwalla, king of the Britons. First of all, he slew Osric in the summer as the latter was rashly besieging him in a strong city, and making a sudden sally with his entire force, he caught Osric off his guard and destroyed him with his whole army. After this, for a full year, he ruled the Northumbrian provinces, not as a victorious king but as a savage tyrant, ravaging them with ghastly slaughter until at length he also destroyed Eanfrid, who had unwisely visited him to negotiate peace accompanied only by twelve picked soldiers. This year is regarded by all good men as wretched and disgraceful, not only on account of the apostasy of the English kings, but also because of the savage tyranny of the British king. Hence all who have recorded the events of this period have agreed to expunge the memory of these apostate kings, and to assign this year to the reign of their successor King Oswald, a man beloved of God. This king, after the death of his brother Eanfrid, advanced with an army small in numbers, but strong in the faith of Christ; and despite Cadwalla's vast forces, which he boasted of as irresistible, the infamous British leader was killed at a place known by the English as Denisesburn, that is, the Brook of Denis.

CHAPTER 2: *Before engaging the heathen in battle, King Oswald sets up a wooden cross: a young man is later healed by a portion of it, and innumerable other miracles take place*
[A.D. 635]

WHEN King Oswald was about to give battle to the heathen, he set up the sign of the holy cross, and kneeling down, asked God that He would grant his heavenly aid to those who trusted in Him in their dire need. It is told that, when the cross had been hurriedly made and a hole dug to receive it, the devout king with ardent faith took the cross and placed it in position, holding it upright with his own hands until the soldiers had thrown in the earth and it stood firm. Then he summoned his army with a loud shout, crying, 'Let us all kneel together, and ask the true and living God Almighty of His mercy to protect us from the arrogant savagery of our enemies, since He knows that we fight in a just cause to save our nation.' The whole army did as he ordered, and advancing against the enemy at the first light of dawn, won the victory that their faith deserved. At this spot where the king prayed innumerable miracles of healing have occurred, which serve as a reminder and testimony to the King's faith. Even to this day many folk take splinters of wood from this holy cross, which they put into water, and when any sick men or beasts drink of it or are sprinkled with it, they are at once restored to health.

The English call this place *Hefenfelth*, meaning 'the heavenly field', and this ancient name was a sure omen of events to come, when the heavenly sign was set up, a heavenly victory won, and heavenly wonders shown. It lies near the northern wall which the Romans built from sea to sea to protect Britain from the attacks of the barbarous peoples. The brothers of the church of Hagulstad,[1] which lies not far away, make a yearly pilgrimage here on the eve of the anniversary of Oswald's death in order to keep vigil for the benefit of his soul, to recite the psalter, and to offer the Holy Sacrifice for him at dawn. And since many people now make this pilgrimage, the brothers have recently built a church on the spot, which has made it doubly honoured and hallowed. This is very fitting, for it seems that there was no evidence of the Christian Faith, no church, and no altar in the whole of Bernicia until the new Christian leader Oswald, moved by his devotion to the Faith, set up the standard of the holy cross before giving battle to his relentless enemies.

I cannot help mentioning one of the many miracles that have taken place at the cross. A few years ago, one of the brothers of the church of Hagulstad named Bothelm, who is still living, was walking unwarily on the ice at night, when he suddenly fell and fractured an arm. He suffered such agonizing pain from it that he could not even raise his hand to his mouth, and hearing that another brother was going next day to the site of the cross, he begged him to bring back

1. Hexham.

a piece of its revered wood, saying that by this means he trusted that God would grant him healing. The brother carried out his request, and as he returned at night when the brothers were seated at their evening meal, he passed the sick man a portion of the old moss that grew on the surface of the cross. Being at table, the brother had nowhere to keep it, so he thrust it next his breast, and when he retired, forgot to take it out. But waking up in the middle of the night, he felt something cold at his side, and putting out his hand to feel what it was, found that his arm was whole and sound as if he had never suffered such great pain.

CHAPTER 3: *Oswald asks the Scots to send him a bishop: when Aidan arrives, he grants him the island of Lindisfarne as his episcopal see* [A.D. 635]

As soon as he became king, Oswald greatly wished that the people whom he ruled should receive the Christian Faith, which had proved so great a support to him in his struggles against the heathen. So he sent to the Scottish chiefs among whom he and his companions had received the sacrament of Baptism when in exile, asking them to send him a bishop who could bring the blessings of the Christian Faith to the English people, and administer the sacraments. His request was granted without delay, and they sent him Bishop Aidan, a man of outstanding gentleness, holiness, and moderation. He was zealous in God's cause, but deficient in knowledge, in that he kept Easter in accordance with the customs of his own nation, which, as I have observed, was between the fourteenth and twentieth days of the moon. For the northern provinces of the Scots and all the Picts observed these customs, believing that they were following the teachings of the holy and praiseworthy father Anatolius, although the true facts are evident to any scholar. But the Scots in the south of Ireland had already conformed to the injunctions of the Bishop of the apostolic see, and observed Easter at the canonical time.

On Aidan's arrival, the king appointed the island of Lindisfarne to be his see as he asked. As the tide ebbs and flows, this place is surrounded by sea twice a day like an island, and twice a day the sand dries and joins it to the mainland. The king always listened humbly and readily to Aidan's advice, and diligently set himself to establish and extend the Church of Christ throughout his kingdom. And while the bishop, who was not yet fluent in the English language, preached the Gospel, it was most delightful to see the king himself interpreting the word of God to his thanes and leaders; for he himself had obtained perfect command of the Scottish tongue during his long exile. Henceforward many Scots arrived daily in Britain, and proclaimed the word of God with great devotion in all the provinces under Oswald's rule, while those of them who were in priest's orders ministered the grace of Baptism to those who believed. Churches were built in several places, and the people flocked gladly to hear the word of God, while the king of his bounty gave money and lands to establish monasteries, and the English, both noble and simple, were instructed by their Scots teachers to observe a regular and disciplined life.

Most of those who came to preach were monks, Aidan himself being a monk of the island of Hii,[1] whose monastery was for a long time the principal monastery of nearly all the northern Scots and Picts, and exercised a widespread authority.* The island itself belongs to Britain, and is separated from the mainland only by a narrow strait; but the Picts living in that part of Britain gave it to the Scots monks long ago, because they received the Faith of Christ through their preaching.

1. Iona.

[A.D. 565]

IN the year of our Lord 565, when Justinian the Younger had succeeded Justinian and ruled as Emperor of Rome, a priest and abbot of outstanding life came from Ireland to preach the word of God in the provinces of the northern Picts, which are separated from those of the southern Picts by a range of steep and desolate mountains.[1]

The southern Picts, who live on this side of the mountains, are said to have abandoned the errors of idolatry long before this date, and had accepted the true Faith through the preaching of Bishop Ninian,* a most reverend and holy man of British race, who had been regularly instructed in the mysteries of the Christian Faith in Rome. Ninian's own episcopal see, named after Saint Martin, and famous for its stately church, is now used by the English, and it is here that his body and those of many saints lie at rest. The place belongs to the province of Bernicia, and is commonly known as *Candida Casa*, the White House, because he built the church of stone, which was unusual among the Britons.

Columba* arrived in Britain in the ninth year of the reign of the powerful Pictish king, Bridius, son of Meilochon (Mailcuin); he converted this island to the Faith of Christ by his preaching and example, and was granted the island of Iona on which to found a monastery. Iona is a small island, with an area of about five hides according to English reckoning, and his successors hold it to this day. It was here that Columba died and was buried at the age of seventy-seven, some thirty-two years after he had come into Britain to preach. Before he came to Britain, he had founded a noble monastery in Ireland known in the Scots language as *Dearmach*, the Field of Oaks,[2] because of the oak forest in which it stands. From both of these monasteries Columba's disciples

1. The Grampians.   2. Derry.

went out and founded many others in Britain and Ireland; but the monastery on the isle of Iona, where his body lies, remains the chief of them all.

Iona is always ruled by an abbot in priest's orders, to whose authority the whole province, including the bishops, is subject, contrary to the usual custom.* This practice was established by its first abbot Columba, who was not a bishop himself, but a priest and monk; his life and sayings are said to have been recorded in writing by his disciples. But whatever type of man he may have been, we know for certain that he left successors distinguished for their purity of life, their love of God, and their loyalty to the monastic rule. They followed doubtful rules in observing the great Feast of Easter, but being so isolated from the rest of the world, there was no one to acquaint them with the synodical decrees about the keeping of Easter; nevertheless, they diligently followed whatever pure and devout customs that they learned in the prophets, the Gospels, and the writings of the Apostles. They held to their own manner of keeping Easter for another 150 years, until the year of our Lord 715.

The most reverend and holy father, Bishop Egbert, an Englishman, who had spent many years of exile in Ireland for love of Christ, and was most learned in the scriptures, and long renowned for his holiness of life, then came and corrected their error, and they changed to the right canonical customs for observing Easter. This error was not, as some imagine, that they kept Easter on the fourteenth day of the moon as do the Jews, but on the Sunday of the wrong week. For as Christians they knew well that the Resurrection of our Lord took place on the first day after the Sabbath, and should always be kept on that day. But being barbarous and simple, they had not learned when this first day after the Sabbath, which is now called the Lord's Day, should occur. But they had not lost the fervent grace of charity, and were therefore worthy to learn the full truth in this matter, in accordance with the Apostle's promise, when he said: "*And if you err in any matter, God Himself will enlighten you.*' But I shall speak of this more fully in its proper place.

CHAPTER 5: *The Life of Bishop Aidan* [DIED A.D. 651]

WHILE the priest Segenius ruled as Abbot of Iona, Aidan was raised to the dignity of the episcopate, and was sent out from this island monastic community to preach the Faith of Christ to the English people. Among other evidences of holy life, he gave his clergy an inspiring example of self-discipline and continence, and the highest recommendation of his teaching to all was that he and his followers lived as they taught. He never sought or cared for any worldly possessions, and loved to give away to the poor whatever he received from kings or wealthy folk. Whether in town or country, he always travelled on foot unless compelled by necessity to ride, and whenever he met anyone, whether high or low, he stopped and spoke to them. If they were heathen, he urged them to be baptized; and if they were Christians, he strengthened their faith, and inspired them by word and deed to live a good life and to be generous to others.

His life is in marked contrast to the apathy of our own times, for all who accompanied him, whether monks or lay-folk, were required to meditate, that is, either to read the scriptures or to learn the Psalms. This was their daily occupation wherever they went, and if, as sometimes happened, he was invited to dine with the king, he went with one or two clerics, and when he had eaten sparingly, he left as soon as possible to read or pray with them. Many devout men and women of that day were inspired to follow his example, and adopted the practice of fasting until None on Wednesdays and Fridays throughout the year, except during the fifty days after Easter. If wealthy people did wrong, he never kept silent out of respect for their position, but corrected them outspokenly. Nor would he offer money to influential people, although he offered them food whenever he entertained them as host. But if the wealthy ever gave him gifts of money, he either distributed it for the needs of the poor, as I have mentioned, or else used it to ransom any who had unjustly been sold as slaves. Many of those whom he had ransomed in this way later became his disciples, and when they had been instructed and trained, he ordained them to the priesthood.

It is said that when King Oswald originally asked the Scots to send a bishop to teach the Faith of Christ to himself and his people, they sent him another man of a more austere disposition. Meeting with no success in his preaching to the English, who refused to listen to him, he returned home and reported to his superiors that he had been unable to teach anything to the nation to whom they had sent him because they were an uncivilized people of an obstinate and barbarous temperament. The Scots fathers therefore held a great conference to decide on the wisest course of action, for although they regretted that the preacher whom they had sent had not been acceptable to the English, they still wished to meet their desire for salvation. Then Aidan, who was present at the conference, said to the priest whose efforts had been unsuccessful: 'Brother, it seems to me that you were too severe on your ignorant hearers. You should have followed the practice of the Apostles, and begun by giving them the milk of simpler teaching, and gradually instructed them in the word of God until they were capable of greater perfection and able to follow the sublime precepts of Christ.' All who were at the conference paid close attention to all he said, and realized that here was a fit person to be made bishop and sent to instruct the ignorant and unbelieving, since he was particularly endowed with the grace of discretion, the mother of virtues. They therefore consecrated him bishop, and sent him to preach. Time was to show that Aidan was remarkable not only for discretion, but for many other virtues as well.

CHAPTER 6: *The wonderful devotion and piety of King Oswald*

HAVING been instructed in the Faith by Bishop Aidan, King Oswald and the English people under his rule not only learned to hope for the kingdom of heaven, which had been unknown to his ancestors, but was also granted by Almighty God, Creator of heaven and earth, a greater earthly kingdom than they enjoyed. For at length he brought under his sceptre all the kingdoms and provinces of Britain speaking the four languages of British, Pictish, Scottish, and English.

Although he wielded supreme power, Oswald was always wonderfully humble, kindly, and generous to the poor and strangers. The story is told how on the Feast of Easter one year, Oswald sat down to dine with Bishop Aidan. A silver dish of rich food was set before him, and Bishop Aidan had just raised his hand to bless the food when the servant who was appointed to relieve the needs of the poor came in suddenly and informed the king that a great crowd of needy folk were sitting in the road outside begging alms of the king. Oswald at once ordered his own food to be taken out to the poor, and the silver dish to be broken up and distributed among them. The bishop, who was sitting beside him, was deeply moved to see such generosity, and taking hold of the king's right hand, exclaimed, 'May this hand never perish.' Later events proved that his prayer was heard, for when Oswald was killed in battle, his hand and arm were severed from his body, and remain uncorrupted to this day. They are preserved as venerated relics in a silver casket at the church of Saint Peter in the royal city, which is called Bebba[1] after a former queen.

Through King Oswald's diplomacy the provinces of Deira and Bernicia, formerly hostile to each other, were peacefully united and became one people. Oswald was nephew to King Edwin by his sister Acha, and it is fitting that so great a

1. Bamburgh.

predecessor should have so worthy a man of his own blood
to maintain his religion and his throne.

CHAPTER 7: *The West Saxons accept the Faith through the
teaching of Birinus and his successors Agilbert and Leutherius* [A.D. 635]

DURING the reign of Cynegils, the West Saxons, anciently known as the Gewissae, accepted the Faith of
Christ through the preaching of Bishop Birinus. He had
come to Britain at the direction of Pope Honorius (I), having
promised the Pope that he would sow the seeds of our holy
Faith in the distant lands beyond the English dominions
where no other teacher had been before him. He was consecrated bishop by Asterius, Bishop of Genoa, at the Pope's
command; but when he had reached Britain and entered the
territory of the Gewissae, he found them completely heathen,
and decided that it would be better to begin to preach the
word of God among them rather than seek more distant
converts. He therefore evangelized that province, and when
he had instructed its king, he baptized him and his people. It
happened at the time that the most holy and victorious
Oswald was present, who greeted King Cynegils as he came
from the font, and offered him an alliance most acceptable
to God, taking him as his godson, and his daughter as wife.
The two kings gave Bishop Birinus the city of Dorcic[1] for
his episcopal see, and there he built and dedicated several
churches, and brought many people to God by his holy
labours. He also died and was buried there; and many years
later, when Hedda* was bishop, his body was translated to
Venta[2] and laid in the church of the blessed Apostles Peter
and Paul.

On the death of Cynegils, his son Cenwalh succeeded to
the throne, but refused to accept the Faith and sacraments of

1. Dorchester.   2. Winchester.

Christ. Not long afterwards he lost his kingdom, for he put away his wife, who was sister of Penda, King of Mercia, and took another woman. This led to war, and Cenwalh was driven out of his kingdom and took refuge with Anna, King of the East Angles. There he lived in exile for three years, during which he learned the Christian Faith and received Baptism. For Anna his host was a good man, and blessed with good and holy children, as I shall mention later.

When Cenwalh had been restored to his kingdom, there arrived in the province a bishop from Gaul named Agilbert, who had been studying the scriptures in Ireland for many years. This bishop came to the king, and voluntarily undertook to evangelize the country. Appreciating his learning and enthusiasm, the king asked him to accept an episcopal see and remain in the province as his chief bishop. Agilbert acceded to the king's request, and presided as bishop for many years. Later, however, the king, who understood only Saxon, grew tired of the bishop's foreign speech, and invited to the province a bishop of his own race called Wini, who had been consecrated in Gaul; and dividing his kingdom into two dioceses, he gave Wini the city of Venta – known by the Saxons as Wintancestir – as his see. This action gravely offended Agilbert, whom the king had not consulted in the matter, and he returned to Gaul, where he became Bishop of Paris and ended his days there at an advanced age. Not many years after Agilbert's departure from Britain, Wini was also driven from his bishopric by the king, and took refuge with Wulfhere, King of Mercia, to whom he offered money for the Bishopric of London, and held it till his death. So for a considerable time the province of the West Saxons remained without any bishop.

During this interval King Cenwalh, who had often lost large areas of his kingdom to his enemies, eventually remembered that as he had formerly been driven from his throne because of his infidelity and had been restored to it after his acceptance of the Christian Faith, so he was now justly deprived of God's protection because his kingdom had no bishop. He therefore sent messengers to Agilbert in Gaul, offering him satisfaction and requesting him to return to his bishopric. But Agilbert sent his regrets, and said that it was impossible for him to return, since he was now responsible for his own bishopric and city of Paris. But not wishing to appear unwilling to help, he sent in his place his nephew, the priest Leutherius,[1] who could be made bishop if the king were agreeable, recommending him as worthy of a bishopric. Both king and people welcomed Leutherius with honour, and asked Theodore, then Archbishop of Canterbury, to consecrate him their bishop. He was accordingly consecrated at Canterbury, and for many years wisely ruled the West Saxon see with the full support of the synod.

CHAPTER 8: *Earconbert, King of Kent, orders the destruction of idols. His daughter Earcongota and his kinswoman Ethelberga dedicate themselves to God as nuns* [A.D. 640]

IN the year of our Lord 640, King Eadbald of Kent departed this life, and his son Earconbert succeeded to the government of the realm, which he ruled most nobly for over twenty-four years. He was the first of the English kings to give orders for the complete abandonment and destruction of idols throughout his realm, and for the observance of the Lenten fast, enforcing his decrees by suitable penalties for disobedience. His daughter Earcongota, who shared her father's zeal, was a nun of outstanding virtue, who served God in a convent in Gaul founded by the noble Abbess Fara at a place called Brie:* for as yet there were few monasteries built in England,* and many who wished to enter conventual life went to France or Gaul for the purpose. Girls of noble family were also sent there for their education, or to be betrothed to their heavenly Bridegroom, especially to the

1. Lothere.

houses of Brie, Chelles, and Andelys; among such girls were
Saethryd, step-daughter of King Anna of East Anglia, just
mentioned, and Ethelberga his own daughter. Although
foreigners, both were of such merit that they became Abbesses
of Brie. Sexberga, Anna's eldest daughter, and wife to King
Earconbert of Kent, had a daughter called Earcongota, who
deserves especial mention.

To this day the people of the district tell stories of the wonderful deeds and miracles of the nun Earcongota, but I must
restrict myself to a brief account of her passing to the heavenly
kingdom. When she felt her death approaching, she visited
the cells of all the infirm servants of Christ, especially those
who were of a great age or were most esteemed for their
holiness of life, and humbly commending herself to their
prayers, she told them how she had received intimation of
her coming death. She told how, in a vision, she had seen a
company of men in white robes entering the monastery, and
when she asked them what they were looking for and what
they wanted, they replied: 'We have been sent to bring away
with us the golden coin that was once brought from Kent.'
And that very night, as dawn drew near, she left the darkness
of this world, and entered the light of heaven. Many brethren
of the monastery,* who lived in separate buildings, said that
they had clearly heard choirs of angels singing, and a sound
like that of a great throng entering the monastery. And when
they came out to discover what it might be, they saw a great
light coming down from heaven, which carried away the
holy soul of Earcongota, freed from the bonds of the body,
to the eternal joys of heaven. Other miracles are reported to
have taken place in the monastery that night; but these I
must leave to others to tell at length. The body of this venerable virgin and spouse of Christ was laid to rest in the church
of the blessed Protomartyr Saint Stephen, and three days
later it was decided to take up the stone slab covering the
grave, and replace the body in a tomb above ground level.
While this was taking place, a perfume of such fragrance rose

from below that it seemed to all the brethren and sisters standing round as though a store of balsam had been unsealed.

Ethelberga, aunt of Earcongota, also preserved the glory of the perpetual virginity beloved by God, and the extent of her holiness became even more apparent after her death. For while she was abbess she began the building of a church in honour of all the Apostles, in which she wished to be buried; but she died when the work was only half completed, and was buried within the church in a spot that she had chosen. After her death the brethren became wholly occupied in other matters, and the building of the church was discontinued for seven years, at the end of which interval they decided to abandon an undertaking that had proved too great for their resources, and to remove the abbess' bones to another church that was already completed and consecrated. When they opened the tomb, they found the body untouched by decay as it had been by the corruption of sinful desires. So having washed it, and clothed it in fresh garments, they removed it to the church of Saint Stephen the Martyr, whose feast-day is kept in the monastery with great splendour on the seventh of July.

CHAPTER 9: *Miraculous cures take place at the site of Oswald's death. A traveller's horse is cured, and a paralytic girl healed*

OSWALD, the most Christian king of Northumbria, reigned for nine years, if we include the fatal year made abhorrent by the callous impiety of the British king Cadwalla and the insane apostasy of the English kings (Osric and Eanfrid): for it has been generally agreed that the names of these apostates should be erased from the list of Christian kings, and the year of their reign ignored. At a later date, Oswald fell in battle at Maserfelth[1] against the heathen king

1. Maserfield.

and people of Mercia, who had also slain his predecessor
Edwin, his death taking place on the fifth of August 642,
when Oswald was thirty-eight years of age.

Oswald's great devotion and faith in God was made evident by the miracles that took place after his death. For at the
place where he was killed fighting for his country against the
heathen, sick men and beasts are healed to this day. Many
people took away earth from the place where his body fell,
and put it in water, from which sick folk who drank it received great benefit. This practice became so popular that as
the earth was gradually removed, a pit was left in which a
man could stand. But it is not to be wondered at that the sick
received healing at the place of his death, for during his lifetime he never failed to provide for the sick and needy, and
to give them alms and aid. Many miracles are reported as
having occurred at this spot, or by means of the earth taken
from it; but it will suffice to mention two, which have been
passed down from our forefathers.

Not long after Oswald's death, a man happened to be
riding near the place when his horse suddenly showed signs
of distress. It stopped and hung its head, foaming at the
mouth, and as its pains increased, it collapsed on the ground.
The rider dismounted, removed the saddle, and waited to
see whether the beast was going to die. At length, having
struggled in great pain for a considerable time, it rolled on to
the spot where the great king had died. Immediately the pain
ceased, and the horse stopped its wild struggles; then, as tired
beasts do, having rolled on its back, it got up completely
recovered, and began to graze. The traveller, an observant
man, concluded that the place where his horse was cured
must possess especial sanctity, and when he had marked it,
he mounted and rode on to the inn where he intended to
lodge. On his arrival he found a girl, the niece of the land-
lord, who had long suffered from paralysis; and when members of the household told him about the girl's disease, he
began to describe to them the place where his horse had been

cured. So they put the girl into a cart, took her to the place, and laid her down. Once there she fell asleep and, on awaking, she found herself restored to health. She asked for water, and washed her face; then she tidied her hair, adjusted her linen headgear, and returned home on foot in perfect health with those who had brought her.

CHAPTER 10: *How the earth from this place has power over fire*

ABOUT this time, a Briton is said to have been crossing the ground where this battle had been fought, and noticing that one spot was more green and beautiful than the rest of the field, he came to the conclusion that there could be no other explanation for this exceptional greenness, but that some person of greater sanctity than anyone else in the army had been slain there. So he took away some of the earth wrapped up in a linen cloth, thinking that it might have power to heal the sick; and proceeding on his journey, arrived that night at a village and entered a house where some neighbours were having a feast. He was welcomed by the owners of the house, and when he had hung the cloth containing the earth on a beam against the wall, he sat down to share their meal. They had sat eating and drinking for a long while around a blazing fire in the centre of the room, when sparks flew up into the roof of the house, which was made of wattles and thatch, and quickly burst into flame. When the fuddled revellers realized this, they rushed out of the burning house in terror, powerless to extinguish the blaze, so that the house burned down, and only the beam from which the earth hung remained whole and untouched by the flames. When they saw this miracle, they were all astonished, and after making careful enquiry, they found that the man had taken the earth from the place where Oswald's blood had been shed. These marvels were reported far and wide, and many folk began to

visit the place each day, and obtained healing for themselves
and their families.

CHAPTER 11: *A heavenly light appears all night over*
Oswald's tomb, and folk are healed from demonic possession

IT would not be right to omit mention of the favours and
miracles that were shown when Oswald's bones were discovered and translated into the church where they are now
enshrined. This took place through the devout interest of
Queen Osthryda of Mercia, daughter of his brother Oswy
who succeeded him on the throne, as I shall mention in due
course.

In the province of Lindsey there is a noble monastery called
Beardeneu[1] which was greatly loved, favoured, and enriched
by the queen and her husband Ethelred, who wished that the
honoured bones of her uncle should be reinterred there. But
when the waggon carrying the bones arrived towards evening at the abbey, the monks were reluctant to admit it, for
although they acknowledged Oswald's holiness, they were
influenced by old prejudices against him even after his death,
because he originally came from a different province, and
had ruled them as an alien king. So it came about that the
king's bones remained outside the gates all night, with a
large awning spread over the waggon in which they lay. But
a sign from heaven showed them that the bones should be
welcomed with respect by all the faithful, for throughout
the night a pillar of light shone skywards from the waggon,
and was seen by nearly all the inhabitants of the province of
Lindsey. Early next morning, therefore, the monks who had
previously refused to admit it, began to pray earnestly that
the holy relics so dear to God should find a resting-place in
the midst. Accordingly the bones were washed and laid in a
casket made for the purpose, which was placed in the church

1. Bardney Abbey, Lincs.

with fitting honour. And to furnish a lasting memorial of the royal saint, they hung the king's banner of purple and gold over his tomb. The water in which the bones had been washed was poured away in a corner of the cemetery, and from that time on the very earth that had received this venerated water had power to expel devils from the bodies of those who were possessed.

Some while later, when Queen Osthryda was staying in the monastery, the venerable Ethelhilda, abbess of a neighbouring house, visited her to pay her respects. This lady, who is still living, is sister of Bishop Ethelwin of Lindsey and of Abbot Aldwin of Bardney, which lies not far away. While she was talking with the queen, the conversation turned to Oswald, and the abbess told her how she had herself seen the light reaching heavenwards from Oswald's relics on that night. And the queen informed her how the dust from the pavement on which the water that had washed the bones had been spilt, had already healed many sick people. The abbess then asked that she might be given some of this healing dust; and when it had been given her, she tied it up in a cloth, and put it into a little casket which she took away with her. Some while later, a guest visited her abbey who was often horribly tormented by an evil spirit during the night hours. This man was hospitably welcomed, and had retired to bed after supper, when he was suddenly possessed by the devil, and began to cry out, grind his teeth, foam at the mouth, and toss his limbs in wild contortions. No one could hold or bind him, so the servant ran and knocked at the abbess' door to inform her. She opened the monastery gate herself, and went out with one of the nuns to the men's quarters, where she called one of the priests to accompany her to the sufferer. On their arrival, they found a crowd already present, none of whom had been able to control the man's wild convulsions. The priest therefore employed exorcisms, but all his efforts were useless. When there seemed no hope of easing his frenzy, the abbess suddenly remembered this dust, and told a servant to go at once and fetch the casket containing it. And as soon as she entered the porch of the house where the possessed man lay, he immediately became silent, laying down his head as though to sleep, and relaxing his whole body. Everyone present stood silent, watching closely to see the outcome of this affair; and after some while, the man who had been so tormented sat up with a deep sigh, saying: 'I am now restored to health, and in my right mind.' They eagerly asked him what had happened, and he replied: 'As soon as the nun carrying the casket approached the porch of the house, all the evil spirits who were tormenting me went away, and I have not seen them since.' Then the abbess gave him a portion of the dust, and after the priest had offered prayers, the man spent a quiet night, and was never again troubled by his old enemy.

CHAPTER 12: *A little boy is cured of ague at Saint Oswald's tomb*

SOME while after this, there was a little boy in the monastery who had been seriously troubled by ague. One day he was anxiously dreading an attack, when one of the brothers came in to him and said: 'My boy, shall I tell you how you may be cured of this complaint? Get up, and go to Oswald's tomb in the church. Remain there quietly and don't stir from it until the time that your fever is due to leave you. Then I will come and fetch you.' The boy did as the brother advised, and was completely free from fever while he sat by the saint's tomb: furthermore, it left him so entirely that it never recurred, either on the second or the third day, or ever after. A brother of that monastery who told me this story added that the boy who had been so miraculously cured is now a young man, and still lives in the monastery. But it need cause no surprise that the prayers of this king, who now reigns with God, should be acceptable to him, since when he was a king

on earth he always used to work and pray fervently for the
eternal kingdom.

It is said that Oswald often remained in prayer from the
early hour of Lauds until dawn, and that through his practice
of constant prayer and thanksgiving to God, he always sat
with his hands palm upwards on his knees. It is also said, and
has since become a proverb, that 'His life closed in prayer';
for when he saw the enemy forces surrounding him and
knew that his end was near, he prayed for the souls of his
soldiers, saying as he fell, 'God have mercy on their souls.'
As I have already mentioned, his bones were taken up and
buried in the Abbey of Bardney; but the king who slew him
ordered that his head, hands, and arms be hacked off and
fixed on stakes. The following year, Oswald's successor
Oswy came to the place with his army, and removed them,
placing the head in the church at Lindisfarne,* and the hands
and arms in his own royal city of Bamborough.

CHAPTER 13: *A man in Ireland is recalled from death's door
by means of Oswald's relics*

THE fame of the renowned Oswald was not confined to
Britain, for the rays of his beneficent light shone far
overseas, and reached Germany and Ireland. The most reverend Bishop Acca* tells how, on a journey to Rome, Bishop
Wilfrid and he stayed awhile with the most holy Willibrord,
now Archbishop of the Frisians, and how he heard him speak
of the miracles that had been done by the relics of the venerated king in his own province. Willibrord also told them that
when he was still a priest in Ireland, and living the life of a
pilgrim out of love for his heavenly home, stories of the
king's holiness were already current far and wide. I include
in this history one of the stories that he told.

'At the time of the great plague that swept Britain and
Ireland,' he said, 'one of its many victims was a scholar of

Scottish race, who was well read in literature, but utterly uninterested and careless in the matter of his eternal salvation. When he realized that his death was near, he began to fear that as soon as he died, his sins would drag him down to hell. As I was in the neighbourhood he sent for me, and said with tears in his voice, sighing and trembling: "You can see how this disease has tightened its hold and brought me to the point of death. I have no doubt that when I die, my soul will immediately be condemned to eternal death and endure all the torments of hell; for although I have made a great study of the scriptures, I have for a long time devoted myself to evil-doing rather than to keeping God's Commandments. But if God's mercy allows me to survive, I solemnly resolve to amend my evil ways, and will completely reform my outlook and way of life in submission to the will of God. I am fully aware that I do not deserve that my life be prolonged, nor can I expect it, unless it pleases God to pardon a wretched sinner through the intercession of those who have served Him faithfully. I have heard the well-known story of your most saintly King Oswald, whose wonderful faith and virtue have become renowned even after his death by the working of miracles. I therefore beg you, if you possess any of his relics, to bring them to me, and perhaps God will have pity on me for his sake." I told him: "I have a portion of the stake to which the king's head was fixed by the heathen after his death, and if you will make a sincere act of faith in God, He of His mercy and through the merits of this great saint may grant you a long term of earthly life, and render you fitted to enter into eternal life." The man then assured me that he had complete faith in Him. Then I blessed some water, and put in it a chip of this oak, and gave it to the sick man to drink. He quickly began to feel better, and having recovered from his illness, he lived many years after. He gave his heart and life entirely to God, and wherever he went he told of the mercy of our kind Creator, and the honour of His faithful servant Oswald.'

CHAPTER 14: *On the death of Paulinus, Ithamar succeeds to his Bishopric of Rochester. An account of the wonderful humility of King Oswin, who was treacherously murdered by Oswy* [A.D. 642–651]

WHEN Oswald departed to the kingdom of heaven, his brother Oswy, a young man of about thirty, succeeded to his earthly crown and ruled for twenty-eight troubled years. He was repeatedly attacked by the pagan king Penda and his Mercians, who had already killed his brother, and also by his own son Alfred and his nephew Ethelwald, son of his brother and predecessor. In the year of our Lord 644, the second year of Oswy's reign, the most reverend father Paulinus, formerly Bishop of York and subsequently Bishop of Rochester, died on the tenth of October, after an episcopate lasting nineteen years, two months, and twenty-one days. He was buried in the sacristy of the church of the blessed Apostle Saint Andrew, which had been founded and built in Rochester by King Ethelbert. In his place Archbishop Honorius consecrated Ithamar, a man of Kent, who was as worthy and learned as his predecessors.

During the first part of his reign, Oswy shared the royal dignity with Oswin, who came of Edwin's royal line, and was son of the above-mentioned Osric. This prince, who was a man of great holiness and piety, ruled the province of Deira most prosperously for seven years, and was deeply loved by all. But Oswy, who ruled the province of Bernicia, which included all the nation north of the Humber, would not live peaceably with him, and when their differences grew more acute, he most treacherously murdered him. For when the kings had raised armies against each other, Oswin realized that his opponent's forces were far stronger than his own, and decided not to risk an engagement, but to await a more favourable opportunity. So he disbanded the army that he had raised at Wilfaresdun, that is, Wilfar's Hill, ten miles north-west of the village of Cataract, and sent all his men to their homes. He himself, accompanied by a single trusted soldier named Tondhere, went back and lay concealed in the house of Earl Hunwald, whom he regarded as his greatest friend. Alas, it was far otherwise: for the earl betrayed Oswin and his man to Oswy, who, amid universal disgust, ordered his commander Ethelwin to put them both to death. This crime took place on the twentieth of August at Ingetlingum in the ninth year of his reign, and here, at a later date, in atonement for this crime, a monastery was built in which prayers were to be offered to God daily for the souls of the two kings, both slayer and slain alike.

King Oswin was a man of handsome appearance and great stature, pleasant in speech and courteous in manner. He was generous to high and low alike, and soon won the affection of everyone by his regal qualities of mind and body, so that nobles came from every province to serve him. But among his other especial endowments of virtue and moderation, the greatest was what one may describe as the singular blessing of humility, of which a single instance will be sufficient.

He had given Bishop Aidan a very fine horse, in order that he could ride whenever he had to cross a river or undertake any difficult or urgent journey, although the bishop ordinarily travelled on foot. Not long afterwards, when a poor man met the bishop and asked for alms, the bishop immediately dismounted and ordered the horse with all its royal trappings to be given to the beggar; for he was most compassionate, a protector of the poor and a father to the wretched. When this action came to the king's ears, he asked the bishop as they were going in to dine: 'My lord bishop, why did you give away the royal horse which was necessary for your own use? Have we not many less valuable horses of other kinds which would have been good enough for beggars, without giving away a horse that I had specially selected for your personal use?' The bishop at once answered, 'What are you saying, Your Majesty? Is this foal of a mare more valuable to you than this child of God?' At this they went in to dinner, and the bishop sat down in his place; but the king, who had come in from hunting, stood warming himself by the fire with his attendants. As he stood by the fire, the king turned over in his mind what the bishop had said; then suddenly unbuckling his sword and handing it to a servant, he impulsively knelt at the bishop's feet and begged his forgiveness, saying: 'I will not refer to this matter again, nor will I enquire how much of our money you give away to God's children.' The bishop was deeply moved, and raising him immediately, assured him of his high regard, begging him to sit down to his food without regrets. At the bishop's request, the king sat down and began to be merry, but Aidan on the contrary grew so sad that he began to shed tears. His chaplain asked him in his own language, which the king and his servants did not understand, why he wept. Aidan replied: 'I know that the king will not live very long, for I have never seen so humble a king as he. I feel that he will soon be taken from us, because this nation is not worthy of such a king.' Not very long afterwards, as I have related, the bishop's foreboding was borne out by the king's death. And Bishop Aidan himself was taken from this world only twelve days after his beloved king, and received the eternal reward of his labours from our Lord on the thirty-first of August 651.

CHAPTER 15: *Bishop Aidan foretells a coming storm, and gives seafarers holy oil to calm the waves* [*c.* A.D. 651]

ALMIGHTY God made known the greatness of Aidan's merits by the evidence of miracles, of which it must suffice to mention three in his memory. A priest named Utta, a truthful and serious man, who was generally respected by all, even by worldly princes, was sent to Kent to bring back Eanfleda as wife for King Oswy: she was the daughter of King Edwin, and had been taken to Kent when her father was killed. Intending to make the outward journey by land

and to return with the princess by sea, he went to Bishop Aidan and asked him to pray for him and his companions as they set out on their long journey. When Aidan had blessed them and commended them to God, he gave them some holy oil, saying: 'When you set sail, you will encounter a storm and contrary winds. Remember then to pour the oil that I am giving you on to the sea, and the wind will immediately drop, giving you a pleasant, calm voyage and a safe return home.' Everything happened as the bishop foretold. In a rising gale, the sailors dropped anchor, hoping to ride out the storm. This proved impossible, for roaring seas broke into the ship from every side, and it began to fill. Everyone felt that his last hour had come, when at last the priest remembered the bishop's words. He took out the flask of oil, and poured some of it over the sea, which immediately ceased its raging as Aidan had foretold. So it came about that the man of God through the spirit of prophecy, although absent, both foretold the storm and calmed its fury. The story of this miracle is no groundless fable, for it was related to me by Cynemund, a most faithful priest of our own church (Jarrow), who had it from the mouth of the priest Utta, on and through whom the miracle was performed.

CHAPTER 16: *Aidan's prayers save the royal city when fired by the enemy* [A.D. 651]

ANOTHER notable miracle of the same father Aidan is told by those in a position to know the facts. While he was bishop, Penda and his enemy army of Mercians spread ruin far and wide throughout Northumbria and reached the very gates of the royal city, which takes its name from Bebba, a former queen. Unable to enter it either by force or after a lengthy siege, Penda attempted to set fire to it. Pulling down all the neighbouring villages, he carried to Bamborough a vast quantity of beams, rafters, partitions, brushwood, and thatch, piling it high around the city wall on the landward side. Directly the wind became favourable, he set fire to this mass, intending to destroy the city. Now while all this was happening, the most reverend Bishop Aidan was living on Farne Island, which lies nearly two miles from the city, and which was his retreat when he wished to pray alone and un-disturbed: indeed, his lonely hermitage can be seen there to this day. When the saint saw the column of smoke and flame rising above the city walls, he is said to have raised his eyes and hands to heaven, saying with grief: 'Lord, see what evil Penda does!' No sooner had he spoken than the wind shifted away from the city, and drove back the flames on to those who had kindled them, so injuring and unnerving them that they abandoned their assault on a city so clearly under God's protection.

CHAPTER 17: *The wooden buttress of the Church against which Aidan leaned as he died is untouched when the rest of the Church is burned down. His spiritual life* [A.D. 651]

DEATH came to Aidan in the sixteenth year of his episco-pate when he was staying at the king's country-house near the capital. Having a church and lodging there, Aidan often used to go and stay at the place, travelling about the surrounding countryside to preach. This was his practice at all the king's country-seats, for he had no personal possessions except his church and a few fields around it. When he fell ill, a tent was erected for him against the west wall of the church, and so it happened that as he drew his last breath, he was leaning against a post that strengthened the outer wall. He passed away on the last day of August, in the seventeenth year of his episcopate, and his body was soon taken across to Lindisfarne Island, and buried in the monks' cemetery. When a larger church, dedicated to the most blessed Prince of the Apostles, was built there some while later, his bones were transferred to it and buried at the right side of the altar in accordance with the honours due to so great a prelate.

Finan, who had also come from the Scottish island of Iona, succeeded him as bishop and held the office for a considerable time. Some years later, Penda, King of Mercia, came and destroyed everything that he found with fire and sword, and he burned down the village and the church where Aidan had died. But, in a wonderful manner, the beam against which he was leaning at his death was the only object untouched by the flames which destroyed everything around it. This miracle was noticed and a church was soon rebuilt on the same site, with the beam supporting the exterior of the structure as before. In a subsequent fire caused by carelessness, the village and church were again destroyed, but even on this occasion the beam remained undamaged. For although the flames licked through the very holes of the pins that secured it to the building in a most extraordinary way, they could not destroy the beam. When the church was rebuilt for the third time, the beam was not employed as an outside support again, but was set up inside the church as a memorial of this miracle, and those who entered used to kneel there and ask God's mercy. Since that day many are known to have obtained the grace of healing at this spot, and many have cut chips of wood from the beam and put them in water, by which means many have been cured of their diseases.

I have dealt at length with the character and life of Aidan, although one cannot commend or approve his inadequate knowledge of the proper observance of Easter; indeed, as I have made clear in my book on the seasons, I strongly disapprove of these practices. None the less, as an impartial historian, I have given an accurate account of his life, commending all that was excellent, and preserving his memory for the benefit of my readers. He cultivated peace and love, purity and humility; he was above anger and greed, and despised pride and conceit; he set himself to keep and to teach the laws of God, and was diligent in study and prayer. He used his priestly authority to check the proud and powerful; he tenderly comforted the sick; he relieved and protected the poor. To sum up in brief what I have learned from those who knew him, he took pains never to neglect anything that he had learned from the writings of the apostles and prophets, and he set himself to carry them out with all his powers.

I greatly admire all these things about Aidan, but I cannot approve or commend his failure to observe Easter at the proper time, whether he did it through ignorance of the canonical times, or in deference to the customs of his own nation. But this in him I do approve, that in all that he believed, worshipped, and taught, his whole purpose was identical with our own, namely the redemption of the human race through the Passion, Resurrection, and Ascension into heaven of the Man Jesus Christ, the Mediator between God and man. He always kept Easter, not as some mistakenly suppose, on the fourteenth moon whatever the day was, as the Jews do, but on the Lord's Day falling between the fourteenth and twentieth days of the moon. He did so because he held that the Resurrection of our Lord took place on the day following the Sabbath, and because, like the rest of Holy Church, he rightly expected our own resurrection to take place on the same day after the Sabbath, which we now call the Lord's Day.

CHAPTER 18: *The life and death of the devout King Sigbert*

[A.D. 635]

AFTER the death of Earpwald, successor to Redwald, the kingdom of East Anglia was ruled by his brother Sigbert, a good and religious man who had been baptized long previously in Gaul while he had been living in exile to escape the hostility of Redwald. When he returned home and became king, he wished to follow the excellent customs of Gaul, and he founded a school for the education of boys.* In this project he was assisted by Bishop Felix who had come to him from Kent, and had provided him with teachers and masters from the school at Canterbury.

King Sigbert became so ardent in his love for the kingdom of heaven that he abandoned the affairs of the kingdom, and entrusted them to his kinsman Ecgric, who had already governed part of the kingdom. He then entered a monastery* that he had founded, and after receiving the tonsure, devoted his energies to winning an everlasting kingdom. A considerable while later, King Penda of Mercia attacked the East Angles who, finding themselves less experienced in warfare than their enemies, asked Sigbert to go into battle with them and foster the morale of the fighting men. When he refused, they dragged him out of the monastery regardless of his protests, and took him into battle with them in the hope that their men would be less likely to panic or think of flight if they were under the eye of one who had once been a gallant and distinguished commander. But mindful of his monastic vows, Sigbert refused to carry anything more than a stick while protected by a well-equipped army, and when the heathen charged, both he and King Ecgric were killed and the army scattered.

These kings were succeeded by Anna son of Eni, an excellent man of royal stock, and father of a distinguished family, of whom I shall give an account in due course. Anna also was later killed by the same pagan king of the Mercians who had slain his predecessors.

CHAPTER 19: *Fursey establishes a monastery in East Anglia: the incorruption of his body after death attests to his visions and holiness* [A.D. 633]

DURING Sigbert's reign there came from Ireland a holy man named Fursey, renowned for his words and doings, and outstanding in virtue. He had made a vow to spend his life as a pilgrim for love of our Lord, and to go wherever God should call him. On his arrival in the province of the East Angles, he was honourably received by the king, and preached the Gospel as he always did. Inspired by the example of his goodness and the effectiveness of his teaching, many unbelievers were converted to Christ, and those who already believed were drawn to greater love and faith in him.

Once when he was ill, God granted Fursey to enjoy a vision, in which he was directed to continue his diligent preaching of the word, and to maintain his accustomed vigils and prayers with indefatigable zeal; for although death is certain, its coming is unpredictable, as our Lord says: '*Be watchful, for you know neither the day nor the hour.*' Stimulated by this vision, Fursey set himself with all speed to build a monastery on a site given him by King Sigbert, and to establish a regular observance in it. This monastery was pleasantly situated in some woods close to the sea, within the grounds of a castle that the English call Cnobheresburg,* meaning Cnobhere's Town. Subsequently, Anna, king of the province, and his nobles endowed the house with finer buildings and gifts.

Fursey was of noble Irish blood, and even more noble in mind than in birth, for from his boyhood he had not only read sacred books and observed monastic discipline, but as is fitting in saints, had also diligently practised all that he learned.

In short, he built a monastery in order to devote himself more freely to sacred studies. There, as the book on his life informs us, he fell ill and entered a trance; and quitting his body from sunset to cockcrow, was privileged to see the choirs of angels, and to hear the songs of the blessed. He used to say that, among other things, he clearly heard them sing: '*The saints shall go from strength to strength*', and '*The God of gods shall be seen in Sion.*' Then he returned to bodily consciousness, but three days later he was again withdrawn from it, and saw not only the great joys of the blessed, but the amazing struggles of evil spirits, who vainly fought to prevent his approach to heaven by constant wicked accusations: nevertheless, under the protection of the angels, he reached his goal. And if any one wishes to learn about these experiences in greater detail, let him read the above-mentioned little book on his life, and I think that he will reap great benefit from it. It describes the deceitful cunning with which the devils misrepresented his actions, words, and even thoughts, as though they were recorded in a book; and it tells of the joyful and sorrowful things that he learned both from the angels and from the saints who appeared among the angels.

I have, however, recorded one happening in this history which may be helpful to many. When Fursey had been carried up to a great height, he was told by his angel guides to look back at the world. As he looked down, he saw what appeared to be a gloomy valley beneath him, and four fires in the air, not far from one another. Asking what these were, the angels told him that they were the fires which were to burn and consume the world. 'One of them is Falsehood, when we do not renounce Satan and all his works as we promised at our Baptism. The next is Covetousness, when we put the love of worldly wealth before the love of God. The third is Discord, when we needlessly offend our neighbours, even in small matters. The fourth is Injustice, when we think it no crime to rob and defraud the weak.' These fires gradually grew together and merged into one vast conflagration, so that Fursey in alarm cried to the angel: 'Master, the fire is coming near me!' To which the angel replied: 'It will not burn you because you did not kindle it; for although it appears as a great and terrible fire, it tests everyone according to his deserts, and will burn away his sinful desires. For every man's body is consumed by unlawful desire, and when death frees him from the body, he must make due atonement for his sins by fire.' Then he saw one of the three angels who had been his guides in both his visions go forward and divide the flames, while the other two flew on each side of him to protect him from harm. He also saw

devils, who flew through the flames stirring up the fires of
war against the just. These evil spirits made accusations
against him, while the good spirits spoke in his defence.
Fursey also saw a greater vision of the heavenly hosts, and of
the saints of his own nation who had once worthily adorned
the dignity of priesthood, and from them he learned many
things of spiritual benefit both to himself and to those who
were ready to listen. And when they had ended speaking and
returned to heaven with the other angelic spirits, there
remained with Fursey the three angels who were to restore
him to his body. As they approached the great fire, the angel
divided the flames as before for him to pass. But when the
man of God came to the passage opened among the flames,
wicked spirits seized one of those whom they had been tormenting in the fire, and thrust him against Fursey, who was
burned on his shoulder and jaw. He recognized this man, and
remembered that he had received some of his clothing when
he died. And when the holy angel quickly took the man and
cast him back into the flames, the malicious devil said: 'Don't
reject one of your own friends, for since you accepted the
property of a sinner, you must share his punishment.' But
the angel defended Fursey, saying: 'He did not accept them
out of greed, but in order to save his soul.' The fire then died
down, and the angel turned to Fursey, saying: 'You lit this
fire, so you were burned: had you not accepted money from
one who died in his sins, you would not have shared his punishment.' And he went on to tell Fursey what should be done
for the salvation of those who repented on their death-bed.
And when Fursey had been restored to his body, he found
that the burn that he had received in his soul had left a permanent and visible scar on his shoulder and jaw, and in this
strange way his body afforded visible evidence of the inward
sufferings of his soul. He continued to set an example of virtue to others in his life and teaching as before, but he would
only relate his visions to those who were moved by penitence
to ask him. An old brother of our monastery, who is still

living, testifies that he once knew a truthful and devout man who had met Fursey in the province of East Anglia, and heard of these visions from his own mouth. He added that although it was a frosty and bitter winter's day, Fursey wore only a thin garment, and as he told his story, he was sweating profusely as though it had been summer, either because of the consolation or terror of his recollections.

To return to my original narrative, when Fursey had preached the word of God among the Irish for many years, he could no longer endure the crowds that thronged him. So he abandoned everything he possessed, and leaving his native island with a few companions, crossed into Britain to the province of the East Angles, where he preached the word of God and built the above-mentioned noble monastery. Having done this with success, he began to long to be rid of all worldly business, even of the affairs of the monastery; and having entrusted the care of souls to his brother Fullan and the priests Gobban and Dicul, he freed himself of all worldly responsibilities, and resolved to end his life as a hermit. Now Fursey had another brother named Ultan, who after many years in a monastery, had adopted the life of a hermit. So Fursey sought him out alone, and for a year shared his life of prayer and austerity, supporting himself by daily manual labour.

At this period, the province was again distressed by the attacks of the heathen, and Fursey, foreseeing that the monastery would be endangered, set his affairs in order and sailed over to Gaul, where he was honourably received by King Clovis (II) and his chamberlain Earconwald, and built a monastery at Latiniacum.* Not long afterwards, when he fell sick and died, the noble Earconwald took his body and placed it in the porch of a church he was building in his home-town of Peronne, until the church itself should be conse-crated. This took place twenty-seven days later, and when the body was taken from the porch to be buried near the altar, it was found to be as free from decay as on the day of his death. Four years later a more suitable chapel was built for his resting-place to the east of the altar, and his still uncorrupt body was transferred to it with great honour. In this chapel God has granted many miracles as evidence of the saint's merits. I have briefly recorded these events and the incorruption of his body, so that the reader may understand more clearly how great a man Fursey was. But he will find a fuller account of Fursey and his companions in the book on his life which I have mentioned.

CHAPTER 20: *On the death of Honorius, Deusdedit succeeds him as Archbishop of Canterbury. The succession of the bishops of East Anglia and Rochester* [A.D. 653]

MEANWHILE Felix, Bishop of the East Angles, died after an episcopate of seventeen years, and Archbishop Honorius consecrated Thomas his deacon from the province of Gyrwas* to succeed him. He died after five years in the bishopric, and was followed by Bertgils, a man of Kent known as Boniface. Archbishop Honorius himself, having run his course, died on the thirtieth of September 653, and after a vacancy of eighteen months, Deusdedit, a South Saxon, was elected to the archiepiscopal see and so became the sixth Archbishop. He was consecrated by Ithamar, Bishop of Rochester, on the twenty-sixth of March (655), and ruled the see until his death nine years, four months, and two days later. And on the death of Ithamar, Deusdedit himself consecrated Damian, a West Saxon, in his place.

CHAPTER 21: *The Province of the Middle Angles, under its king Peada, becomes Christian* [A.D. 653]

ABOUT this time, the Middle Angles, ruled by their king Peada, son of Penda, accepted the true Faith and its sacraments. Peada, who was a noble young man, kingly both in name and person, whom his father had appointed to the throne of his people, went to King Oswy of Northumbria and requested the hand of his daughter Alchfleda in marriage. Oswy, however, would not agree to this unless the king and his people accepted the Christian Faith and were baptized. So when Peada had received instruction in the true Faith, and had learned of the promises of the kingdom of heaven and of man's hope of resurrection and eternal life to come, he said that he would gladly become a Christian, even if he were refused the princess. He was chiefly influenced to accept the Faith by King Oswy's son Alfrid, who was his kinsman and friend, and had married his sister Cyneberga, daughter of King Penda.

Accordingly, Peada was baptized by Bishop Finan, together with his companions, thanes, and servants, at a well-known village belonging to the king known as At-Wall.* Then taking with him four priests, chosen for their learning and holy life, to instruct and baptize his people, he returned home full of joy. These priests were Cedd, Adda, Betti, and Diuma, all of whom were English except Diuma, who was a Scot. As I have said, Adda was brother of Utta, a well-known priest and Abbot of Gateshead. On their arrival in the province with the king, these priests preached the word of God and found a ready hearing, both noble and common folk alike coming in great numbers daily to renounce their idols and receive Baptism.

King Penda himself did not forbid the preaching of the Faith to any of his Mercians who wished to listen, but he hated and despised any whom he knew to be insincere in their practice of Christianity once they had accepted it, and said that any who failed to obey the God in whom they professed to believe were despicable wretches. This Christian mission was begun two years before Penda's death. And when Penda was killed, and was succeeded by the Christian King Oswy, as I shall tell later, Diuma, one of these four priests, was consecrated Bishop of the Middle Angles and

Mercians by Bishop Finan, since a shortage of priests made it necessary for one bishop to preside over the two peoples.* During his short episcopate, Diuma converted many to the Faith, and died among the Middle Angles in the district known as Infeppingum. He was succeeded by Ceollach, a Scot who relinquished the see after a short time and returned to the Isle of Iona which is the chief and mother-house of many Scots monasteries. His successor was Bishop Trumhere, a devout man trained in an English monastery, but consecrated bishop by the Scots. This took place during the reign of King Wulfhere, of whom I shall speak later.

CHAPTER 22: *The East Saxons, who had apostatized from the Faith under King Sigbert, are re-converted by the preaching of Cedd* [A.D. 653]

ABOUT this time, the East Saxons, who had once rejected the Faith and driven out Bishop Mellitus, again accepted it under the influence of King Oswy. For Sigbert their king, successor to Sigbert the Small, was a friend of Oswy, and often used to visit him in Northumbria. Oswy used to reason with him how gods made by men could not be gods, and how a god could not be made from a log or block of stone, the rest of which might be burned, or made into articles of everyday use, or possibly thrown away as rubbish to be trampled underfoot and reduced to dust. He showed him how God is of boundless majesty, invisible to human eyes, almighty, Creator of heaven and earth and of the human race. He told him that he rules and will judge the world in justice, abiding in eternity, not in base and perishable metal; and that it should be rightly understood that all who know and do the will of their Creator will receive an eternal reward from him. King Oswy advanced these and other arguments during friendly and brotherly talks with Sigbert, who was at length convinced; and having obtained the consent and support of his friends, all accepted the Faith and were baptized with him by Bishop Finan in the king's village of At-Wall, so named because it stands close to the wall which the Romans once built to protect Britain, about twelve miles from the eastern coast.

Having now become a citizen of the kingdom of heaven, Sigbert returned to his earthly capital after asking Oswy to send him teachers to convert his people to the Faith of Christ and baptize them. Accordingly the king sent to the province of the Middle Angles and summoned the man of God, Cedd, whom he despatched with another priest as companion to evangelize the East Saxons. And when these priests had visited the entire province and established a strong Christian community, Cedd returned home to Lindisfarne for consultations with Bishop Finan. When the latter learned the great success of his preaching, he invited two other bishops to assist him, and consecrated Cedd Bishop of the East Saxons. And when Cedd had been raised to the dignity of bishop, he returned to his province and used his increased authority to promote the work already begun. He built churches in several places, and ordained priests and deacons to assist in teaching the Faith and baptizing the people, especially in the city which the Saxons call Ythancestir,* and that called Tileburg.[1] The former place stands on the bank of the River Pante, the latter on the River Thames. Here Cedd established communities of the servants of Christ, and taught them to maintain the discipline of the regular life so far as these untutored folk were then capable of doing.

To the great joy of the king and all his people, the Gospel of eternal life made daily headway throughout the province for a considerable time until, at the instigation of the Enemy of all good men, the king was murdered by his own kinsman. This horrid crime was committed by two brothers, who on being asked their motive, had no answer to make except that they hated the king because he was too lenient towards his

1. Tilbury.

enemies, and too readily forgave injuries when offenders asked pardon. This then was the fault for which the king was killed, that he sincerely observed the teachings of the Gospel. Yet in this undeserved fate, he was overtaken by punishment for his real fault, as the man of God had once foretold. For one of the earls who murdered him had contracted an illicit marriage which the bishop had been unable to prevent or correct, and had therefore excommunicated him, forbidding anyone to enter his house or eat at his table. But the king had disregarded this ban, and had accepted the earl's invitation to a feast. As he was leaving the house, the bishop met him, and the king immediately dismounted from his horse and fell trembling at his feet, begging pardon for his fault. The bishop also dismounted in great anger, and touching the prostrate king with the staff in his hand, exercised his pontifical authority and said: 'I tell you, that since you have refused to avoid the house of a man who is lost and damned, this very house will be the place of your death.' However, since the death of this religious king was due to his loyal obedience to Christ's commandments, we may believe that it atoned for his earlier offence and increased his merits.

Sigbert was succeeded as king by Suidhelm, son of Sexbald, who had been baptized by Cedd in the province of the East Angles at the king's country-seat of Rendlesham, that is, Rendil's House: his godfather was Ethelwald, King of the East Angles.

CHAPTER 23: *Cedd receives the site for a monastery from King Ethelwald, and hallows it to our Lord with prayer and fasting: his death* [A.D. 659]

DURING his episcopate among the East Saxons, God's servant Cedd often visited his own province of Northumbria to preach. Ethelwald, son of King Oswald, who ruled the province of Deira, knowing Cedd to be a wise, holy, and

honourable man, asked him to accept a grant of land to found
a monastery, to which he himself might often come to pray
and hear the word of God, and where he might be buried:
for he firmly believed that the daily prayers of those who
would serve God there would be of great help to him. The
king's previous chaplain had been Cedd's brother, a priest
named Caelin, a man equally devoted to God, who had ministered the Word and Sacraments to himself and his family,
and it was through him that the king came to know and love
the bishop. In accordance with the king's wishes, Cedd chose
a site for the monastery among some high and remote hills,
which seemed more suitable for the dens of robbers and
haunts of wild beasts than for human habitation. His purpose in this was to fulfil the prophecy of Isaiah: '*in the haunts
where dragons once dwelt shall be pasture, with reeds and rushes*',
and he wished the fruit of good works to spring up where
formerly lived only wild beasts, or men who lived like the
beasts.

The man of God wished first of all to purify the site of the
monastery from the taint of earlier crimes by prayer and
fasting, and make it acceptable to God before laying the
foundations. He therefore asked the king's permission to
remain there throughout the approaching season of Lent,
and during this time he fasted until evening every day except
Sunday according to custom. Even then, he took no food but
a morsel of bread, an egg, and a little watered milk. He
explained that it was the custom of those who had trained
him in the rule of regular discipline to dedicate the site of any
monastery to God with prayer and fasting. But ten days
before the end of Lent a messenger arrived to summon him
to the king, so in order that the king's business should not
interrupt the work of dedication, Cedd asked his brother the
priest Cynebil to complete this holy task. The latter readily
consented, and when the period of prayer and fasting came
to an end, he built the monastery now called Laestingaeu,[1]

1. Lastingham, near Whitby.

and established there the observance of the usages of Lindisfarne where he had been trained.

When Cedd had been bishop of the province and administered the affairs of the monastery for many years through his chosen representatives, he happened to visit the monastery during a time of plague, and there fell sick and died. He was first buried in the open, but in the course of time a stone church was built, dedicated to the blessed Mother of God, and his body was reinterred in it on the right side of the altar.

The bishop bequeathed the abbacy of the monastery to his brother Chad, who subsequently became a bishop as I shall record later. The four brothers I have mentioned – Cedd, Cynebil, Caelin, and Ceadda[1] – all became famous priests of our Lord, and two became bishops, which is a rare occurrence in one family. When the brethren of Cedd's monastery in the province of the East Saxons heard that their founder had died and been buried in the province of Northumbria, about thirty of them came wishing, God willing, either to live near the body of their Father, or to die and be laid to rest at his side. They were kindly welcomed by their brothers and fellow-soldiers of Christ, and all of them died there of the plague with the exception of one little boy who was preserved from death by the prayers of his Father Chad. Many years afterwards, this boy, who applied himself to the study of the Scriptures, learned that he had never been baptized, so he at once sought salvation in the waters of the font, and was subsequently admitted to the priesthood, proving himself a support to many in the Church. I have no doubt that, when the boy visited the tomb of his beloved Father, he was saved from death by his prayers, in order that he might escape eternal death, and by his witness exercise a ministry of life and salvation to the other brethren.

1. Usually known as Chad.

AT this period King Oswy was subjected to savage and intolerable attacks by Penda, the above-mentioned King of the Mercians who had slain his brother. At length dire need compelled him to offer Penda an incalculable quantity of royal regalia and presents as the price of peace, on condition that he returned home and ceased to devastate the provinces of his kingdom. But the treacherous king refused to consider his offer, and declared his intention of wiping out the entire nation from the highest to the humblest in the land. Accordingly Oswy turned for help to the mercy of God, who alone could save the land from its barbarous and godless enemy; and he bound himself with an oath, saying: 'If the heathen refuses to accept our gifts, let us offer them to the Lord our God.' So he vowed that if he were victorious, he would offer his daughter to God as a consecrated virgin, and give twelve estates to build monasteries. This done, he gave battle with an insignificant force to the pagan armies, which are said to have been thirty times greater than his own, and comprised thirty battle-hardened legions under famous commanders. Oswy and his son Alchfrid, trusting in Christ as their leader, met them, as I have said, with very small forces; his other son Egfrid was at the time held hostage at the court of Queen Cynwise in the province of Mercia. But Oswald's son Ethelwald, who should have helped them, had gone over to the enemy and was fighting in Penda's army against his own kin and country, although during the actual battle he withdrew and awaited the outcome in a place of safety. When battle had been joined, the pagans suffered defeat, and the majority of Penda's commanders and allies were killed, including Ethelhere, brother and successor of King Anna of the East Angles, who had been responsible for the war, and who fell with all his men. This battle was fought close by the River Winwaed, which at the time was swollen by heavy rains, and had flooded the surrounding country: as a result, many more were drowned while attempting to escape than perished by the sword.

In fulfilment of his vow to the Lord, King Oswy gave thanks to God for his victory, and dedicated his daughter Aelffleda, who was scarcely a year old, to his service in perpetual virginity. He also gave twelve small grants of land, where heavenly warfare was to take the place of earthly, and to provide for the needs of monks to make constant intercession for the perpetual peace of his nation. Six of these lay in the province of Deira, and six in Bernicia, each of ten hides in extent, making one hundred and twenty in all. The daughter whom King Oswy had in this way dedicated to God entered the monastery of Hereteu[1] or Hart's Island, at that time ruled by Abbess Hilda. Two years later, the Abbess acquired a property of ten hides at Streanaeshalch,[2]* where she founded a monastery in which the king's daughter became firstly a novice and later a mistress of the monastic life, until at sixty years of age this holy virgin departed to the wedding-feast and embrace of her heavenly Bridegroom. In the church of this monastery, dedicated to the holy Apostle Peter, both she, her father Oswy, her mother Eanfleda, her mother's father Edwin, and many other noble folk are buried. To the great benefit of both nations, King Oswy brought this campaign to a close in the region of Loidis[3] on the fifteenth of November in the thirteenth year of his reign. Not only did he deliver his people from the hostile attacks of the heathen, but cut off the head of the wicked king, and converted the Mercians and their neighbours to the Christian Faith.

The first Bishop of Mercia, together with Lindisfarne and the Middle Angles, was the above-mentioned Diuma, who died and was buried among the Middle Angles. The second

1. Hartlepool.   2. Whitby.   3. Leeds.

was Ceollach, who resigned the bishopric, and returned to his native Ireland, for both he and Diuma were Irish. The third was Trumhere, an Englishman trained and ordained by the Scots, who was abbot of the monastery of Ingetlingum.[1] As I have said, this was the place where King Oswin had been killed, and where his kinswoman Queen Eanfleda, in expiation for his unjust death, petitioned King Oswy to grant God's servant Trumhere, who was also a near relative of the king, land on which to build a monastery; in this way, prayer could be offered for the eternal salvation of both kings, slayer and slain alike. For three years after the death of Penda, King Oswy ruled both Mercia and the other southern provinces; he also subjected the Picts to English rule.

At this time he granted Peada, son of Penda, who was his kinsman, the Kingdom of South Mercia, which consisted of five thousand hides of land and was divided by the River Trent from North Mercia, which consisted of seven thousand hides. In the following spring, however, during the Festival of Easter Peada was foully assassinated through the treachery, it is said, of his own wife. And three years after Penda's death, the Mercian leaders Immin, Eafa, and Eadbert rebelled against Oswy and proclaimed as king Wulfhere, son of Penda, a youth whom they had kept hidden; and having driven out the representatives of a king whom they refused to acknowledge, they boldly recovered their liberty and lands. Free under their own king, they gave willing allegiance to Christ their true King, so that they might win his eternal kingdom in heaven. King Wulfhere ruled the Mercians for seventeen years, and as I have said, had Trumhere as his first bishop. The second bishop was Jarman; the third, Chad; the fourth, Wynfrid; all these in turn held the bishopric of Mercia under King Wulfhere.

1. Gilling, near Richmond.

WHEN Bishop Aidan departed this life, he was succeeded in the Bishopric by Finan, who had been consecrated and sent by the Scots. He built a church in the Isle
of Lindisfarne, his see, constructing it not of stone, but of
hewn oak thatched with reeds after the Scots manner. It
was later dedicated by the most reverend Archbishop Theodore in honour of the blessed Apostle Peter. But Eadbert, a
later Bishop of Lindisfarne, removed the thatch, and covered
both roof and walls with sheets of lead.

About this time there arose a great and recurrent controversy on the observance of Easter, those trained in Kent and
Gaul maintaining that the Scottish observance was contrary
to that of the universal Church. The most zealous protagon-
ist of the true Easter was a Scot named Ronan, who had been
trained in theology and law in Gaul and Italy. He disputed
against Finan and convinced many, or at least persuaded
them to make more careful enquiry into the truth. But he
entirely failed to move Finan, a hot-tempered man whom
reproof made more obstinate, and openly hostile to the truth.
James, formerly the deacon of the venerable Archbishop
Paulinus, of whom I have spoken, kept the true and Catholic
Easter with all whom he could persuade to adopt the right
observance. Also Queen Eanfleda and her court, having as
chaplain a Kentish priest named Romanus who followed the
Catholic customs, observed the customs she had seen in Kent.
It is said that the confusion in those days was such that Easter
was kept twice in one year, so that when the King had ended
Lent and was keeping Easter, the Queen and her attendants
were still fasting and keeping Palm Sunday. During Aidan's
lifetime these differences of Easter observance were partially
tolerated by everyone, for it was realized that although he
was in loyalty bound to retain the customs of those who sent
him, he nevertheless laboured diligently to cultivate the

faith, piety, and love that marks out God's saints. He was therefore rightly loved by all, even by those who differed from his opinion on Easter, and was held in high respect not only by ordinary folk, but by Honorius of Canterbury and Felix of East Anglia.

When Finan, who followed Aidan as bishop, died, he was succeeded by an Irishman, Colman, under whom an even more serious controversy arose about Easter and the rules of Church discipline. This dispute began to trouble the minds and consciences of many people, who feared that they might have received the name of Christian in vain. The matter came to the notice of King Oswy and his son Alchfrid, and the former preferred the Scots teaching, having been instructed and baptized by the Scots, and having a complete grasp of their language. But Alchfrid, who had been instructed in the Faith by Wilfrid – a very learned man who had gone to Rome for his theological studies, and spent a long time at Lyons under Dalfin, Archbishop of Gaul, from whom he had received the tonsure – rightly regarded Wilfrid's teaching as superior to all the traditions of the Scots. He had therefore given him a monastery with forty hides of land at Inhrypum,[1] which he had given not long previously to the adherents of the Scottish customs; but since, when offered the alternative, these preferred to give up the place rather than alter their customs, he then offered it to Wilfrid, whose life and teaching made him a worthy recipient. About this time, Agilbert, Bishop of the West Saxons, whom I have mentioned, had come to visit the province of Northumbria. He was a friend both of King Alchfrid and Abbot Wilfrid, and at the king's request he made Wilfrid a priest in his monastery. He also had with him a priest named Agatho. And when discussion arose on the questions of Easter, the tonsure, and various other church matters, it was decided to hold a synod to put an end to this dispute at the monastery of Streanaeshalch, which means The Bay of the Beacon, then ruled by the Abbess Hilda, a woman

1. Ripon.

devoted to God. Both kings, father and son, came to this
synod, and so did Bishop Colman with his Scots clergy, and
Bishop Agilbert with the priests Agatho and Wilfrid. James
and Romanus supported the latter, while Abbess Hilda and
her community, together with the venerable bishop Cedd,
supported the Scots. Cedd, who as already mentioned had
long ago been ordained by the Scots, acted as a most careful
interpreter for both parties at the council.

King Oswy opened by observing that all who served the
One God should observe one rule of life, and since they all
hoped for one kingdom in heaven, they should not differ in
celebrating the sacraments of heaven. The synod now had
the task of determining which was the truest tradition, and
this should be loyally accepted by all. He then directed his
own bishop Colman to speak first, and to explain his own
customs and their origin. Then Colman said: 'The Easter
customs which I observe were taught me by my superiors,
who sent me here as a bishop; and all our forefathers, men
beloved of God, are known to have observed these customs.
And lest anyone condemns or rejects them as wrong, it is
recorded that they owe their origin to the blessed evangelist
Saint John, the disciple especially loved by our Lord, and all
the churches over which he presided.' When he had concluded these and similar arguments, the king directed Agilbert to explain the origin and authority of his own customs.
Agilbert replied: 'May I request that my disciple the priest
Wilfrid be allowed to speak in my place? For we are in full
agreement with all those here present who support the traditions of our Church, and he can explain our position in the
English language more competently than I can do through
an interpreter.' When Wilfrid had received the king's permission to speak, he said: 'Our Easter customs are those that
we have seen universally observed in Rome, where the
blessed Apostles Peter and Paul lived, taught, suffered, and
are buried. We have also seen the same customs generally
observed throughout Italy and Gaul when we travelled

through these countries for study and prayer. Furthermore, we have found them to be observed in many different countries and languages at the same time, in Africa, Asia, Egypt, Greece, and throughout the world wherever the Church of Christ has spread. The only people who are stupid enough to disagree with the whole world are these Scots and their obstinate adherents the Picts and Britons, who inhabit only a portion of these two islands in the remote ocean.' In reply to this statement, Colman answered: 'It is strange that you call our customs stupid when they rest on the authority of so great an Apostle, who was considered worthy to lean on our Lord's breast, and whose great wisdom is acknowledged throughout the world.' Wilfrid replied: 'Far be it from us to charge John with foolishness, for he literally observed the Law of Moses at a time when the Church was still greatly influenced by the synagogue, and the Apostles were not able immediately to abrogate the observances of the Law once given by God. It was for this reason that all converts to the Faith had to forsake idols, which are an invention of the Devil, lest they gave offence to believers who were Jews. For the same reason Paul circumcised Timothy, offered sacrifice in the Temple, and shaved his head at Corinth with Aquila and Priscilla, with the sole intention of avoiding offence to the Jews. For James said to Paul: "*You see, brother, how many thousands among the Jews have believed, and all of them zealously observe the Law.*" But today, as the Gospel spreads throughout the world, it is unnecessary and undesirable for the faithful to be circumcised or to offer animals to God in sacrifice. John, following the customs of the Law, at first used to keep the Feast of Easter on the evening of the fourteenth day of the first month, whether it fell on the Sabbath or on any other day. But when Peter preached in Rome, remembering that it was on the day after the Sabbath that our Lord rose from the dead and gave the world the hope of resurrection, he realized that Easter should begin at moonrise on the evening of the fourteenth day of the full

moon. This was in accordance with the Law, and was John's
own practice. And if the Lord's Day, then called the day after
the Sabbath, fell on the following day, he began to observe
Easter the same evening, as we do today. But if the Lord's
Day did not fall on the day following the fourteenth day of
the moon, but on the sixteenth, seventeenth, or any other
day up to the twenty-first, he waited until that day, and on
the Sabbath evening preceding it he began the observance
of the Easter Festival. This evangelical and apostolical tradition does not abrogate but fulfil the Law, which ordained
that the Passover be kept between the eve of the fourteenth
and twenty-first days of the moon of that month. And this is
the custom of all the successors of blessed John in Asia since
his death, and is also that of the world-wide Church. This is
the true and only Easter to be observed by the faithful. It was
not newly decreed by the Council of Nicaea, but reaffirmed
by it, as Church history records. It is quite apparent to us,
Colman, that you follow neither the example of John, as you
imagine, nor that of Peter, whose tradition you deliberately
contradict. Your keeping of Easter agrees neither with the
Law nor the Gospel. For John, who kept Easter in accordance with the decrees of Moses, did not keep to the first day
after the Sabbath; but this is not your practice, for you keep
Easter only on the first day after the Sabbath. Peter kept
Easter between the fifteenth and twenty-first days of the
moon; you do not, for you keep it between the fourteenth
and twentieth days of the moon. As a result, you often begin
Easter on the evening of the thirteenth day, which is not
mentioned in the Law. Nor did our Lord, the Author and
Giver of the Gospel, eat the old Passover or institute the
Sacrament of the New Testament to be celebrated by the
Church in memory of His Passion on that day, but on the
fourteenth. Furthermore, when you keep Easter, you expressly exclude the twenty-first day, which the Law of Moses
particularly ordered to be observed. Therefore, I repeat, you
conform neither to John nor Peter, the Law nor the Gospel,

in your keeping of our greatest Festival.'

Colman in reply said: 'Do you maintain that Anatolius, a holy man highly spoken of in Church history, taught contrary to the Law and the Gospel, when he wrote that Easter should be kept between the fourteenth and twentieth days of the moon? Are we to believe that our most revered Father Columba and his successors, men so dear to God, thought or acted contrary to Holy Scripture when they followed this custom? The holiness of many of them is confirmed by heavenly signs, and their virtues by miracles; and having no doubt that they are Saints, I shall never cease to emulate their lives, customs, and discipline.'

'It is well established that Anatolius was a most holy, learned, and worthy man,' answered Wilfrid; 'but how can you claim his authority when you do not follow his directions? For he followed the correct rule about Easter, and observed a cycle of nineteen years; but either you do not know of this general custom of the Christian Church, or else you ignore it. He calculated the fourteenth day of the moon at Easter according to the Egyptian method, making it the evening of the fifteenth day; similarly, he assigned the twentieth to Easter Sunday, regarding it after sunset as the twenty-first day. But it appears that you do not realize this distinction, since you sometimes keep Easter before full moon, that is, on the thirteenth day. And with regard to your Father Columba and his followers, whose holiness you imitate and whose rules and customs you claim to have been supported by heavenly signs, I can only say that when many shall say to our Lord at the day of judgement: "*Have we not prophesied in Thy name, and cast out devils, and done many wonderful works?*" the Lord will reply, "*I never knew you.*" Far be it from me to apply these words to your fathers, for it is more just to believe good rather than evil of those whom one does not know. So I do not deny that they were true servants of God and dear to Him, and that they loved Him in primitive simplicity. Nor do I think that their ways of keeping

Easter were in any way harmful, so long as no one came to show them a more perfect way. Nevertheless, I feel certain that if any Catholic adviser had come to them, they would readily have accepted his guidance, since we know that they readily observed such of God's ordinances as they already knew. But you and your colleagues are most certainly guilty of sin if you reject the decrees of the Apostolic See and the universal Church which are confirmed by these Letters. For although your Fathers were holy men, do you imagine that they, a few men in a corner of a remote island, are to be preferred before the universal Church of Christ throughout the world? And even if your Columba – or, may I say, ours also if he was the servant of Christ – was a Saint of potent virtues, can he take precedence before the most blessed Prince of the Apostles, to whom our Lord said: "*Thou art Peter, and upon this rock I will build my Church, and the gates of hell shall not prevail against it, and to thee I will give the keys of the kingdom of heaven*"?'

When Wilfrid had ended, the king asked: 'Is it true, Colman, that these words were spoken to Peter by our Lord?' He answered: 'It is true, Your Majesty.' Then the king said: 'Can you show that a similar authority was given to your Columba?' 'No,' replied Colman. 'Do you both agree', the king continued, 'that these words were indisputably addressed to Peter in the first place, and that our Lord gave him the keys of the kingdom of heaven?' Both answered: 'We do.' At this, the king concluded: 'Then, I tell you, Peter is guardian of the gates of heaven, and I shall not contradict him. I shall obey his commands in everything to the best of my knowledge and ability; otherwise, when I come to the gates of heaven, he who holds the keys may not be willing to open them.'*

All present, both high and low, signified their agreement with what the king had said, and abandoning their imperfect customs, readily accepted those which they had learned to be better.

IN this way the controversy was terminated, the company dispersed, and Agilbert returned home. Colman, seeing his teachings rejected and his following discounted, took away with him all who still dissented from the Catholic Easter and tonsure* – for there was no small argument about this as well – and returned to Ireland in order to consult his compatriots on their future course of action. Cedd, on the other hand, having abandoned the Scots' customs and accepted the Catholic, returned to his own bishopric. This Synod took place in the year of our Lord 664, which was the twenty-second year of King Oswy's reign, and the thirtieth anniversary of the coming of the Scots bishops to England, Aidan having held his bishopric for seventeen years, Finan for ten, and Colman for three.

On Colman's return to his own land, the servant of God, Tuda, became bishop of the Northumbrians in his place. He had been trained and consecrated bishop by the southern Scots, and had worn the ecclesiastical tonsure according to the customs of the province, and observed the Catholic Easter customs. He was a good devout man, but ruled the diocese only for a short time. He had arrived from Scotland during Colman's episcopate, and taught the truths of the Faith diligently in word and deed. Then Eata, abbot of the monastery of Mailros,[1] a gentle man and greatly revered, was appointed Abbot of Lindisfarne to rule the brethren who elected to remain there when the Scots withdrew. It is said that before Colman left, he asked and obtained this favour from King Oswy, because Eata had been one of the English boys whom Aidan received into the monastery to be taught the Christian Faith when he first became bishop; for the king had high regard for Bishop Colman's singular good sense.

1. Melrose.

Not long afterwards, Eata was raised to the bishopric of the church of Lindisfarne. On his departure, Colman took with him a portion of the bones of the most reverend Father Aidan, and deposited some of them in the church over which he had ruled, directing that they be enshrined in the sacristy.

So frugal and austere were Colman and his predecessors that when they left the monastery there were very few buildings except the church; indeed, no more than met their bare requirements. They had no property except cattle, and whenever they received any money from rich folk, they immediately gave it to the poor; for they had no need to acquire money or provide lodging for important people, since such only visited the church in order to pray or hear the word of God. Whenever opportunity offered, the king him-self used to come with only five or six attendants, and when he had visited the church to pray, he used to leave. But if they happened to remain for a meal, they were content with the plain daily food of the brothers and asked nothing more, for the sole concern of these teachers was to serve God, not the world; to satisfy the soul, not the belly. Accordingly the religious habit was held in high esteem, and whenever any priest or monk paid a visit, he was joyfully welcomed by all as the servant of God. And if anyone met him on the road, they ran to him and bowed, eager to be signed by his hand or receive a blessing from his lips. Whenever he spoke, he was given an attentive hearing, and on Sundays the people flocked to the churches and monasteries, not to obtain food, but to hear the word of God taught. When a priest visited a village, the people were quick to gather in some cottage to hear the word of life, for priests and clerics always came to a village solely to preach, baptize, visit the sick, and, in short, to care for the souls of its people. They were so free from the sin of avarice that none of them would accept lands or gifts for the building of monasteries unless expressly directed to do so by the secular authorities. This was the general practice for many years among the churches of Northumbria. But enough has been said on such matters.

CHAPTER 27: *Egbert, an Englishman of holy life, becomes a monk in Ireland*

IN the same year of our Lord 664 an eclipse of the sun occurred about ten o'clock in the morning on the third of May, and a sudden plague which first decimated the southern parts of Britain, and later spread into Northumbria, brought widespread death to its people. Bishop Tuda fell a victim to this plague, and was buried with honour in the monastery of Paegnalaech; this plague was equally destructive in Ireland. At this period there were many English nobles and lesser folk in Ireland who had left their own land during the episcopates of Bishops Finan and Colman, either to pursue religious studies or to lead a life of stricter discipline. Before long, some of these devoted themselves to the monastic life, while others preferred to travel, studying under various teachers in turn. The Scots welcomed them all kindly, and, without asking for any payment, provided them with books and instructors.

Among the English nobles were Ethelhun and Egbert, two young men of outstanding ability. The former was brother of Ethelwin, a man no less dear to God, who at a later date also travelled to study in Ireland, and after a full course of instruction, returned home and was made Bishop of Lindsey, where he enjoyed a long and illustrious episcopate. These two young men, who were studying in the monastery which the Scots call Rathmelsigi,[1] having lost all their companions either through the plague or through their dispersal to other places, were themselves stricken by the same disease and fell dangerously ill. And I am told by an old and most dependable priest, who says that he was informed by the

1. Melfont.

youth himself, that Egbert,* believing himself about to die, left the infirmary one morning, and sitting down in a place by himself, began seriously to examine his past life. Tears fell from his eyes as he sorrowfully recalled his sins, and he begged God from the bottom of his heart not to let him die until he could atone for the offences of his boyhood and youth, and acquire greater merit by good deeds. He also made a vow that he would remain an exile and never return to his native island of Britain; and that, unless prevented by sickness, in addition to the canonical hours of prayer, he would recite the entire Psalter daily to the praise of God and observe a whole day's fasting each week. When he had ended his vows and prayers, he returned to the infirmary where he found his companion asleep; and lying down on his pallet, he composed himself to rest. When he had lain there a short while, his friend awoke, and looking at him, said: 'O brother Egbert, what have you done? I was hoping that we should enter eternal life together; but now I know that what you have prayed for will be granted.' For he had learned in a vision what his friend had prayed for, and that his prayer was heard. In short, Ethelhun died the following night, but Egbert threw off the disease, recovered, and lived for many years. He became a worthy ornament of the priestly order, and, as he had prayed, lived a life of great merit, entering the kingdom of heaven at the age of ninety in the year of our Lord 729. Egbert led a life of great humility, gentleness, purity, simplicity, and clemency. He brought great blessings both to his own nation, and to the Picts and Scots among whom he exiled himself, setting them an example of holy life. He was indefatigable in teaching, he corrected them with authority, and generously distributed whatever he received from the rich. In addition to his earlier vows, he ate only one meal a day during Lent, allowing himself a scanty ration of bread and milk; for he used to keep the previous day's fresh milk in a flask, and having skimmed off the cream next day, he drank what was left with a little bread. He practised a similar abstinence for forty days before Christmas, and as many after the Feast of Pentecost.

CHAPTER 28: *On Tuda's death, Wilfrid is consecrated bishop in Gaul and Chad in Wessex, to be bishops in the Province of Northumbria* [A.D. 665]

MEANWHILE King Alfrid (of Deira) sent the priest Wilfrid to the King of the Gauls* to be consecrated bishop of himself and his people. That king sent him for consecration to Agilbert who, as I have said, had been made Bishop of Paris after his return from Britain. Summoning several other bishops to the royal country-seat at Compiègne, he consecrated Wilfrid with great splendour. But since Wilfrid remained overseas for a considerable time after his consecration, King Oswy meanwhile, following his son's example, sent the priest Chad to Canterbury to be consecrated Bishop of York. He was a holy man, modest in his ways, learned in the Scriptures, and one who was careful to practise all that he found in them. He was a brother of the above-mentioned most reverend Bishop Cedd, and was Abbot of Lastingham. The king sent with Chad the priest Eadhed, who, during the reign of Egfrid, later became Bishop of Ripon. On arriving in Kent, they found that Archbishop Deusdedit had died, and that no successor had yet been appointed. They therefore went on to Bishop Wini in the province of the West Saxons, who consecrated Chad as bishop with the assistance of two British bishops.* These did not keep Easter at the canonical time, which, as I have often observed, is between the fourteenth and twentieth days of the moon. For at that time Wini was the only bishop in all Britain who had been canonically consecrated bishop.

As a bishop, Chad immediately devoted himself to maintain the truths of the Church, and set himself to practise humility and continence, and to study. After the example of the Apostles, he travelled on foot and not on horseback when he went to preach the Gospel, whether in towns, the countryside, cottages, villages, or castles, for he was one of Aidan's disciples, and always sought to instruct his people by the same methods as Aidan and his own brother Cedd. And when Wilfrid returned to Britain as a bishop, he introduced into the English churches many Catholic customs, with the result that the Catholic Rite daily gained support, and all the Scots remaining in England either conformed to it, or returned to their own land.

CHAPTER 29: *The priest Wighard is sent from Britain to Rome to be made archbishop: letters from the apostolic Pope tell of his death there* [A.D. 655]

AT this time, the most noble English kings Oswy of Northumbria and Egbert of Kent conferred together on the state of the Church in England, for Oswy, although educated by the Scots, was fully aware that the Roman Church was the Catholic and Apostolic Church. With the choice and approval of the holy English Church, the two kings accepted the priest Wighard, one of Archbishop Deusdedit's clergy, a good man well fitted to be a bishop, and sent him to Rome to be consecrated bishop, so that when he had received the rank of Archbishop, he could consecrate Catholic bishops for the churches of the English throughout Britain. Wighard arrived in Rome, but died before he could be consecrated, and the following letter was sent to Oswy in Britain:

'To our son, the most excellent Lord Oswy, King of the Saxons, from Bishop Vitalian, servant of the servants of God.

'We have read Your Excellency's welcome letter, in which we recognize your very sincere devotion and fervent desire for eternal life. And we know how you have been converted to the true and apostolic Faith by the guiding hand of God, and trust that, as you now reign over your own nation, so you will one day reign with Christ. Your nation is fortunate to have a king so wise and devoted to the worship of God, who not only adores God himself, but labours day and night to lead all his people to the Catholic Apostolic Faith, and to save his own soul. Who cannot help being glad when they hear such encouraging news? And who will not be delighted at such high understanding? For your nation has come to believe in Christ our mighty God in fulfilment of the words of God's prophets, as Isaiah says: "*In that day there shall be a root of Jesse, which shall stand as a sign of the people; to him shall the Gentiles seek.*" And again: "*Listen, O isles, unto Me, and hearken, ye people, from far.*" And a little later he says: "*It is a small thing that thou shouldst be My servant, to raise up the tribes of Jacob, and to restore the preserved of Israel. I will also give thee for a light to the Gentiles, that thou mayest be My salvation to the ends of the earth.*" And again: "*Kings shall see, princes also shall arise and worship.*" And later: "*I have given thee for a covenant of the people, to establish the earth and possess the desolate heritages; that thou mayest say to the prisoners, Go forth; to them that are in darkness, Show yourselves.*" And again: "*I, the Lord, have called thee in righteousness, and will hold thine hand, and will keep thee, and give thee for a light to the Gentiles, and for a covenant of the people; to open the blind eyes, to bring out the prisoner from prison, and them that sit in darkness from the prison-house.*"

'Here you may see, most excellent son, how clearly the prophets declare that not only you, but all nations shall believe in Christ the Maker of all things. It must therefore be the task of Your Majesty, as a living member of Christ, always to observe the holy precepts of the Prince of the Apostles, both in keeping Easter, and in everything transmitted to us by the holy Apostles Peter and Paul, who, like two heavenly bodies, light the world, and whose teaching gives daily guidance to the hearts of all believers.'

And after some observations on the uniform keeping of Easter throughout the world, the Pope continues:

'In view of the lengthy journey involved, we are not at

present able to discover a man wholly suitable to be your bishop, as you request in your letters. But as soon as such a man can be found, we will give him instructions and send him to your country, so that under God's guidance, through his own witness and the teachings of God, he may uproot the snares of the Enemy throughout your island. We gratefully acknowledge the gifts sent by Your Highness to the blessed Prince of the Apostles in tribute to his immortal memory, and pray for your own safety and that of your Christian clergy. But the bearer of your gifts has departed this life, and is buried in the Church of the Apostles. We are deeply distressed that he should have died here. We have directed, however, that the blessings of the Saints – that is, relics of the blessed Apostles Peter and Paul, and of the holy martyrs Laurence, John, and Paul, Gregory and Pancras – be given to the bearers of this letter for delivery to Your Excellency. By the same bearers we send our spiritual daughter, your queen, a cross with a golden key made from the fetters of the blessed Apostles Peter and Paul, whose sacred labours are the boast of the entire apostolic see wherever its holy deeds shine and blossom in the sight of God. We trust that Your Highness will soon fulfil our hope, and dedicate your whole island to Christ our God, Redeemer of the human race and your own sure Protector, who will support all your efforts to draw together a new people in Christ, and establish them in the Catholic and Apostolic Faith. For Scripture says: " *Seek first the kingdom of God and His righteousness, and all these things shall be added to you*"; and you assuredly seek, and will obtain our mutual desire, that is, the conversion of all your islands. We greet Your Excellency with fatherly affection, constantly praying that God of His mercy will assist you and yours in all good works, so that you may reign with Christ in the world to come. May Heaven's grace preserve Your Excellency in health.'

The next book will provide a more suitable place to tell who was wisely chosen and consecrated in place of Wighard.

CHAPTER 30: *During a plague the East Saxons lapse into idolatry, but are quickly recalled from their errors by Bishop Jarman* [A.D. 665]

AT the same time, the kings Sighere and Sebbi succeeded Suidhelm, of whom I have spoken, as rulers of the East Saxons under Wulfhere, King of Mercia. While the plague caused a heavy death-roll in the province, Sighere and his people abandoned the mysteries of the Christian Faith, and relapsed into paganism. For the king himself, together with many of the nobles and common folk, loved this life and sought no other, having no belief in a future life. Hoping for protection against the plague by this means, they therefore began to rebuild the ruined temples and restore the worship of idols. But Sebbi his fellow-king and colleague held loyally to the Faith which he and his people had accepted, and, as will appear later, remained faithful and ended his days happily.

As soon as King Wulfhere learned that part of the province had apostasized from the Faith, he sent Bishop Jarman, Trumhere's successor, to correct their error and recall the province to the true faith. I am told by a priest who accompanied him on his journey and shared his preaching, that Jarman proceeded with great discretion, for he was a good devout man who travelled far and wide, and succeeded in bringing back both king and people to the right way. As a result, they abandoned or destroyed the temples and altars they had erected, and opened the churches, glad to confess the name of Christ whom they had denied, and more ready to die with him believing in the Resurrection than to continue living among their idols in the degradation of apostasy. Their task accomplished, these priests and teachers then returned home full of joy.

BOOK FOUR

CHAPTER 1: *On the death of Archbishop Deusdedit, Wighard is sent to Rome to be consecrated in his stead: on the latter's death there, Theodore is consecrated Archbishop and sent to Britain with Abbot Hadrian* [A.D. 664]

O N the fourteenth of July in the above-mentioned year when an eclipse was quickly followed by plague, and during which Bishop Colman was refuted by the unanimous decision of the Catholics and returned to his own country, Deusdedit the sixth Archbishop of Canterbury died. Earconbert, King of Kent, died on the same day, and was succeeded by his son Egbert, who reigned for nine years. The See of Canterbury was then vacant for a considerable time, until Wighard, an English priest with great experience in church administration, was sent to Rome by the common consent of Egbert and King Oswy of Northumbria, with the request that he be consecrated Archbishop of the English Church. This I have already briefly noted in an earlier book. At the same time the two kings sent presents to the apostolic Pope, including many gold and silver vessels. On his arrival in Rome, where Vitalian was ruling the apostolic see, Wighard explained to the Pope the reason for his journey, but shortly afterwards he and nearly all of his companions fell victim to a plague that broke out at the time.

The apostolic Pope therefore took advice on the situation, and made careful enquiry as to whom he could send as Archbishop of the English Church. Not far from Naples in Campania is the monastery of Niridan,* whose Abbot Hadrian, a native of Africa, was very learned in the Scriptures, experienced in ecclesiastical and monastic administration, and a great scholar in Greek and Latin. So the Pope summoned Hadrian, and directed him to accept the bishopric and go to Britain. Hadrian excused himself on the grounds that he was not fitted for such high dignity, but said that he could recommend another, whose learning and age were more suited to the office of bishop. He proposed to the Pope the monk Andrew, who was chaplain to a neighbouring convent of women, and was considered as worthy of a bishopric by all who knew him; but Andrew excused himself on the grounds of ill health. Then Hadrian was again pressed to accept the bishopric, but he asked for a delay in order to make a fresh attempt to find a more suitable man.

At this time there was in Rome a monk named Theodore, a native of Tarsus in Cilicia, who was well known to Hadrian. He was learned both in sacred and secular literature, fluent in Greek and Latin, of proved integrity, and of the mature age of sixty-six. Hadrian, therefore, suggested the name of Theodore to the Pope, who agreed to consecrate him, but made it a condition that Hadrian himself should accompany him to Britain, since he had already travelled through Gaul twice on various missions, and had both a better knowledge of the road and sufficient men of his own available. The Pope also ordered Hadrian to give full support to Theodore in his teaching, and to ensure that he did not introduce into the Church which he was to rule any Greek customs which conflicted with the teachings of the true Faith. On receiving the sub-diaconate, Theodore waited four months for his hair to grow so that he could receive the circular tonsure, for hitherto he had worn the tonsure of the holy Apostle Paul in conformity to Eastern custom. He was then consecrated bishop by Pope Vitalian on Sunday the 26th of March 668, and on the 27th of May he set out for Britain, accompanied by Hadrian.

The travellers crossed by sea to Massilia,[1] and thence overland to Arles, where they delivered Pope Vitalian's letters of

1. Marseilles.

commendation to John, Archbishop of that city, who gave
them hospitality until Ebrin, Chamberlain of the king's
palace, gave them a permit to travel wherever they wished.
Theodore then went on to Agilbert, Bishop of Paris, of
whom I have already spoken, who welcomed him kindly
and entertained him for a considerable time. Hadrian meanwhile went first to Emme, Bishop of Sens, and then to Faro,
Bishop of Meaux, and made lengthy stays with them since
the approach of winter obliged travellers to remain quietly
wherever they could. When messengers informed King
Egbert that the bishop whom they had requested from Rome
was now in Gaul, he at once sent his High Reeve Redfrid to
escort him; and when the Reeve arrived, he obtained Ebrin's
permission to escort Theodore to the port of Quentavic.[1]
Here exhaustion compelled Theodore to rest for a while, but
as soon as he began to recover, he took ship for Britain. But
Hadrian was detained by Ebrin, who suspected that he bore
some message from the Emperor to the kings of Britain,
which might be to the disadvantage of the kingdom for
whose interests he was largely responsible. But when he
ascertained that Hadrian had in fact no such mission, he
released him and allowed him to follow Theodore. And as
soon as Hadrian arrived, Theodore appointed him abbot of
the monastery of blessed Peter the Apostle, where, as I have
said, the Archbishops of Canterbury are buried. For when
he left Rome the apostolic Pope had instructed Theodore to
provide for him in his diocese, and give him a suitable place
to live with his followers.

1. Étaples.

CHAPTER 2 : *Theodore makes a general visitation: the English churches begin to receive instruction in Catholic truth, and sacred study is fostered. Putta succeeds Damian as Bishop of Rochester* [A.D. 669]

THEODORE arrived in his see on Sunday May 27th in the second year after his consecration, and held it for twenty-one years, three months, and twenty-six days. Soon after his arrival, he visited every part of the island occupied by the English peoples, and received a ready welcome and hearing everywhere. He was accompanied and assisted throughout his journey by Hadrian, and he taught the Christian way of life and the canonical method of keeping Easter. Theodore was the first archbishop whom the entire English Church obeyed, and, as I have observed, since both he and Hadrian were men of learning both in sacred and secular literature, they attracted a large number of students, into whose minds they poured the waters of wholesome knowledge day by day. In addition to instructing them in the holy Scriptures, they also taught their pupils poetry, astronomy, and the calculation of the church calendar. In proof of this, some of their students still alive today are as proficient in Latin and Greek as in their native tongue. Never had there been such happy times as these since the English settled in Britain, for the Christian kings were so strong that they daunted all the barbarous tribes. The people eagerly sought the new-found joys of the kingdom of heaven, and all who wished for instruction in the reading of the Scriptures found teachers ready at hand.

The knowledge of sacred music, hitherto limited to Kent, now began to spread to all the English churches. With the exception of the deacon James, already mentioned, the first singing-master in the Northumbrian churches was Eddi, known as Stephen, who was invited from Kent by the most reverend Wilfrid, the first bishop of English blood* to teach the English Church the Catholic way of life.

During his visitation, Theodore consecrated bishops in suitable places, and with their assistance he corrected abuses wherever he found them. When he informed Bishop Chad that his consecration was irregular,* the latter replied with the greatest humility: 'If you consider my consecration as bishop to have been irregular, I willingly resign the office, for I have never thought myself worthy of it. Although unworthy, I accepted it solely under obedience.' At this humble reply, Theodore assured him that he had no wish to deprive him of his office, and completed his consecration according to Catholic rites. About the time that Deusdedit died and a successor for the See of Canterbury was sought for, consecrated, and sent, Wilfrid was also sent from Britain for consecration. Returning before Theodore, he ordained certain priests and deacons in Kent, pending the archbishop's arrival in his own see. Shortly afterwards Theodore himself came to Rochester, where the see had been vacant ever since the death of Damian, and there consecrated Putta as its bishop. He was a man of simple life, who was well acquainted with church affairs, but had little experience in worldly matters. He was a most skilled exponent of the Roman chant, which he had studied under the disciples of blessed Pope Gregory.

CHAPTER 3: *Chad is appointed Bishop of Mercia: his life, death, and burial* [c. A.D. 667]

THE Mercians at this time were ruled by King Wulfhere, who on the death of Jarman, asked Theodore to provide him and his people with a bishop. Theodore, however, did not wish to consecrate a new bishop for them, and asked King Oswy to accept Chad as their bishop. The latter was then living quietly in his monastery at Lastingham, while Wilfrid ruled the Bishopric of York, which consisted of all the lands of the Northumbrians and Picts to the borders of Oswy's realms. The most reverend Bishop Chad always pre-

ferred to undertake his preaching missions on foot rather
than on horseback, but Theodore ordered him to ride whenever he undertook a long journey. He was most reluctant to
forgo this pious exercise which he loved, but the archbishop,
who recognized his outstanding holiness and considered it
more proper for him to ride, himself insisted on helping him
to mount his horse. So Chad received the Bishopric of
Mercia and Lindisfarne, and administered the diocese in
great holiness of life after the example of the early Fathers.
King Wulfstan gave him fifty hides of land to build a monastery at Adbearw – that is, At the Wood – in the province
of Lindsey, and evidences of the regular observance that he
established remain to this day.

Chad established his episcopal seat in the town of Lyccid-
felth,[1] where he also died and was buried, and where the succeeding bishops of the province have their see to this day.
There he built himself a house near the church where he used
to retire privately with seven or eight brethren in order to
pray or study whenever his work and preaching permitted.
When he had ruled the church of the province with great
success for two and a half years, divine providence ordained
a time such as is spoken of in Ecclesiastes: ' *There is a time to
cast away stones, and a time to gather them together.*' For heaven
sent a plague which, bringing bodily death, bore away the
living stones of the Church to the temple in heaven. And
when death had freed many members of the revered bishop's
church from the burden of the flesh, the hour drew near when
Chad himself was to pass out of this world to our Lord. One
day he was alone in his house with a brother whose name was
Owini, his other companions having had occasion to return
to the church. This Owini was a monk of great virtue, who
had renounced the world with the pure intention of winning
a heavenly reward, so that he was altogether a fit person to
receive a revelation of God's secrets, and one whose word
everyone could trust. He had accompanied Queen Ethelfrid

1. Lichfield.

from East Anglia, and had been her chief thane and steward
of her household. Growing in devotion to the Faith, he
decided to renounce the world, which he did in no half-
hearted fashion; for he gave away all his possessions, put on
a simple garment, and carrying an axe and trowel, set off for
the reverend father Chad's monastery at Lastingham. This
he did to show that he was not entering the monastery for
the sake of an idle life, as some do, and he demonstrated this
in practice; for whenever he found himself unable to meditate
on the Scriptures with profit, he undertook a larger amount
of manual labour. In short, recognizing his reverence and
devotion, the bishop admitted him to the monastery among
the brethren, and whenever they were engaged in study, he
used to busy himself in essential tasks out of doors. One day,
while Owini was working outside and the other brethren
were in church, the bishop was reading and praying alone in
his oratory. Suddenly, as he afterwards related, he heard the
sound of sweet and joyful singing coming down from heaven
to earth. The sound seemed at first to emanate from the south-
east, gradually coming closer to him until it centred over the
roof of the oratory where the bishop was at prayer. It then
entered the oratory, and seemed to fill both it and the surrounding air. He listened closely to what he heard, and after
about half an hour, the song of joy rose from the roof of the
oratory, and returned to heaven as it had come with inexpres-
sible sweetness. Owini stood astonished for a while, turning
over in his mind what this might portend, when the bishop
threw open the oratory window, and in his customary way
clapped his hands to summon him indoors. When he hurried
in, the bishop said: 'Go at once to the church, and fetch seven
of the brethren here, and come back with them yourself.'
On their arrival, he first urged them to live in love and peace
with each other and with all the faithful, and to be constant
and tireless in keeping the rules of monastic discipline that he
had taught them and they knew him to observe, and those
that they had learned from the lives and teachings of former

abbots. He then announced that his own death was drawing near, saying: 'The welcome guest who has visited many of our brethren has come to me today, and has deigned to summon me out of this world. Therefore return to the church, and ask the brethren to commend my passing to our Lord in their prayers. And let each prepare for his own passing by vigils, prayers, and good deeds, for no man knows the hour of his death.' Having said this and much besides, he gave them his blessing, and they left him sadly; but the brother who had heard the heavenly music came back alone and flung himself to the ground, saying: 'Father, I beg you to let me ask you a question.' 'Ask what you wish', Chad replied. 'Tell me, I pray,' he asked, 'what was the glad song that I heard coming down from heaven upon this oratory, and that later returned to heaven?' 'Since you have heard the singing and were aware of the coming of the heavenly company,' Chad answered, 'I command you in the name of our Lord not to tell anyone of this before my death. For they were angelic spirits, who came to summon me to the heavenly reward that I have always hoped and longed for, and they have promised to return in seven days and take me with them.' All took place as he had been told, for Chad was quickly attacked by a disease which steadily grew worse until the seventh day. Then he prepared for death by receiving the Body and Blood of our Lord, his holy soul was released from the prison-house of the body, and, one may rightly believe, was taken by the angels to the joys of heaven. Nor is it strange that he regarded death with joy as the Day of the Lord, for he had always been careful to prepare for his coming.

In addition to Chad's many virtues of continence, humility, zeal in preaching, voluntary poverty, and many others, he was so filled with the fear of God and so mindful of his last end in all that he did, that I was told by one of his monks named Trumhere – who was my tutor in the Scriptures, and had been trained in the monastery under Chad's direction –

that if a gale arose while he was reading or doing anything else, he would at once call upon God for mercy, and pray him to show mercy on mankind. And if the wind increased in violence, he would close his book and prostrate himself on the ground, praying even more earnestly. But if there was a violent storm of wind and rain, or the earth shook with thunder and lightning, he would go to the church, and say prayers and psalms continuously until the tempest had passed. When his monks asked him why he did this, Chad replied: 'Have you not read, "*The Lord thundered from heaven, and the Highest gave His voice. He sent out His arrows and scattered them; He shot forth lightnings and discomfited them*"? For God stirs the air and raises the winds; He makes the lightning flash and thunders out of heaven, to move the inhabitants of the earth to fear Him, and to remind them of judgement to come. He shatters their conceit and subdues their presumption by recalling to their minds that awful Day when heaven and earth will flame as He comes in the clouds with great power and majesty to judge the living and the dead. Therefore we should respond to His heavenly warnings with love and fear,' said Chad. 'And whenever He raises His hand in the trembling air as if to strike, yet spares us still, we should hasten to implore His mercy, examining our inmost hearts and purging the vileness of our sins, watchful over our lives lest we incur His just displeasure.'

This brother's account of the bishop's death agrees with the evidence of the above-mentioned most reverend Father Egbert, who lived the monastic life in Ireland with Chad when they were both youths, constantly occupied in prayer, fasting, and meditation on the sacred scriptures. But when Chad returned to his own country, Egbert remained an exile for God's sake until the end of his life. A long time afterwards, Hygbald, a very holy and austere man who was an abbot in the province of Lindsey, came to visit him. And while they were discussing the lives of the early Fathers and delighting to imitate them as was fitting in holy men, the name of the most holy Bishop Chad was mentioned. Whereupon Egbert said: 'I know a man still living in this island who, when the bishop died, saw the soul of his brother Cedd descend from heaven accompanied by angels, and carry away his soul to the heavenly kingdom.' Whether he was speaking of himself or another is uncertain, but the truth of a statement by so great a man cannot be doubted.

Chad died on the second of March (672), and was first buried close by Saint Mary's church, but when the church of the most blessed Peter, Prince of the Apostles, was built later, his body was transferred to it.* In both of these places, frequent miracles of healing attested to his virtues. More recently, a mentally deranged tramp arrived one evening, and passed the night in church unknown to the watchmen. And in the morning, to the amazement and delight of all, he left the place in his right mind, which shows that he had been granted healing by the goodness of God. Chad's tomb is in the form of a little wooden house, covered, with an aperture in the side through which those who visit it out of devotion to him may insert their hand and take out some of the dust. They mix this in water, and give it to sick men or beasts to drink, by which means their ailment is quickly relieved and they are restored to health.

In Chad's place Theodore consecrated Wynfrid, a good and modest man, who like his predecessors, presided over the provinces of the Middle Angles, Mercians, and Lindisfarne, all of which were subject to King Wulfhere, who was still living. Winfrid was one of his predecessor's clergy, and had been his deacon for a considerable time.

CHAPTER 4: *Bishop Colman leaves Britain, and founds two monasteries in Scotland, one for the Scots, and another for the English whom he had taken with him* [A.D. 667]

MEANWHILE the Scots bishop Colman left Britain, taking with him all the Scots he had collected at Lindisfarne, together with about thirty English whom he had trained in the monastic life. Leaving some brethren in his own church, he first visited the isle of Hii[1], from which he had originally been sent to preach the word to the English. He subsequently retired to a small island off the west coast of Ireland known in the Scots tongue as Inisboufinde, meaning the Isle of the White Heifer. On his arrival, he founded a monastery, and established there the monks of both races whom he had gathered. But a dispute arose among them in the summer when the Scots went off to wander around places they knew instead of assisting at harvest. Then, as winter approached, they came back and demanded to share whatever the English monks had gathered. Colman sought a remedy for this dispute, and after a widespread search, discovered a site suitable for a monastery on one of the Irish islands which the Scots call Mageo.* Here he bought a small tract of land from the nobleman who owned the island, who made it a condition of sale that the monks who settled there should pray for him. So a monastery was built with the help of the nobleman and all the neighbours, and Colman established the English monks there, leaving the Scots on the original island. This monastery is still occupied by English monks, and has grown from small beginnings into a great place. It is usually known as Mageo, and nowadays, under an improved constitution,* it houses a distinguished community of monks drawn from the English provinces. After the example of the venerable Fathers, they live devoutly and austerely by the labour of their own hands, and observe a Rule under a canonically elected abbot.

1. Iona.

IN the year of our Lord 670, two years after Archbishop Theodore's arrival in Britain, King Oswy of Northumbria fell sick and died at the age of fifty-eight. At this time the King held the apostolic Roman see in such high esteem that, had he recovered from his illness, it was his intention to travel to Rome and end his life among its holy places, and he had persuaded Bishop Wilfrid to conduct him on the journey with the promise of a considerable gift. He died on February 15th, leaving his son Egfrid to succeed him as king. In the third year of the latter's reign, Theodore summoned a council of bishops and many other teachers of the Church who both understood and loved the canonical statutes of the Fathers. As befitted his authority as archbishop, when they were assembled, he began by charging them to observe whatsoever things were conducive to the peace and unity of the Church. The decisions of the Council are in the following form:

'In the name of the Lord God and our Saviour Jesus Christ, who reigns in eternity and rules His Church through the same Lord Jesus Christ. It was thought right that we should assemble in accordance with the custom of ancient canons to transact the necessary affairs of the Church. We therefore assembled on the 24th day of September, the first indiction, at Hertford; that is, myself, Theodore, though unworthy, Bishop of the See of Canterbury by the authority of the apostolic see; our fellow-bishop and brother the most reverend Bisi, Bishop of the East Angles; also our brother the Bishop Wilfrid, Bishop of the Northumbrian people, who is represented by his own proxies. Also present were our brothers and fellow-bishops Putta, Bishop of the Kentish fortress of Rochester; Eleutherius, Bishop of the West Saxons, and Winfrid, Bishop of the province of Mercia. When all the above had assembled and taken their places in due order, I said: "My dearest brothers, for the love and reverence you bear our Redeemer, I beg that we may all deliberate in harmony for our Faith, preserving inviolate the decrees and definitions of our holy and respected Fathers." I then proceeded to speak at length on the need for charity, and the preservation of the Church's unity. And having concluded my discourse, I asked each in turn whether they agreed to observe all the canonical decrees of the ancient Fathers. To which all our fellow-priests replied: "We agree gladly, and we will readily and willingly obey whatever is laid down in the canons of the holy Fathers." I then produced the said book of canons, and publicly showed them ten chapters which I had marked in certain places, because I knew them to be of the greatest importance to us, and I asked that all should devote careful attention to them.

'*Chapter 1.* "That we all unite in observing the holy day of Easter on the Sunday after the fourteenth day of the moon of the first month."

'*Chapter 2.* "That no bishop intrude into the diocese of another, but confine himself to the guidance of the people committed to his charge."

'*Chapter 3.* "That no bishop shall interfere in any way with monasteries dedicated to God, nor take anything from them forcibly."

'*Chapter 4.* "That monks shall not wander from place to place, that is, from monastery to monastery, except with letters dimissory from their own abbot; and that they keep the promise of obedience which they made at the time of their profession."

'*Chapter 5.* "That no clergy shall leave their own bishop and wander about at will, nor be received anywhere without letters of commendation from their own bishop. And should such a person, once received, refuse to return when so directed, both receiver and received shall incur excommunication."

'*Chapter 6.* "That bishops and clergy when travelling shall be content with whatever hospitality is offered them; and that it is unlawful to exercise any priestly function without permission from the bishop in whose diocese they are."

'*Chapter 7.* "That a synod be held twice a year." In view of various obstacles, however, it was unanimously agreed that we should meet once a year on the first of August at Clofeshoch.[1]

'*Chapter 8.* "That no bishop claim precedence over another out of ambition: seniority of consecration shall alone determine precedence."

'*Chapter 9.* It was generally determined, "That more bishops shall be consecrated as the number of the faithful increases." But we shall take no action in the matter for the present.

'*Chapter 10.* On marriages: "That lawful wedlock alone is permissible; incest is forbidden; and no man may leave his lawful wife except, as the gospel provides, for fornication. And if a man puts away his own wife who is joined to him in lawful marriage, he may not take another if he wishes to be a good Christian. He must either remain as he is, or else be reconciled to his wife."

'These decrees are drawn up and defined by our common consent, and in order that no occasion for unedifying controversy or differences between ourselves may arise, it has been thought right that each of us should ratify our decisions by his own signature. I have dictated this expression of our decisions to Titillus our secretary to be written down, and this has been done in the month and indiction mentioned above. Therefore, if anyone shall presume in any way to disregard or disobey these decisions confirmed by our agreement and ratified by our signatures, according to canonical decrees, let him take notice that he incurs suspension from every priestly function and exclusion from our fellowship.

1. Clovesho (probably near London).

'May divine grace preserve us all in safety, who live in the unity of His Holy Church.'

This synod took place in the year of our Lord 673, in July of which year King Egbert died and was succeeded by his brother Lothere, who reigned eleven years and seven months. Bisi, Bishop of the East Angles, who is said to have attended this synod, was successor to Boniface, of whom I have spoken, and was a man of great holiness and devotion; for when Boniface died in the seventeenth year of his episcopate, Theodore consecrated Bisi in his place. And when severe illness prevented him from administering his diocese, two bishops,* Aecci and Bedwin, were chosen and consecrated to carry out his duties, and from then until the present day this province has had two bishops.

CHAPTER 6: *Winfrid is deposed, and Sexwulf appointed to his see: Earconwald is made Bishop of the East Saxons*

NOT long afterwards Archbishop Theodore, displeased at some disobedience on the part of Bishop Winfrid of Mercia, deposed him from the bishopric which he had held only a few years, and appointed in his place Sexwulf, founder and abbot of the monastery of Medeshamstead[1] in the Gyrwas country. On his deposition, Winfrid retired to his own monastery of Ad Barve[2], and lived a most holy life there until his death.

Theodore also made Earconwald Bishop of the East Saxons, whose kings were the above-mentioned Sebbi and Sighere, with London as his see city. Both before and after his consecration as bishop, Earconwald is said to have lived so holy a life that heaven still affords proofs of his virtues. To this day, the horse-litter in which he travelled when ill is preserved by his disciples, and continues to cure many folk troubled by fevers and other complaints. Sick people are cured when

1. Now Peterborough.   2. Barton on Humber.

placed in or near the litter, and chips cut from it bring speedy relief when taken to the sick.

Before he became bishop, Earconwald had built two well-known monasteries, one for himself and the other for his sister Ethelberga, and had established an excellent regular discipline in both houses. His own monastery stood by the river Thames at Ceorteseig[1] – meaning Ceorot's island–in Surrey. The convent where his sister was to rule as mother and instructress of women devoted to God was at Berecingum[2] in the province of the East Saxons. Entrusted with the affairs of this convent, she always bore herself as befitted the sister of a bishop, upright of life, and as heavenly miracles attest, constantly planning for the needs of her community.

CHAPTER 7: *A heavenly light indicates where the bodies of the nuns of Barking should be buried*

IN this convent many proofs of holiness were evident, which many people have recorded from the testimony of eyewitnesses in order that the memory of them might edify future generations; I have therefore been careful to include some in this history of the Church. When the plague that I have mentioned was at its height, it attacked the men's part of the monastery, and daily carried off some to meet their God. The watchful Mother of the Community therefore began to ask the sisters of the convent where they wished their bodies to be buried, and where the cemetery should be made when the plague should enter the enclosure where these servants of God lived separately from the men, and snatch them out of this world in the same catastrophe. But when her frequent enquiries of the sisters had elicited no definite reply, both she and the whole Community received a very clear indication of the wishes of heaven. For one night when they had finished singing the morning psalms* of praise to

1. Chertsey.   2. Barking.

God, these servants of Christ left the oratory to visit the graves of the brothers who had departed this life. And as they were singing their customary praises to our Lord, a light from heaven like a great sheet suddenly appeared and shone over them all, so alarming them that they broke off their singing in consternation. After a short while, this brilliant light, which seemed brighter than the noonday sun, rose and travelled to the south side of the convent westward of the oratory, and having remained over that area for a time, withdrew heavenwards in the sight of them all. This occurrence left no doubt in their minds that the light, which was to guide or receive the souls of Christ's servants into heaven, had also indicated the spot where their bodies were to rest and await the day of resurrection. So brilliant was this light that one of the older brothers, who was in the oratory at the time with another younger brother, reported next morning that the rays of light penetrating the chinks of doors and windows seemed brighter than the brightest daylight.

CHAPTER 8: *A little boy, dying in the convent, announces the approaching death of one of the sisters. A nun, about to depart this life, sees a glimpse of future glory*

IN this convent lived a little boy named Aesica, not more than three years ago, who, being so young, had been brought up and taught by these women vowed to God. Attacked by the plague and about to die, he three times called the name of one of Christ's virgins as though she were present, saying: 'Eadgyth! Eadgyth! Eadgyth!' Then he left this present world, and passed to eternal life. The nun whose name he had called with his dying breath was at once stricken where she was by the same disease, and departed this life, following the child who had called her to the kingdom of heaven.

Again, one of the servants of God was brought to her last

hour by this disease, and in the middle of the night she began
to call to those who attended her to put out the lamp that
burned by her bed. But in spite of her repeated requests, none
of them paid any attention. At length she said: 'I know that
you think that my mind is wandering, but I assure you that
it is not so. I tell you truthfully that I see the house filled with
such brilliant light that your lamp only appears as darkness
to me.' And when they still disregarded her request and made
no reply, she said again: 'Let the lamp burn as long as you
wish, but I assure you that it gives me no light. My light will
come to me when dawn draws near.' She then told them
how a man of God, who had died the same year, had appeared
to her and informed her that at daybreak she would depart
to eternal light. The reality of this vision was quickly confirmed, for the nun died at dawn.

CHAPTER 9: *Signs from heaven appear when the Mother of
the Community departs this life* [A.D. 664]

WHEN Ethelburga, the devout Mother of this God-
fearing Community, was herself about to be taken
out of this world, one of the sisters whose name was Tortgith
saw a wonderful vision. This nun had lived for many years
in the convent, humbly and sincerely striving to serve God,
and had helped the Mother to maintain the regular observances by instructing and correcting the younger sisters. In
order that her strength might be *'made perfect in weakness'* as
the Apostle says, she was suddenly attacked by a serious
disease. Under the good providence of our Redeemer, this
caused her great distress for nine years, in order that any
traces of sin that remained among her virtues due to ignorance or neglect might be burned away in the fires of prolonged suffering. Leaving her cell one night at first light of
dawn, this sister saw distinctly what appeared to be a human
body wrapped in a shroud and shining more brightly than

the sun. This was raised up and carried out of the house where the sisters lived. She observed closely to see how this shining body was raised, and saw what appeared to be cords brighter than gold which drew it upwards until it entered the open heavens and she could see it no longer. When she thought about this vision, there remained no doubt in her mind that some member of the Community was shortly to die, and that her soul would be drawn up to heaven by her good deeds as though by golden cords. And so it proved not many days later, when God's beloved Ethelburga, the Mother of the Community, was set free from her bodily prison. And none who knew her holy life can doubt that when she departed this life the gates of our heavenly home opened at her coming.

In the same convent there was also a nun of noble family in the world, who was yet more noble in her love for the world to come. For many years she had been so crippled that she could not move a single limb; and hearing that the venerable abbess' body had been carried into the church until its burial, she asked to be carried there, and bowed herself towards it in an attitude of prayer. Then she spoke to Ethelburga as though she were still alive, and begged her to pray to God on her behalf, and ask him of his mercy to release her from her continual pain. Her request received a swift reply, for twelve days later she was set free from the body, and exchanged her earthly troubles for a heavenly reward.

Three years after the death of this lady, Christ's servant Tortgith was so wasted away by the disease that I mentioned earlier that her bones scarcely held together, until finally, as death drew near, she lost the use of her limbs and even of her tongue. After three days and nights in this condition, she was suddenly refreshed by a vision from heaven, opened her eyes, and spoke. Looking up to heaven, she began to address the vision that she saw: 'I am so glad that you have come; you are most welcome.' She remained silent for awhile, as if awaiting an answer from the person whom she saw and spoke to; then, seeming a little displeased, she said: 'This is not happy news.' After an interval of silence, she spoke a third time: 'If it cannot be today, I beg that it may not be long delayed.' Then she kept silent a little while, and ended: 'If this decision is final and unalterable, I implore that it may not be delayed beyond the coming night.' When she had finished, those around her asked her to whom she had spoken. 'To my dearest Mother Ethelburga', she replied; and from this they understood that she had come to announce that the hour of her passing was near. So after a day and a night, her prayers were answered, and she was delivered from the burden of the body, and entered the joys of eternal salvation.

CHAPTER 10: *A blind woman regains her sight while praying in the convent burial-ground*

ETHELBURGA was succeeded in the office of abbess by a devout servant of God named Hildilid, who ruled the convent with great energy until extreme old age, promoting observance of the regular discipline, and making provision for the needs of the Community. Owing to the restricted space on which the convent was built, she decided that the bones of Christ's servants buried there, both men and women, should be exhumed and transferred to a single tomb within the church of the blessed Mother of God. And whoever wishes to read about the wonderful things that happened there will find in the book which is the source of my information how a bright, heavenly light was often seen there, and how a wonderfully fragrant scent was often evident.

It would not be right to omit mention of a miraculous cure which this same book records as having taken place in the cemetery of this God-fearing Community. In the neighbourhood there lived a nobleman whose wife was afflicted by a gradual loss of sight, which daily grew worse until she could no longer see the faintest glimmer of light. When she had been totally blind for some while, it suddenly occurred to her that if she were taken to the convent of these holy nuns and prayed before the relics of the saints, she might recover her lost sight. She lost no time in putting this inspiration into effect. Professing a firm belief that she would be healed, she was taken by her maids to the near-by convent and guided to the burial ground, where she remained a long while on her knees in prayer. Her petition was quickly granted, for as she rose from prayer and before she left the place, her sight was restored. And whereas she had been led there by the hands of her maids, she returned home unaided and full of delight. It might almost seem that she had lost her bodily sight solely in order that its restoration might show how great a light is enjoyed by the saints in heaven, and how great a power their virtues possess.

CHAPTER 11: *Sebbi, King of the East Saxons, ends his days as a monk*

THE same little book informs us that Sebbi, a man who dearly loved God and of whom I have already spoken, ruled the kingdom of the East Saxons at this time. He devoted himself to religious exercises, frequent prayer, and acts of mercy, and he preferred a retired, monastic life to all the riches and honours of a kingdom. In fact, had not his wife absolutely refused to be separated from him, he would long before have abdicated and entered a monastery. For this reason many people thought and often said that a man of such disposition should have been a bishop rather than a king. When this soldier of Christ had reigned for thirty years, he was attacked by the serious disease that was to cause his death. He therefore urged his wife that, since they could no longer enjoy or serve the world, they should both devote themselves to the service of God. Having obtained her reluctant consent, the king went to Waldhere, Bishop of

London, successor to Earconwald, and with his blessing
received the monastic habit that he had so long desired. He
brought the bishop a considerable sum of money to be distributed among the poor, and kept nothing at all for himself,
wishing to be *poor in spirit* for the sake of the kingdom of
heaven.

As his malady gained ground and he felt the day of his
death approaching, Sebbi, who was a man of a regal nature,
became apprehensive that the sufferings of a painful death
might cause him to do or say something unbecoming to his
dignity. He therefore summoned the Bishop of London, in
which city he was living, and asked that none but the bishop
and two attendants might be present at his death. The bishop
readily promised this, and not long afterwards this godly
man saw in his sleep a comforting vision, which removed his
anxiety on this score, and revealed to him on what day he
was to depart this life. As he subsequently related, he saw
three men in bright robes come to him, one of whom sat
down in front of his pallet while his companions remained
standing and enquired about the condition of the sick man
they had come to visit. The first man replied that his soul
would leave his body without pain in a splendour of light,
and that he would die in three days' time. Both of these things
happened as he had learned in the vision; for on the third day
at the hour of None, he seemed suddenly to fall into a light
sleep, and breathed out his spirit without any feeling of pain.

A stone sarcophagus had been made ready for the burial,
but when they came to lay his body in it, they found it a
hand's breadth too long for the sarcophagus. So they chiselled
out sufficient stone to add a further two fingers in length to
it, but it still proved too short to receive the body. In this
quandary, they wondered whether to look for another coffin,
or whether, if possible, to shorten the body by bending the
knees until it fitted the sarcophagus. But an amazing thing
happened, undoubtedly caused by providence, that rendered
both these alternatives unnecessary; for in the presence of the

bishop and of Sighard, son of the monk-king – who became
king jointly with his brother Suefred – and a considerable
number of men, the sarcophagus was suddenly found to be
the correct length for the body, so that a pillow could be
placed at the head, while the feet rested four fingers short of
the end of the sarcophagus. Sebbi was buried in the church
of the blessed Apostle of the Gentiles,* through whose
teachings he had learned to aspire to heavenly things.

CHAPTER 12: *Hedda succeeds Eleutherius as Bishop of the
West Saxons: Cuichelm succeeds Putta in the See of
Rochester, and is himself succeeded by Gefmund. The suc-
cession of the Northumbrian bishops*

ELEUTHERIUS was the fourth Bishop of the West Saxons,
Birinus being the first, Agilbert the second, and Wini the
third. On the death of Cenwalh, during whose reign
Eleutherius was made bishop, his aldermen undertook the
government of the realm, dividing it between them and
ruling ten years. Eleutherius died during this interregnum,
and was succeeded in the bishopric by Hedda, who had been
consecrated by Theodore in the city of London. During
Hedda's episcopate, Cadwalla deposed and removed these
aldermen, and assumed control himself; but after a reign of
two years, desire for the kingdom of heaven moved him to
resign his powers, and, as I shall record more fully later, he
went away to end his days in Rome.

In the year of our Lord's incarnation 676, Ethelred, King
of the Mercians, ravaged Kent with his wicked soldiery, pro-
faning churches and monasteries without fear of God or
respect to religion, and among the rest, he destroyed the city
of Rochester, Putta's see, the bishop being absent at the time.
But as soon as he learned that his church was looted and
destroyed, Putta went to Sexwulf, Bishop of the Mercians,
who granted him a church and a small plot of land, where he

ended his days quietly, and made no attempt to re-establish his see. As I have said, he was more at home in religious than in worldly matters, and therefore served God only in his own church, travelling about wherever invited to teach church music. Theodore consecrated Cuichelm as Bishop of Rochester in his place, but after a short time he resigned this destitute see and withdrew elsewhere, Gebmund taking his place as bishop.

In the month of August 678, in the eighth year of Egfrid's reign, a star known as a comet appeared, which remained visible for three months, rising in the morning and emitting what seemed to be a tall column of bright flame. In the same year a dispute arose between King Egfrid and the most reverend Bishop Wilfrid, who was driven from his diocese, and two bishops were appointed to preside over the Northumbrian churches in his place. These were Bosa, Bishop of Deira, and Eata, Bishop of Bernicia; the former had the city of York as his see, and the latter had Hagulstad[1] or Lindisfarne. Both of them were monks before their elevation to the episcopate. At the same time Eadhed was made bishop of the province of Lindsey, which King Egfrid had recently annexed after Wulfhere's defeat and flight. So for the first time this province had its own bishop, the second being Ethelwin; the third, Edgar; and the fourth, Cynebert, the present bishop. Before Eadhed, Sexwulf had been bishop not only of Lindsey, but also of the Mercians and Middle Angles; when he was expelled from Lindsey, he continued to preside over the other two provinces. Eadhed, Bosa, and Eata were consecrated at York by Archbishop Theodore, who, three years after Wilfrid's departure, consecrated two others, Tunbert to the See of Hagulstad – Eata remaining at Lindisfarne – and Trumwin to be bishop of those Picts* who were then subject to English rule. When Ethelred recovered the province of Lindsey, Eadhed returned and was appointed by him as Bishop of Ripon.

1. Hexham.

D RIVEN out of his see, Wilfrid spent a considerable time travelling in various parts, and also went to Rome. When he returned to Britain, the hostility of King Egfrid made it impossible for him to return to his own province or diocese, but nothing could deter him from preaching the Gospel. He therefore made his way to the province of the South Saxons, which stretches west and south from Kent as far as Wessex, and covers an area of seven thousand hides. As the province was still pagan, Wilfrid preached the Christian Faith there, and administered the baptism of salvation. Ethelwalh its king had been baptized in Mercia not long previously under the influence of King Wulfhere, who was present at his baptism and became his godfather at the font. In token of their relationship, Wulfhere gave him two provinces, the Isle of Wight and the province of Meanware* in the territory of the West Saxons. With the king's approval and greatly to his satisfaction, the bishop baptized the leading thanes and soldiers of the province, while the remainder of the people were baptized either then or subsequently by the priests Eappa, Padda, Burghelm, and Odda. Queen Ebba, who had already received baptism in her own province of the Hwiccas, was the daughter of Eanfrid, brother of Eanher, both of whom were Christians, as were their people; otherwise the whole South Saxon province was ignorant of the Name and Faith of Christ. There was, however, a Scots monk named Dicul, who had a very small monastery at a place called Bosanham[1], surrounded by woods and the sea, where five or six brothers served the Lord in a life of humility and poverty: but none of the natives were willing to follow their way of life or listen to their teaching.

By preaching to these folk, Bishop Wilfrid not only delivered them from the penalty of eternal damnation, but also

1. Bosham, near Chichester.

saved them from a cruel and horrible extinction in this life. For no rain had fallen in the province for three years prior to his arrival, and a terrible famine ensued which reduced many to an awful death. It is said that frequently forty or fifty emaciated and starving people would go to a precipice, or to the sea shore, where they would join hands and leap in, to die by the fall or by drowning. But on the very day that the nation received the baptism of faith, a soft but ample rainfall refreshed the earth, restoring greenness to the fields and giving a happy and prosperous season. Having once abandoned their earlier superstition and rejected idolatry, '*the heart and flesh of all rejoiced in the living God*', and they came to understand how He who is true God, had of his divine mercy granted them both spiritual and material blessings. For when Wilfrid had first arrived in the province and found so much misery from famine, he taught the people to obtain food by fishing; for although fish were plentiful in the sea and rivers, the people had no knowledge of fishing, and caught only eels. So the bishop's men collected eel-nets from all sides and cast them into the sea, where, by the aid of God's grace, they quickly caught three hundred fishes of various kinds. These they divided into three portions, giving a hundred to the poor, a hundred to those who had lent their nets, and retaining a hundred for their own needs. By this good turn the bishop won the hearts of all, and the people began to listen more readily to his teaching, hoping to obtain heavenly blessings through the ministry of one to whom they already owed these material benefits.

At this time, King Ethelwalh granted the most reverend Bishop Wilfrid eighty-seven hides of land so that he could maintain his exiled companions. This land lay at Selsey, known as the Isle of the Sea-Calf, a place surrounded by the sea on all sides except to the west, where there is an approach about a sling's cast in width. A place of this description is known as a *peninsula* by the Latins, and as a *chersonese* by the Greeks. Bishop Wilfrid accepted this land, and having built

a monastery there, established the regular life, most of the
monks being his own companions: his successors occupy the
place to this day. Until the death of King Egfrid five years
later, Wilfrid performed all the duties of a bishop in these
parts, and was held in high esteem by all. And since the king
had given him not only the land, but all the property and
inhabitants on it, Wilfrid instructed and baptized them all in
the Faith of Christ. Among them were two hundred and
fifty male and female slaves, all of whom he released from
the slavery of Satan by baptism; granting them their freedom, and releasing them from the yoke of human slavery as
well.

CHAPTER 14: *A fatal epidemic is halted by the intercession of
King Oswald*

CERTAIN proofs of heaven's especial favour are said to
have been shown to this monastery, for once the tyranny
of the Devil had been overthrown, the rule of Christ began.
I have thought it fitting to preserve the memory of one of
these stories, often told me by the very reverend Bishop
Acca, who said that it was vouched for by some very reliable
brethren of the monastery.

About the time that this province accepted the Faith of
Christ, a dangerous epidemic struck many provinces of
Britain. When, by God's dispensation, it reached the monastery, ruled at the time by the most religious priest of Christ,
Eappa, it swept from this life many of the brethren, some of
whom had come with the bishop, while others were South
Saxons recently converted to the Faith. The brethren therefore decided to observe a three-day fast and implore God in
his mercy to show pity on them, that he would preserve
those who were in danger of death by disease, and deliver the
souls of those already departed this life from eternal damnation.

In the monastery at this time lived a little Saxon boy, who had recently been converted to the Faith; this child caught the disease, and for a long time had been confined to bed. About the second hour on the second day of prayer and fasting, he was alone in the place where he lay sick, when, under divine providence, the most blessed Princes of the Apostles deigned to appear to him; for he was a boy of innocent and gentle disposition, who sincerely believed the truths of the Faith that he had accepted. The Apostles greeted him very lovingly, and said: 'Son, put aside your present fear of death, for today we are going to take you with us to the kingdom of heaven. But first of all you must wait until the Masses are said, and you have received the Viaticum of the Body and Blood of our Lord. Then you shall be set free from sickness and death, and carried up to the endless joys of heaven. So call the priest Eappa, and tell him that our Lord has heard your prayers, and regarded your fasting and devotion with favour. No one else in this monastery and its possessions is to die, and all who are now suffering from this disease will recover and be restored to their former health. You alone are to be set free by death today, and shall be taken to heaven to see the Lord Christ whom you have served so faithfully. God in his mercy has granted you this favour at the intercession of the devout King Oswald, so beloved by God, who once ruled the people of Northumbria with outstanding devotion as their earthly king, and whose Christian piety has won him an everlasting kingdom. For today is the anniversary of the king's death in battle at the hands of the heathen, when he was taken up to the joys of the souls in heaven and enrolled among the company of the Saints. If the brethren will consult the chronicles that record the burials of the dead, they will find that this is the day on which he departed this life, as we have said. So let them say Masses at all the altars of the monastery, either in thanksgiving for God's answer to their prayers, or in commemoration of King Oswald the former ruler of their nation, who has prayed for them as strangers of his own race. Let all the brethren assemble in church, and join in offering the heavenly Sacrifice; and let them end their fast and take food to restore their strength.'

When the boy had called Eappa and told him all that the Apostles had said, the priest particularly asked him to describe the clothes and appearance of these men who had appeared to him. 'They wore wonderful robes,' the boy replied, 'and their faces were very kindly and handsome, such as I have never seen before. I did not believe that there could be men so distinguished and wonderful. One of them was tonsured like a priest, and the other had a long beard; and they said that one of them was Peter and the other Paul, and that they were servants of our Lord and Saviour Jesus Christ, sent by Him to protect our monastery.' The priest then believed the boy's statement, and went off at once to consult his chronicle, where he found that King Oswald had indeed been killed on that very day. So he summoned the brethren, ordered a meal to be prepared, Masses to be said, and all the brethren to communicate as usual. He also directed that a particle of the Lord's Offering should be taken to the sick boy at the time of the holy Sacrifice.

A little while later the same day the boy died, and his death proved the truth of what Christ's Apostles had told him. In further confirmation of his statement, no one except himself died in the monastery at that time. Many who heard about this vision were wonderfully inspired to implore God's mercy in every trouble, and to adopt the wholesome remedy of fasting. And from that time the heavenly birthday of Christ's warrior King Oswald was commemorated each year by the offering of Masses, not only in this monastery but in many other places as well.

CHAPTER 15: *King Cadwalla of the Gewissae kills King Ethelwalh and devastates his province with plundering and slaughter*

MEANWHILE Cadwalla, a daring young man of the royal house of the Gewissae, exiled from his own country, came with an army and killed King Ethelwalh, wasting the province with slaughtering and plunder. But the last king's ealdormen Berthun and Andhun soon drove him out, and administered the country in turn. The former was subsequently killed by Cadwalla when he became king of the Gewissae, and the province was reduced to a worse state of subjection. Similarly Ini, who succeeded Cadwalla, held the province in subjection for several years. For this reason, it had no bishop of its own during all this period; for when Wilfrid its first bishop had been recalled home, it became dependent on the Bishop of the Gewissae, that is, the West Saxons, whose see was at Winchester.

CHAPTER 16: *The Isle of Wight receives Christian settlers. Two young princes of the island are killed immediately after Baptism* [A.D. 686]

AFTER Cadwalla became king of the Gewissae, he captured the Isle of Wight, whose people were all heathen, and deliberately exterminated all the natives, replacing them by settlers from his own province. Although not yet baptized, he is said to have bound himself by an oath to dedicate a quarter of the land and spoils to the Lord if he conquered the island, and he fulfilled this oath by offering it for God's use to Bishop Wilfrid, who chanced to have left his own people in order to visit the island at this time. By English reckoning, the island has an area of twelve hundred hides, so that the bishop was given three hundred hides of land. This share he entrusted to Bernwin, one of his clerks who was his own sister's son, and he appointed a priest named Hiddila to preach and administer Baptism to all who sought salvation.

It would not be right to omit mention of two young princes, brothers of Atwald, king of the island, who were especially favoured by God's grace, and became the first natives of the island to believe and be saved. On the approach of the invaders, these princes escaped from the island and crossed to the adjoining province of the Jutes. Here they were guided to a place called At-the-Stone,[1] where they hoped to remain hidden from the victorious king; but they were betrayed and ordered to be put to death. This was reported to the priest Cynebert, Abbot of Hreutford, that is, the Ford of Reeds;[2] so he sought out the king, who was living in seclusion in the district while he recovered from wounds received while fighting in the Isle of Wight, and begged him that, if it was necessary for these lads to die, he might first be allowed to instruct them in the mysteries of the Christian Faith. The king consented to this, and when Cynebert had taught them the word of truth, he baptized them in the fount of salvation, and assured their entry into the kingdom of heaven. So when the executioner arrived, they met bodily death gladly, in the firm faith that through it their souls would pass to eternal life. So last of all the provinces of Britain, the Isle of Wight accepted the Faith of Christ, but owing to its subjection to an alien rule, it had no bishop or see of its own until the time of Daniel, who is now Bishop of the West Saxons.

The Isle of Wight lies opposite the boundary between the South Saxons and the Gewissae, and is separated from it by three miles of sea, known as the Solent. In this strait, two ocean tides that flow around Britain from the boundless northern seas meet in daily opposition off the mouth of the River Homelea.[3] This enters the sea after flowing through the lands of the Jutes who live in the Gewissae country; and when

1. Stoneham, Hants.   2. Redbridge.
                  3. The Hamble.

the turbulence ceases, they flow back into the ocean whence they spring.

CHAPTER 17: *Theodore presides over a synod held in the Plain of Heathfield (Hatfield)* [A.D. 680]

ABOUT this time, Theodore learned that the faith of the Church at Constantinople was greatly disturbed by the heresy of Eutyches.* Wishing to preserve the English Church that he ruled untainted by this error, he summoned a large number of venerable bishops and teachers to a conference; and when he had carefully ascertained their individual beliefs, he found them all united in support of the Catholic Faith. He therefore took pains to record this fact in a synodical letter, to serve as a reminder and guide to future generations. This letter opens as follows:

'In the Name of our Lord and Saviour Jesus Christ. On the seventeenth of October in the tenth year of the reign of our most devout lord Egfrid, King of the Northumbrians; in the sixth year of King Ethelfrid of the Mercians; in the seventeenth year of King Aldwulf of the East Anglians; and in the seventh year of King Lothair of Kent. Under the presidency of Theodore, by the grace of God Archbishop of the island of Britain and of the City of Canterbury, we the venerable bishops of the island of Britain assembled in conclave at the place which the Saxons call Heathfield, having the most holy Gospels before us, hereby unite to proclaim the true and orthodox faith. This same faith our Lord Jesus Christ delivered in the flesh to His disciples, who saw Him in person and heard His teaching. This is now set forth in the Creed of the holy fathers, and by all the sacred General Councils, and by the united voice of the accredited doctors of the Catholic Church. We follow them in devotion and right faith, professing our belief in their divinely inspired teachings; and we unite with the holy fathers in acknowledging the Father, the

229

Son, and the Holy Spirit, the Trinity consubstantial in Unity, and Unity in Trinity, that is, One God subsisting in three consubstantial Persons of equal glory and honour.'

And after a great deal more to this effect, in which they affirm their confession of the true Faith, the letter of this holy synod continues: 'We accept the decisions of the five holy General Councils of the blessed fathers who were acceptable to God; that is, the Council of three hundred and eighteen bishops assembled at Nicaea, which condemned Arius and his impious teachings; the Council of one hundred and fifty bishops at Constantinople, which condemned the senseless teachings of Macedonius and Eudoxius; the first Council of two hundred bishops at Ephesus, which condemned the wicked teachings of Nestorius; the Council of three hundred and sixty bishops at Chalcedon, which condemned the teaching of Eutyches and Nestorius; and the fifth Council at Constantinople in the reign of Justinian the younger, which condemned Theodorus, Theodoret, the epistles of Ibas, and the teachings of Cyril.'

Shortly after this, the letter continues: 'We also accept the decisions of the Council held in Rome* under the blessed Pope Martin in the ninth year and eighth indiction of the reign of the most pious Emperor Constantine (IV). We adore our Lord Jesus Christ as they adored Him, neither adding nor withholding anything; we sincerely and formally anathematize those whom they anathematized, and accept those whom they accepted. And we glorify God the Father, who is without beginning, and His only-begotten Son, begotten of the Father before all worlds, and the Holy Spirit ineffably proceeding from the Father and the Son, as proclaimed by all the holy Apostles, prophets, and teachers whom we have already mentioned. And we who have all joined with Archbishop Theodore in proclaiming the Catholic Faith affix our signatures hereto.'

AMONG those who signed the affirmation of the Catholic Faith at this Synod was the venerable John, Arch-cantor of the church of the holy Apostle Peter and Abbot of the monastery of Saint Martin, who had recently come from Rome under instructions from Pope Agatho with the most reverend Abbot Benedict, of whom I have spoken. For when Benedict had built a monastery in Britain near the mouth of the River Wear[1] in honour of the blessed Prince of the Apostles, he travelled to Rome with his colleague and companion Ceofrid, who later succeeded him as abbot of the monastery. As he had made several earlier visits to Rome, he was received with honour by Pope Agatho of blessed memory, from whom he asked and obtained a letter of privilege, granted with his apostolic authority, which confirmed the independence of the monastery that he had founded, for he knew this to accord with the wishes of King Egfrid, with whose approval and grant he had built the monastery.

Benedict received Abbot John and conducted him to Britain, where he was to teach his monks the chant for the liturgical year as it was sung at Saint Peter's, Rome. In accordance with the Pope's instructions, Abbot John taught the cantors of the monastery the theory and practice of singing and reading aloud, and he put into writing all that was necessary for the proper observance of festivals throughout the year. His teachings are still followed in this monastery, and many copies have been made for other places. John's instruction was not limited to the brethren of this monastery alone, for all who were proficient singers came from nearly all the monasteries of the province to hear him, and he received many invitations to teach elsewhere.

In addition to his task of teaching singing, and reading, John had also been directed by the apostolic Pope to make

1. Monkwearmouth.

careful enquiries about the faith of the English Church, and
to report on it when he returned to Rome. And he had
brought with him the decisions of the Council recently held
in Rome by blessed Pope Martin and one hundred and five
bishops, which particularly condemned those who taught
that only one will operated in Christ, and he handed this over
for a transcript to be made in the monastery of the most
religious Abbot Benedict. Those who supported such views
had caused great confusion in the Church of Constantinople
at the time, but by God's help they were exposed and refuted.
For this reason, Pope Agatho wished to be informed on the
state of the Church in Britain as well as in other provinces,
and whether it was free from contamination by heretics, so
he entrusted this mission to the most reverend Abbot John,
who had already been ordered to visit Britain. After the
above-mentioned Synod had been summoned for the purpose in Britain, the Catholic Faith was shown to be held untainted by all, and a copy of its decisions was given to John to
take back to Rome.

Not long after crossing the sea, on his return journey to his
own country, John fell sick and died; and out of devotion to
Saint Martin, of whose monastery he was abbot, his friends
carried his body to Tours, where he was buried with great
honour. For on his journey to Britain he had been courteously welcomed there by the brethren, who begged him to
visit them again on his return to Rome. They also provided
him with brothers to accompany him on his journey and help
him in his appointed task. And although he died on his journey, John's testimony to the Catholic Faith of the English
was taken on to Rome, where it was received with great
satisfaction by the apostolic Pope, and by all who read it.

KING EGFRID married Etheldreda,* a daughter of Anna, King of the East Angles, of whom I have often spoken; he was a very devout man, noble in mind and deed. Before her marriage to Egfrid, Etheldreda had been married to Tonbert, a prince of the South Gyrwas, but he died shortly after the wedding and she was given to King Egfrid. Although she lived with him for twelve years, she preserved the glory of perpetual virginity, which fact is absolutely vouched for by Bishop Wilfrid of blessed memory, of whom I made enquiry when some people doubted it. He said that Egfrid promised to give estates and much money to anyone who could persuade the queen to consummate the marriage, knowing that she loved no man so well as himself. But there is no doubt that the same thing could happen in our own day, when reliable histories record it as having happened on several occasions in the past through the grace of the same Lord who has promised to remain with us until the end of the world. For the miraculous preservation of her body from corruption in the tomb is evidence that she had remained untainted by bodily intercourse.

For a long time Etheldreda begged the king to allow her to retire from worldly affairs and serve Christ the only true King in a convent. And having at length obtained his reluctant consent, she entered the convent of the Abbess Ebba, King Egfrid's aunt, at Coludi,[1] where she received the veil and clothing of a nun from the hands of Bishop Wilfrid. A year later she was herself made Abbess of Elge,[2] where she built a convent and became the virgin mother of many virgins vowed to God, displaying the pattern of a heavenly life in word and deed. It is said that from the time of her entry into the convent, she never wore linen but only woollen garments, and that she washed in hot water only before the

1. Coldingham.   2. Ely.

greater festivals such as Easter, Pentecost, and the Epiphany, and then only after she and her assistants had helped the other servants of Christ to wash. She seldom had more than one meal a day except at the greater festivals or under urgent necessity, and she always remained at prayer in the church from the hour of Matins until dawn unless prevented by serious illness. Some say that she possessed the spirit of prophecy, and that in the presence of all the community, she not only foretold the plague that was to cause her death, but also the number who would die of it in the convent. She was taken to Christ in the presence of her nuns seven years after her appointment as abbess, and in accordance with her instructions, she was buried among them in the wooden coffin in which she died.

Etheldreda was succeeded in the office of abbess by her sister Sexburga,* who had been wife of King Earconbert of Kent. Seventeen years after Etheldreda's burial, this abbess decided to exhume her bones, place them in a new coffin, and transfer them into the church. She therefore directed some of the brethren to search for stone to make this coffin. And since the Isle of Ely was surrounded on all sides by sea and fens and had no large stones, they took a boat and came to a small ruined city not far distant which the English call Grantchester. After a short while they discovered near the city walls a white marble sarcophagus of very beautiful workmanship* with a close-fitting lid of similar stone; and realizing that God had prospered their journey, they returned thanks to him, and brought it back to the convent.

When the tomb of the holy and virginal spouse of Christ was opened and her body brought to light, it was found as free from decay as if she had died and been buried that very day; this is vouched for by Bishop Wilfrid and many other knowledgeable persons. But even fuller proof is given by the physician Cynefrid, who was present both at her death and exhumation, and who stated that during her last illness she had a large tumour under the jaw. He said: 'I was asked to open the tumour and drain away the poisonous matter in it. I did this, and for two days she seemed somewhat easier, so that many thought that she would recover from her illness. But on the third day her earlier pain returned, and she was taken from this world, and exchanged all pain and death for everlasting life and health. When her bones were to be taken up out of the grave so many years later, a pavilion was raised over it, and the whole community stood around it chanting, the brothers on one side, and the sisters on the other. The abbess herself, with a few others, went in to take up and wash the bones, when we suddenly heard her cry out in a loud voice, "Glory to the Name of the Lord!" Shortly afterwards they opened the door of the pavilion and called me in. There I saw the body of the holy virgin taken from its grave and laid on a bed as though asleep, and when they had uncovered her face, they showed me that the incision which I had made had healed. This astounded me, for in place of the open gaping wound with which she was buried, there remained only the faint mark of a scar. All the linen cloths in which the body had been wrapped appeared as fresh and new as on the day when they had been placed around her pure body.'

It is said that when she was affected by this tumour and pain in her jaw and neck, she welcomed pain of this kind, and used to say: 'I realize very well that I deserve this wearisome disease in my neck, because I remember that when I was a girl, I used to wear the needless burden of jewellery. And I believe that God in His goodness wishes me to endure this pain in my neck so that I may be absolved from the guilt of my needless vanity. So now I wear a burning red tumour on my neck instead of gold and pearls.' At the touch of these robes devils were expelled from the bodies of those whom they possessed, and other complaints were sometimes cured. And the coffin in which she was first buried is said to have cured diseases of the eye, relieving pain and failing sight in those who placed their heads on the coffin as they prayed.

When the sisters had washed the virgin's body and clothed it in new robes, they carried it into the church and laid it in the sarcophagus which had been brought, where it is held in great veneration to this day. This same sarcophagus was found to fit the virgin's body in a marvellous way, as though it had been especially made for her, and the place cut out for the head exactly fitted the measurements of her own.

Ely lies in the province of the East Angles, an area of about six hundred hides. As I have said, it resembles an island surrounded by water and marshes, and it derives its name from the vast quantity of eels that are caught in the marshes. And the servant of Christ wished to have her monastery in this place because, as already mentioned, her forbears came from the province of the East Angles.

CHAPTER 20: *A hymn in honour of Etheldreda*

O TRINITY, who thro' the ages long
    Has ruled the spheres, give aid to this my song.
Let Maro wars extol – of peace I sing,
And praise the gracious gifts of Christ our King.
No rape of Helen forms my present theme,
Or idle tale for venal, shallow men:
Such foolish tales I shun, and here proclaim
The gifts of God that raise our hearts again.
See! God most high resigns His royal throne,
Descends to earth, and enters Mary's womb;
To free the sons of men from all their tears
A spotless Virgin her Creator bears,
The Gate of Heaven, thro' which its radiance pours.
Now sing, O choirs of virgins, of your Queen,
The peerless one whose like has ne'er been seen,
To whose high honour countless flowers arise
To follow her and imitate her ways.
Fair Agatha stands firm amid the flame;
Eulalia, too, prefers their sting to shame.

Strong in her faith, the virgin Thecla stands;
Euphemia faces beasts with prayerful hands.
Sweet Agnes smiles to greet the deadly thrust;
Cecilia meets her death and keeps her trust.
High triumph waits the faithful, trusting heart;
God's loving care no worldly power can part.
Now Etheldreda shines on these our days,
And sheds the light of grace upon our ways.
Sprung of a royal and illustrious line,
She brings yet nobler gifts to Christ her King.
A glorious queen, a starry sceptre she
Receives from Him, a well-won dignity.
What earthly prince a worthy groom would be
When Christ makes her His bride eternally?
In Mary's heavenly train you move in grace,
And, in her pattern, bear a royal race.
Twelve years you reigned a queen to your royal lord,
Then took the veil, and gave yourself to God.
Renowned for holy deeds, this blessed saint
Returned her life to God still free from taint.
For sixteen years her body, sealed away,
Remained untarnished by the tomb's decay.
Thine was the power, O Christ, that did maintain
Her holy body and its robes from stain.
The direful dropsy and disease depart
When her fair garments touch the ailing part.
And Satan, Eve's seducer, burns with hate
As this victorious virgin seals his fate.
Chaste bride of Christ, what glory rings you now
As heaven and earth your name and graces show!
Raise high the torches! Light the Bridegroom's road:
Prepare a joyful welcome for our God!
Take up the harp, and sing a sweet new song –
Repeat its happy chorus, saintly throng!
None from the Lamb's own flock can e'er remove
The souls close-bound to Him by chains of love.

CHAPTER 21: *Archbishop Theodore makes peace between King Egfrid and King Ethelred* [A.D. 679]

IN the ninth year of his reign, King Egfrid fought a great battle near the river Trent against King Ethelred of Mercia, in which Egfrid's brother Elfwin was killed. The latter was a young man of about eighteen, who was much loved in both provinces since Ethelred had married his sister Osthryth. This gave every indication of causing fiercer strife and more lasting hatred between the two kings and their peoples, until Archbishop Theodore, the beloved of God, trusting in God's help, smothered the flames of this awful peril by his wholesome advice. As a result, peace was restored between the kings and peoples, and no further bloodshed occurred, but the customary heavy compensation* was paid to King Egfrid for his brother's death. So peace was maintained between these kings and their peoples for many years.

CHAPTER 22: *A prisoner's chains fall off when Masses are sung on his behalf* [A.D. 679]

IN the above battle in which Elfwin was killed, a remarkable thing occurred which I should not fail to mention since it will further the salvation of many. During the battle, a young thane named Imma belonging to Elfwin's forces was struck down, and lay apparently dead all that day and the following night among the bodies of the slain. At length he recovered consciousness, sat up, and bandaged his wounds as well as he could; then when he had rested awhile, he got up and tried to find some friends to help him. While so engaged he was found and captured by men of the enemy forces, and taken before their leader, who was an ealdorman of King Ethelred. When asked his identity, he was afraid to reveal that he was a soldier, and answered that he was a poor married peasant who had come with others to bring provisions

to the army. The ealdorman ordered him to be given shelter
and treatment for his wounds; and when he began to recover,
he ordered him to be chained to prevent his escape. But this
proved impossible, for no sooner had those who chained him
left than the fetters fell off.*

Now this young man had a brother named Tunna who
was a priest, and abbot of a monastery that is still called
Tunnacester after him. And when he heard that his brother
had been killed in battle, he went to see whether he could
find his body. Finding another very similar to him, he concluded that it was his; so he took the body back to his monastery, gave it honourable burial, and offered many Masses
for the repose of his brother's soul. And it was on account of
these Masses that, as I have said, when anyone tried to chain
him, he was immediately set free. The ealdorman, whose
prisoner he was, was astonished, and asked why he could not
be bound, and whether he possessed any written charms like
those mentioned in fables. He replied: 'I know nothing about
such things, but I have a brother who is a priest in my own
province, and I am sure that, thinking me killed, he has said
many Masses for me; and were I now in another life, my soul
would be freed from its pains by his prayers.' After a considerable time in the ealdorman's custody, those who observed the young man closely realized from his appearance,
clothing, and speech that he was no common peasant as he
said, but of noble birth. The ealdorman then sent for him
privately, and pressed him to disclose his identity, promising
that he would do him no harm if he told him the truth about
who he was. On this assurance, the young man revealed that
he was a king's thane. At this the ealdorman said: 'I realized
by all your answers that you were no peasant, and you deserve to die, because all my brothers and kinsmen were killed
in that battle: but I will not put you to death because I have
given you my promise.'

As soon as Imma recovered, the ealdorman sold him to a
Frisian in London, who took him away, but found that he

was unable to fetter him. And when various kinds of fetters had been put on him and none could hold him, his buyer gave him permission to ransom himself if he could. It was at the hour of Terce, when Masses were usually said, that his chains were most frequently loosed. Promising either to return or to send his ransom money, Imma went to King Lothair of Kent, who was nephew to the above Queen Etheldreda, because he had once been one of the queen's thanes. From him he obtained the money for his ransom, and sent it to his master as he had promised.

When Imma returned to his own country, he visited his brother and gave him a full account of all his troubles, and how he had been helped in them, and he thus learned that his chains had been loosed at the times when Mass was being said on his behalf. He also realized how he had received comfort and strength from heaven in many other dangers through the prayers of his brother and his offering of Christ's saving Sacrifice. He related his experiences to many people, who were inspired to greater faith and devotion, and gave themselves to prayer, almsgiving, and offering the Holy Sacrifice to God for the deliverance of their friends who had departed this life; for they understood how this saving Sacrifice availed for the eternal redemption of soul and body.

This story was told me by those who had heard it from the mouth of the man to whom these things had happened, so that I have no hesitation about including it in this history of the Church as it was related.

CHAPTER 23: *The life and death of Abbess Hilda* [A.D. 680]

IN the following year, that is the year of our Lord 680, Hilda, abbess of the monastery of Whitby, a most religious servant of Christ, passed away to receive the reward of eternal life on the seventeenth of November at the age of sixty-six, after a life full of heavenly deeds. Her life fell into two equal parts, for she spent thirty-three years most nobly in secular occupations, and dedicated the remainder of her life even more nobly to our Lord in the monastic life. She was nobly born, the daughter of Hereric, nephew to King Edwin, with whom she received the Faith and sacraments of Christ through the preaching of Paulinus of blessed memory, first bishop of the Northumbrians, and she preserved this Faith inviolate until she was found worthy to see him in heaven.

When she decided to abandon the secular life and serve God alone, she returned to the province of the East Angles, whose king was her kinsman; for having renounced her home and all that she possessed, she wished if possible to travel on from there into Gaul, and to live an exile for our Lord's sake in the monastery of Cale.[1] In this manner she hoped the more easily to attain her eternal heavenly home, for her sister Hereswith, wife of Aldwulf, King of the East Angles, was living there as a professed nun and awaiting her eternal crown. Inspired by her example, Hilda remained in the province a full year, intending to join her overseas; but when Bishop Aidan was recalled home, he granted her one hide of land on the north bank of the River Wear, where she observed the monastic rule with a handful of companions.

After this, Hilda was made abbess of the monastery of Heruteu,[2] founded not long previously by Heiu, a devout servant of Christ who is said to have been the first woman in the province of Northumbria to take vows and be clothed as a nun, which she did with the blessing of Bishop Aidan. But soon after establishing the monastery she left for the town of Calcaria, which the English call Calcacestir,[3] and settled there. Then Christ's servant Hilda was appointed to rule this monastery, and quickly set herself to establish a regular observance as she had been instructed by learned men; for Bishop Aidan and other devout men, who knew her and admired her innate wisdom and love of God, often used to visit and advise her.

1. Chelles, near Paris.   2. Hartlepool.   3. Possibly Tadcaster.

When she had ruled this monastery for some years, constantly occupied in establishing the regular life, she further undertook to found or organize a monastery at a place known as Streaneshalch, and carried out this appointed task with great energy. She established the same regular life as in her former monastery, and taught the observance of justice, devotion, purity, and other virtues, but especially in peace and charity. After the example of the primitive Church, no one there was rich or poor, for everything was held in common, and none possessed any personal property. So great was her prudence that not only ordinary folk, but kings and princes used to come and ask her advice in their difficulties. Those under her direction were required to make a thorough study of the Scriptures and occupy themselves in good works, in order that many might be found fitted for Holy Orders and the service of God's altar.

Subsequently, five bishops were chosen from this monastery – Bosa, Hedda, Oftfor, John, and Wilfrid – all of them men of outstanding merit and holiness. As already mentioned, Bosa was consecrated Bishop of York; Hedda became Bishop of Dorchester; and I shall tell in due course how John became Bishop of Hexham, and Wilfrid Bishop of York. Meanwhile I wish to speak of Oftfor, who having devoted himself to reading and studying the Scriptures in both Hilda's monasteries, wished to win greater perfection, and travelled to Kent in order to visit Archbishop Theodore, of blessed memory. When he had continued his studies under him for some while, he decided to visit Rome, which in those days was considered an act of great merit. On his return to Britain he visited the province of the Hwiccas, then ruled by King Osric, where he remained a long time, preaching the word of faith and setting an example of holy life to all who met and heard him. At this time Bosel, bishop of the province, was in such ill health that he was unable to carry out his duties, and Oftfor was therefore unanimously elected bishop in his place. At the request of King Ethelred, he was consecrated by Bishop Wilfrid of blessed memory, who was acting as Bishop of the Middle Angles, since Theodore had died, and as yet no bishop had been appointed to succeed him. Tatfrid, predecessor of the man of God Bosel, an energetic and very learned man of great ability, had been elected bishop while a monk in Hilda's monastery, but met an untimely death before he could be consecrated.

Christ's servant Abbess Hilda, whom all her acquaintances called Mother because of her wonderful devotion and grace, was not only an example of holy life to members of her own community, for she also brought about the amendment and salvation of many living far distant, who heard the inspiring story of her industry and goodness. Her life was the fulfilment of a dream which her mother Bregusyth had when Hilda was an infant, during the time that her husband Hereric was living in banishment under the protection of the British king Cerdic, where he was poisoned. In this dream she fancied that he was suddenly taken away, and although she searched everywhere, she could find no trace of him. When all her efforts had failed, she discovered a most valuable jewel under her garments, and as she looked closely, it emitted such a brilliant light that all Britain was lit by its splendour. This dream was fulfilled in her daughter, whose life afforded a shining example not only to herself, but to all who wished to live a good life.

When Hilda had ruled this monastery for many years, it pleased the Author of our salvation to try her holy soul by a long sickness, in order that, like the Apostle, her strength might be perfected in weakness. She was attacked by a burning fever that racked her continually for six years; but during all this time she never ceased to give thanks to her Maker, or to instruct the flock committed to her both privately and publicly. For her own example taught them all to serve God rightly when in health, and to render thanks to him faithfully when in trouble or bodily weakness. In the seventh year of her illness she suffered interior pains, and her last day came.

About dawn she received the Viaticum of the holy Communion, and when she had summoned all the servants of Christ in the monastery, she urged them to maintain the gospel peace among themselves and with others. And while she was still speaking, she joyfully welcomed death, and, in the words of our Lord, passed from death to life.

That same night it pleased Almighty God to make her death known by means of a vision in a monastery some considerable distance away, which she had founded that year at Hackness. In this place there was a devout nun named Begu, who had vowed herself to God in virginity in the monastic life over thirty years previously. As she was resting in the sisters' dormitory, she suddenly heard the well-known note of the bell that used to wake and call them to prayer when any of the sisters had died. Opening her eyes, as she thought, she saw the roof open, and a great light pour in from above. While she gazed into this light, she saw the soul of God's servant Hilda borne up to heaven in the midst of the light accompanied and guided by angels. Then she awoke, and seeing the other sisters lying around her, realized that what she had seen was either a dream or a vision. Rising at once in alarm, she ran to Frigyth, who was Prioress at the time, and with many sighs and tears told her that their Mother the Abbess Hilda had departed this life, and that she had seen her surrounded by angels in a great light, and ascending to the abode of eternal light to join the company of the saints in heaven. When she had heard the nun's story Frigyth roused all the sisters, and when she had gathered them into the church, she enjoined them to pray and recite the psalter for the soul of their Mother. They did this for the remainder of the night, and at daybreak some brothers arrived from the monastery where she had died with news of her passing. The sisters replied that they already knew, and when they explained how and when they had heard it, it was evident that her death had been revealed to them by means of the vision at the very hour that the brothers said she had died. In this way the mercy of heaven ordained that while some of her Community attended her death-bed, the others were made aware of her soul's entry into eternal life, although these monasteries are about thirteen miles apart.

It is also said that Hilda's death was revealed in a vision to one of the sisters in the same monastery where the servant of God passed away. This sister, who loved her dearly, saw her soul ascend to heaven in the company of angels, and immediately awoke the servants of Christ with her and told them to pray for her soul: this was even before the rest of the Community knew of her death, which was only made known to them early in the morning. At this time the nun was with certain other servants of Christ in a remote part of the monastery, where novices were admitted to test their vocation until they were fully instructed and admitted to membership of the Community.

CHAPTER 24: *A brother of the monastery is found to possess God's gift of poetry* [A.D. 680]

IN this monastery of Whitby there lived a brother whom God's grace made remarkable. So skilful was he in composing religious and devotional songs, that he could quickly turn whatever passages of Scripture were explained to him into delightful and moving poetry in his own English tongue. These verses of his stirred the hearts of many folk to despise the world and aspire to heavenly things. Others after him tried to compose religious poems in English, but none could compare with him, for he received this gift of poetry as a gift from God and did not acquire it through any human teacher. For this reason he could never compose any frivolous or profane verses, but only such as had a religious theme fell fittingly from his devout lips. And although he followed a secular occupation until well advanced in years, he had never learned anything about poetry: indeed, whenever all those present at a feast took it in turns to sing and entertain the company, he would get up from table and go home directly he saw the harp approaching him.

On one such occasion he had left the house in which the entertainment was being held and went out to the stable, where it was his duty to look after the beasts that night. He lay down there at the appointed time and fell asleep, and in a dream he saw a man standing beside him who called him by name. 'Caedmon', he said, 'sing me a song.' 'I don't know how to sing', he replied. 'It is because I cannot sing that I left the feast and came here.' The man who addressed him then said: 'But you shall sing to me.' 'What should I sing about?' he replied. 'Sing about the Creation of all things', the other answered. And Caedmon immediately began to sing verses in praise of God the Creator that he had never heard before, and their theme ran thus: 'Let us praise the Maker of the kingdom of heaven, the power and purpose of our Creator, and the acts of the Father of glory. Let us sing how the eternal God, the Author of all marvels, first created the heavens for the sons of men as a roof to cover them, and how their almighty Protector gave them the earth for their dwelling place.' This is the general sense, but not the actual words that Caedmon sang in his dream; for however excellent the verses, it is impossible to translate them from one language into another without losing much of their beauty and dignity. When Caedmon awoke, he remembered everything that he had sung in his dream, and soon added more verses in the same style to the glory of God.

Early in the morning he went to his superior the reeve, and told him about this gift that he had received. The reeve took him before the abbess, who ordered him to give an account of his dream and repeat the verses in the presence of many learned men, so that they might decide their quality and origin. All of them agreed that Caedmon's gift had been given him by our Lord, and when they had explained to him a passage of scriptural history or doctrine, they asked him to

render it into verse if he could. He promised to do this, and
returned next morning with excellent verses as they had
ordered him. The abbess was delighted that God had given
such grace to the man, and advised him to abandon secular
life and adopt the monastic state. And when she had admitted
him into the Community as a brother, she ordered him to be
instructed in the events of sacred history. So Caedmon stored
up in his memory all that he learned, and after meditating on
it, turned it into such melodious verse that his delightful ren-
derings turned his instructors into his audience. He sang of
the creation of the world, the origin of the human race, and
the whole story of Genesis. He sang of Israel's departure from
Egypt, their entry into the land of promise, and many other
events of scriptural history. He sang of the Lord's Incarnation, Passion, Resurrection, and Ascension into heaven, the
coming of the Holy Spirit, and the teaching of the Apostles.
He also made many poems on the terrors of the Last Judgement, the horrible pains of Hell, and the joys of the kingdom
of heaven. In addition to these, he composed several others
on the blessings and judgements of God, by which he sought
to turn his hearers from delight in wickedness, and to inspire
them to love and do good. For Caedmon was a deeply religious man, who humbly submitted to regular discipline, and
firmly resisted all who tried to do evil, thus winning a happy
death.

When the time of his death drew near, he was subject to
physical weakness for fourteen days, although it was not serious enough to prevent his walking or talking the whole
time. Close by there was a house to which all who were sick
or likely to die were taken, and towards nightfall on the day
when he was to depart this life, Caedmon asked his attendant
to prepare a bed for him in this house. The latter was surprised
at this request, because he did not appear likely to die yet;
nevertheless, he did as he was asked. So Caedmon went to the
house, and conversed happily and cheerfully with those who
were already there; and when it was past midnight, he asked:

'Is the Eucharist in the house?'* 'Why do you want the Eucharist?' they enquired; 'you are not likely to die, when you are talking so cheerfully to us, and seem to be in perfect health.' 'Nevertheless', he said, 'bring me the Eucharist.' And taking It in his hands, Caedmon asked whether they were all charitably disposed towards him, and whether they had any complaint or ill-feeling against him. They replied that they were all most kindly disposed towards him, and free from all bitterness. Then in turn they asked him whether he were kindly disposed towards them. At once he answered: 'Dear sons, I am at peace with all the servants of God.' Then when he had fortified himself with the heavenly Viaticum, he prepared to enter the other life, and asked how long it was before the brothers were roused to sing God's praises in the Night Office. 'Not long', they replied. 'Good, then let us wait until then', he answered; and signing himself with the holy Cross, he laid his head on the pillow, and passed away quietly in his sleep. So, having served God with a simple and pure mind, and with quiet devotion, he left the world and departed to his presence with a peaceful death. His tongue, which had sung so many noble verses in praise of his Maker, uttered its last words in his praise as he signed himself with the Cross and commended his soul into his hands. For, as I have already said, Caedmon seems to have had a premonition of his death.

CHAPTER 25: *A man of God sees a vision portending the destruction of Coldingham monastery by fire*

A{T this time, the monastery of nuns called Coludi,[1] which I have already mentioned, was burned down through carelessness. However, all who knew the facts were fully aware that it happened because of the wickedness of its members, and in particular of those who were supposed to

1. Coldingham.

be in authority. But God's mercy gave them a warning of punishment, and if they had followed the example of the Ninevites in fasting, prayers, and tears, they could have averted the anger of the just Judge.

In this monastery lived a Scot named Adamnan, who led a life so devoted to God in prayer and austerity that he took no food or drink except on Sundays and Thursdays, and often spent the entire night in vigil and prayer. He had originally adopted this severe life from necessity, to overcome his evil inclinations, but as time went on, this necessity became his custom. During his youth he had committed some crime for which, when he came to his senses, he was thoroughly ashamed, and dreaded punishment by the strict Judge. So he visited a priest from whom he hoped to learn a way of salvation, confessed his sins to him, and asked for advice how he might escape God's anger in time to come. When he had heard his confession, the priest said: 'A severe wound calls for an ever more severe remedy. Therefore spend your time as far as possible in fasting, reciting the psalter, and prayer, so that you may avert God's anger in confession, and deserve to find His mercy.' Already deeply smitten in conscience and longing for speedy release from the inward fetters of the sin that burdened him, he replied: 'I am still young and strong in body, and I will readily undergo whatever penance you impose on me, if only I may be saved at Judgement Day. Even if you order me to remain standing in prayer all night, or to remain the whole week fasting, I will do it.' But the priest answered: 'To remain the whole week without food is too severe a penance: it will be sufficient if you fast for two or three days. Do this until I return shortly, when I will explain more fully what you should do, and how long you should continue this penance.' So, having prescribed the extent of his penance, the priest went away, but for some reason he travelled to Ireland, which was his native land, and never returned to him as he had arranged. But Adamnan bore in mind his directions and his own promise, and earnestly applied himself to penance, holy vigils, and fasting. He took food only on Sundays and Thursdays, as I have said, and ate nothing on the other days of the week. And when he heard that his priest had left for Ireland and died there, he continued to observe the austerity that he had imposed; for having accepted it in fear of God as atonement for his sin, he continued it undaunted out of love for God and in hope of a heavenly reward.

When he had followed this way of life for a considerable time, it happened one day that he had travelled some distance from the monastery accompanied by one of the brothers. On the return journey, as they were approaching the monastery, the man of God burst into tears, and his face betrayed the sorrow of his heart. Seeing this, his companion enquired the reason, and he replied: 'The time is near when all the public and private buildings that you see in front of you will be burned to ashes.' When his companion heard this, he went and informed Ebba, the Mother of the Community, as soon as he reached the monastery. She was naturally alarmed, and summoning Adamnan, pressed him to tell her how he knew such a thing. He answered: 'One night recently I was occupied in keeping vigil and reciting the psalter, when a stranger suddenly appeared beside me, and I was greatly startled. He told me not to be afraid, and spoke kindly to me, saying, "You do well to employ these night hours of rest in vigil and prayer instead of indulging in sleep." I answered, "I am aware that I have great need of wholesome vigils and earnest prayer to God to pardon my sins." He said, "You are right, and many besides yourself need to atone for their sins by good works, and to set themselves free to seek their eternal welfare by abstaining from worldly occupations. But there are very few who do this, for I have visited every part of this monastery, and entered every building and dormitory. Nowhere have I found anyone except yourself concerned with their eternal salvation. All of them, men and women alike, are either sound asleep, or else awake only in order to do evil. Even the

cells, which were built for prayer and study, are now converted into places for eating, drinking, gossip, or other
amusements. When they have leisure, even the nuns vowed
to God abandon the propriety of their calling and spend their
time weaving fine clothes, which they employ to the peril of
their souls, either to adorn themselves like brides, or to
attract attention from strange men. For this reason a heavy
and well-deserved punishment is about to fall on this place
and its people in the form of a terrible fire."' The abbess
asked: 'Why did you not reveal this to me earlier?' Adamnan
replied: 'I hesitated to do so out of regard for you, lest it
should cause you grave distress: but let it be some comfort to
you that this calamity will not happen in your own time.'
Once the vision became known, the Community was somewhat alarmed for a few days, and began to abandon wrong-
doing and undergo penance. But after the death of the abbess,
they relapsed into their earlier sins and became even more
wicked. And when they thought themselves at peace and
secure, the predicted judgement fell on them.

My informant in all these events was my fellow-priest,
Edgils, who was living in the monastery at the time. And
when the majority of the inhabitants had left the ruined
monastery, he lived a long while in our own monastery, and
died there. I have thought it desirable to include this in my
history to warn the reader of the workings of God, and how
terrible He is in his dealings with the sons of men. Let us
beware lest at some time we should indulge in the pleasures
of the flesh, and pay such scant heed to the judgements of
God that we incur his sudden anger. For we shall either be
justly and severely punished by losses in this world, or else
be even more strictly judged, and carried away to eternal
perdition.

CHAPTER 26: *On the death of King Egfrid and King Lothere*

IN the year of our Lord 684, King Egfrid of the Northumbrians sent an army into Ireland under the command of Beort, who brutally harassed these inoffensive people who had always been so friendly to the English, and in his hatred he spared neither churches nor monasteries. The islanders resisted force by force as well as they could, and implored the merciful aid of God, praying Heaven long and earnestly to avenge them. And although those who curse may not enter the kingdom of God, one may well believe that those who were justly cursed for their wickedness quickly suffered the penalty of their guilt at the hands of God their Judge. For in the following year King Egfrid, ignoring the advice of his friends and in particular of Cuthbert, of blessed memory, who had recently been made bishop, rashly led an army to ravage the province of the Picts. The enemy pretended to retreat, and lured the king into narrow mountain passes, where he was killed with the greater part of his forces on the twentieth of May in his fortieth year and the fifteenth of his reign.* As I have said, his friends had warned him against this campaign; but in the previous year he had refused to listen to the reverend Father Egbert, who begged him not to attack the Irish who had done him no harm; and this was his punishment, that he now refused to listen to those who tried to save him from destruction.

Henceforward the hopes and strength of the English realm began to waver and decline, for the Picts recovered their own lands that had been occupied by the English, while the Scots living in Britain and a proportion of the Britons themselves regained their freedom, which they have now enjoyed for about forty-six years. Many of the English at this time were killed, enslaved, or forced to flee from Pictish territory. Among them, the most reverend man of God Trumwine, who had been appointed their bishop, withdrew with his

people from the monastery of Abercurnig which was situated in English territory, but stood close to the firth that
divides the lands of the English from those of the Picts.
Wherever he could, he recommended his own people to
friends in various monasteries, and himself chose to live in
the often-mentioned monastery of Whitby. There, for
several years, he lived an austere life with a few of his own
folk, to the benefit of many besides himself. On his death, he
was buried in the church of blessed Peter the Apostle with the
honours due to his life and dignity. The royal nun Aelffleda,
with her mother Eanfleda whom I mentioned earlier, ruled
the monastery at this period: and when Bishop Trumwine
came, she found him a great help in the administration of the
monastery and a great comfort in her own life. Egfrid's successor on the throne was Alfrid, a man well-read in the
Scriptures, who was said to be brother of Egfrid and son of
King Oswy. He ably restored the shattered fortunes of the
kingdom, though within smaller boundaries.

On the sixth of February in the same year of our Lord 685,
King Lothere of Kent died after a reign of twelve years, his
brother Egbert having reigned nine years. He was wounded
in battle against the South Saxons, whom Edric, son of
Egbert, had raised against him, and he died as his wound was
being dressed. This Edric succeeded him and reigned a year
and a half; on his death, various alien kings and usurpers
plundered the kingdom for a while, until Wictred, son of
Egbert, its rightful king, established himself on the throne,
and freed the nation from foreign invasion by his devotion
and diligence.

CHAPTER 27: *Cuthbert, a man of God, is made bishop: his
life and teaching as a monk* [A.D. 685]

IN the year of his death, King Egfrid appointed as Bishop
of Lindisfarne the holy and venerable Cuthbert, who for
many years had lived a solitary life in great austerity of mind

and body on a tiny island known as Farne, which lies off the coast about nine miles from the church. From his earliest boyhood he had always longed to enter the religious life, and was clothed and professed as a monk when a youth. He first entered the monastery of Melrose on the banks of the River Tweed, then ruled by Abbot Eata the gentlest and simplest of men, who later became Bishop of the church of Hagulstad or Lindisfarne, as already noted: the prior of Melrose was Boisil, a priest of great virtues and prophetic spirit. Cuthbert humbly submitted himself to the direction of Boisil, who gave him instruction in the Scriptures, and showed him an example of holy life.

When Boisil departed to our Lord, Cuthbert was made prior in his place, and trained many men in the monastic life with masterly authority and by his personal example. He did not restrict his teaching and influence to the monastery, but worked to rouse the ordinary folk far and near to exchange their foolish customs for a love of heavenly joys. For many profaned the Faith that they professed by a wicked life, and at a time of plague some had even abandoned the Christian sacraments and had recourse to the false remedies of idolatry, as though they could expect to halt a plague ordained of God by spells, amulets, and other devilish secret arts. Following Boisil's example, in order to correct such errors he often used to leave the monastery, sometimes on horseback but more frequently on foot, and visit the neighbouring towns, where he preached the way of truth to those who had gone astray. In those days, whenever a clerk or priest visited a town, English folk always used to gather at his call to hear the Word, eager to hear his message, and even more eager to carry out whatever they had heard and understood. But Cuthbert was so skilful a speaker, and had such a light in his angelic face, and such a love for proclaiming his message, that none presumed to hide their inmost secrets, but openly confessed all their wrong-doing; for they felt it impossible to conceal their guilt from him, and at his direction they made proper atonement for the sins that they confessed. He used to visit and preach mainly in the villages that lay far distant among high and inaccessible mountains which others feared to visit, and whose barbarity and squalor daunted other teachers. Cuthbert, however, gladly undertook this pious task, and taught with such patience and skill that when he left the monastery, it would sometimes be a week, sometimes two or three, and occasionally an entire month before he returned home, remaining in the mountains to guide the peasants heavenward by his teachings and virtuous example.

When this venerable servant of our Lord had spent many years in the monastery of Melrose and become renowned for his wonderful acts of virtue, the most reverend Abbot Eata transferred him to Lindisfarne to instruct the brethren there in the observance of regular discipline, both in his official capacity and by his personal example. For the most reverend Father Eata was then Abbot of Lindisfarne as well. And in ancient times, the bishop and his clergy used to reside at Lindisfarne with the abbot and his monks, the latter being regarded as part of the bishop's household. For Aidan, first Bishop of Lindisfarne, himself a monk, brought monks with him and established the regular life there. The blessed Father Augustine is known to have done the same earlier in Kent, which is shown in the letter addressed to him by the most reverend Pope Gregory, which I included earlier: 'Since you, my brother, are subject to monastic rule and may not live apart from your clergy of the English Church, which by God's help has lately been brought to the Faith, you are to follow the way of life practised by our forefathers of the primitive Church, who did not regard any property as personal, but shared all things in common.'

CHAPTER 28: *Cuthbert becomes a hermit: his prayers obtain a spring from dry ground, and a crop from seed sown out of season*

THEN Cuthbert, as I have said, added to his merits, and carried out his intention to live a life of solitary contemplation and silence. But as I wrote a full account of his life and virtues both in heroic verse and prose a few years ago, it may suffice to record here a single incident. When he was about to leave for the island, he assured the brethren: 'If God's grace will enable me to live in this place and support myself by my own labour, I shall gladly remain there; but if it proves otherwise, I will soon return to you.' Now the island had no water, corn, or trees, and being the haunt of evil spirits was very ill-suited to human habitation. But when the man of God came, he ordered the evil spirits to withdraw, and the island became quite habitable. And when he had expelled these hostile forces, the brethren helped him to build a tiny dwelling surrounded with a ditch, and such essential buildings as an oratory and a communal shelter. He then directed the brethren to dig a well in the floor of the house, although the ground was hard and stony, and there seemed no hope whatever of finding a spring. But they did so, and through the faith and prayers of God's servant it was found full of water next day; and by the kindness of heaven, this spring still provides an ample supply for those who come here. Cuthbert also asked for farming implements and wheat to be brought him; but although he prepared the ground and sowed at the right season, not a single shoot or blade appeared by summer. So when the brethren paid their accustomed visit, he asked them to bring some barley, in case the nature of the soil and the laws of the divine Giver required that a crop of this grain should be sown. This he planted as soon as it was brought, but after the proper season, when there was no hope of its maturing; nevertheless, a rich crop quickly sprang up, and gave the man of God the much desired opportunity to support himself by his own labour.

Cuthbert served God in solitude for many years, and the embankment that surrounded his hut was so high that he could see nothing but the heavens for which he longed so ardently. Then it came about that a great Synod was held under the presidency of Archbishop Theodore of blessed memory, and in the presence of King Egfrid. This assembled near the river Alne at a place called Twyford, or the Two Fords, and the whole company unanimously elected Cuthbert as bishop of the church of Lindisfarne. But although many messengers and letters were sent to him, nothing would induce him to abandon his hermitage. At length the king in person, accompanied by the most holy Bishop Trumwine and other devout and distinguished men, took boat to the island. There they were joined by many of the Lindisfarne brethren, and the whole company knelt before him and begged him with tears to consent, until eventually they drew him, also in tears, from his retreat, and brought him to the Synod. Still profoundly reluctant, he at length bowed to the unanimous decision of the whole assembly, and was persuaded to accept episcopal dignity. He was chiefly influenced to do so by the words of God's servant Boisil, who had foretold all that was to happen to him, and how he would become a bishop. His consecration did not take place at once; but after the winter, which was then approaching, it was performed at York on Easter Day in the presence of King Egfrid by the Primate Theodore of blessed memory, assisted by six other bishops. In the first instance, Cuthbert was appointed to the Bishopric of Hagulstad, in place of Tunbert who had been deposed: but since he much preferred to rule the church of Lindisfarne where he had been trained, it was arranged that Eata should return to the See of Hagulstad, to which he had originally been appointed, and that Cuthbert should undertake responsibility for the church of Lindisfarne. As bishop he followed the example of the blessed Apostles, and enhanced his dignity by his holy actions, protecting his people

by his constant prayer, and inspiring them to heavenly things
by his salutary teachings. As is most valuable in a teacher, he
first practised whatever he taught others to do. Above all
else, he was afire with heavenly love, unassumingly patient,
devoted to unceasing prayer, and kindly to all who came to
him for comfort. He regarded the labour of helping the
weaker brethren with advice as equivalent to prayer, remembering that he who said, '*Thou shalt love the Lord thy God*',
also said, '*Love thy neighbour.*' His self-discipline and fasting
were exceptional, and through the grace of contrition, he
was always intent on the things of heaven. Lastly, whenever
he offered the sacrifice of the Saving Victim to God, he
offered his prayers to God in a low voice, and with tears
welling up from the depths of his heart.

CHAPTER 29: *Cuthbert foretells his own death to the hermit
Heribert* [A.D. 687]

WHEN he had spent two years in his bishopric, Cuthbert
returned to his island hermitage, God having made
known to him that the day of his death was drawing near, or
rather, the day of his entry into that life which alone may be
called life. In his usual simple way, he mentioned this fact to
some people at the time in somewhat veiled terms, which
they only understood later, but to others he spoke openly.

There was a priest of praiseworthy life named Heribert,
who had for a long time enjoyed a spiritual friendship with
the man of God. He lived the life of a hermit on an island in
a great lake which is the source of the river Derwent, and used
to visit Cuthbert each year to seek his advice on matters of
eternal salvation. Hearing that Cuthbert was at the city of
Lugubalia,[1] he went to visit him as usual, wishing to be ever
more fervently inspired to heavenly desires by his salutary
guidance. As each in turn discoursed on the joys of the

1. Carlisle.

heavenly life, Cuthbert said among other things: 'Brother Heribert, remember that whatever you wish to ask or tell me, you must do before we part, because we shall not see one another again in this world. For I know that the day of my death is approaching, and I shall soon leave this earthly dwelling.' At these words, the other fell at his feet with sighs and tears, saying: 'In the Name of our Lord, I beg you not to leave me! Remember that I am your most devoted friend, and ask God of His mercy to grant that as we have served Him together on earth, we may pass away to the heavenly vision together. You know how I have always tried to live as you directed, and whenever I have sinned out of ignorance or frailty, I have at once tried to make amends in any way you enjoined.' So the bishop prostrated himself in prayer, and soon received inward intimation that God had granted his request. 'Rise, my brother, and do not weep. Be glad, for God in His mercy has heard our prayer.'

Subsequent events proved the truth of this prophecy, for when they parted, they never saw one another again in this life, and before long, on the twentieth of March, their souls left their bodies on the same day, and were borne by angels to see the beatific vision in the kingdom of heaven. But Heribert was first tried by a long illness, and one may believe that God's mercy decreed this in order that if his merits were inferior to those of blessed Cuthbert, the chastening of a long illness might supply whatever was lacking: in this way, he would be made equal in grace with his intercessor, and in departing this life at the same time, merit to enter into the same state of eternal blessedness.

The most reverend Father Cuthbert died on Farne Island, earnestly requesting the brethren to bury him in this place where he had served God so long. But at length he yielded to their entreaties, and consented that his body should be taken back to Lindisfarne and buried within the church. This was accordingly done, and the venerable Bishop Wilfrid held the see for a year until a successor could be appointed.

Subsequently Eadbert was consecrated, a man who was well
known for his knowledge of the Scriptures, his obedience to
God's Commandments, and especially for his generosity.
For each year, in accordance with the Law, he used to give a
tenth of all beasts, grain, fruit, and clothing to the poor.

CHAPTER 30: *After eleven years in the grave, Cuthbert's
body is found incorrupt. His successor departs this life soon
afterwards* [A.D. 698]

IN order to make more widely known the height of glory
attained after death by God's servant Cuthbert, whose illustrious life on earth had been marked by so many miracles
prior to his death, Divine Providence guided the brethren to
exhume his bones. After eleven years, they expected to find
his flesh reduced to dust and the remains withered, as is usual
in dead bodies; and they proposed to place them in a new
coffin on the same site but above ground level, so that he
might receive the honours due to him. When they informed
Bishop Eadbert of their wish, he gave approval and directed
that it should take place on the anniversary of his burial. This
was done, and when they opened the grave, they found the
body whole and uncorrupt as though still living, and the
limbs flexible as though he were asleep rather than dead.
Furthermore, all the vestments in which he was clothed
appeared not only spotless, but wonderfully fresh and fair.
The brothers were awestruck at this sight, and hastened to
inform the bishop of their discovery. At the time, the latter
was living alone at some distance from the church in a place
surrounded by the sea, where he always used to spend Lent
and the forty days before the Nativity of our Lord in fasting, prayer, and penitence. It was here that his venerable predecessor Cuthbert had served God in solitude for a period
before he went to Farne Island.

The brothers brought some of the garments in which the

holy body had been clothed to the bishop, who received
these gifts with gratitude, and as he listened to their account
of the miracle, he lovingly kissed the garments as though
they were still on the father's body. 'Clothe the body in new
garments', he said, 'in place of those that you have removed,
and place it in the coffin you have prepared. I have certain
knowledge that the grave hallowed by so great and heavenly
a miracle will not remain empty for long. And blessed is the
man to whom our Lord, the Author and Giver of all bliss,
shall grant the privilege of resting in it.' When the bishop had
said this and more to the same effect in a trembling voice with
tears and deep feeling, the brethren carried out his instructions; and having clothed the body in fresh garments, they
laid it in a new coffin, which they placed on the pavement of
the sanctuary.

Not long afterwards, God's beloved Bishop Eadbert was
attacked by an illness that rapidly grew more serious, and in
a short time he departed to our Lord, on the sixth of May.
Whereupon the brethren laid his body in the tomb of the
blessed Father Cuthbert, and above it they placed the coffin
containing the uncorrupt body of the Father. The miracles
of healing that take place from time to time at the tomb bear
witness to the holiness of them both, and I have recorded
some instances in my book on his life. And in this present
history I have included further examples that have recently
come to my knowledge.

CHAPTER 31: *A brother is cured of paralysis at Cuthbert's
tomb*

IN the monastery was a brother named Badudegn, who is
still living, and who served for a considerable time in the
guest-house. All the brethren and visitors testify that he was
a very devout and religious man, who did his appointed task
solely for the sake of a heavenly reward. One day he had

washed the cloaks used in the guest-house in the sea. As he
was returning homewards, he had a sudden seizure, and fell
to the ground, where he lay prostrate for some while before
he could rise. When at last he got up, he found that one side
of his body was paralysed from head to foot, and made his
way home with the greatest difficulty leaning on a stick.
The disease gradually increased, and at nightfall became even
more serious, so that next day he could hardly rise or walk
without help. Crippled as he was, he conceived the excellent
plan of making his way to the church as best he could to visit
the tomb of the most reverend Father Cuthbert. There on
bended knee he would implore God's mercy either to heal
his disease if this were to his good, or else to give him grace
to bear his affliction calmly and with patience should Divine
Providence decree that he endure it longer. Acting on this
resolve and supporting his feeble limbs with a staff, he entered
the church and prostrated himself before the body of the man
of God, earnestly praying that, at Cuthbert's intercession,
our Lord would show mercy. As he prayed he fell into a deep
sleep, and as he subsequently related, seemed to feel a great,
broad hand rest on the seat of the pain in his head. At this
touch, the entire area of his body affected by the disease was
gradually eased of its pain, and health was restored right
down to the feet. He soon awoke and rose completely cured,
and gave thanks to God for his recovery, afterwards telling
the brethren what had happened to him. And to their great
joy he returned to the duties that he had always carried out so
faithfully, as though chastened by the scourge of suffering.

The garments that had clothed Cuthbert's hallowed body
both before and after his death continued to possess healing
virtues, as anyone may read in the book of his life and
miracles.

I CANNOT omit mention of a cure that took place through his relics three years ago, and was told me by the very brother to whom it happened. It occurred in a monastery which was in course of construction near the river Dacore,[1] from which it took its name, and whose head was the devout Abbot Suidbert. In this house lived a young man who developed a tumour on his eyelid which daily increased in size, and threatened to destroy the eye. Although the physicians applied poultices to reduce it, they had no success: some advised cutting it out, while others opposed this, fearing graver complications. So the brother suffered great pain for a long time, and felt that no human skill could prevent the loss of his eye, whose condition was deteriorating daily, when he was suddenly cured by the goodness of God and by means of the relics of the most holy father Cuthbert. This came about because, when the brethren found his body uncorrupt after many years in the grave, they had taken some of his hair to provide relics for their friends, and to show as evidence of this miracle.

Thridred, one of the priests of the monastery and now its abbot, had a small portion of these relics in his possession at the time. And one day, when he went into the church and opened the casket of relics in order to give a portion to a friend who had requested it, the young man with the diseased eye happened to be present. Having given a suitable portion to his friend, Thridred handed the remainder to the young man to replace in their casket. Moved by a fortunate impulse, the latter took the hairs of holy Cuthbert's head in his hand and applied them to his eyelid, attempting to soften and reduce the swelling by holding them there for a while. He then replaced the relics in their casket as he had been directed, believing that his eye would soon be cured by the application

1. Dacre, near Penrith.

of the man of God's hair. Nor was his faith in vain. For, as he tells, it was then about Terce, and thenceforward he was busy about the day's duties until nearly Sext, when he suddenly felt his eye, and found both it and the lid sound, as though there had never been any deformity or swelling on it.

BOOK FIVE

CHAPTER I: *The hermit Ethelwald, Cuthbert's successor, calms a storm by his prayer when some brethren are in danger at sea*

CUTHBERT, the man of God who had lived a solitary life on Farne Island before he became a bishop, was succeeded by a venerable man named Ethelwald. The latter, who had received the priesthood many years previously in the monastery of Ripon, adorned the office worthily by his doings. To illustrate his virtue and the kind of life that he led more clearly, I will relate a miracle of his that was told me by one of the brethren for whose benefit it was performed; this was the venerable priest and servant of Christ Guthfrid, who subsequently became abbot, and ruled the church of Lindisfarne where he had been brought up.

'I came with two other brothers to Farne Island,' he said, 'wishing to speak with the most reverend Father Ethelwald. We were greatly inspired by his discourse, and when we had asked his blessing and were returning homewards, while we were in the middle of the sea, the calm weather that was favouring our crossing suddenly changed. There followed a storm of such ferocity and violence that sail and oars were useless, and we expected nothing but death. Having struggled unavailingly against the wind and waves for a long time, we looked back to see whether it were practicable to fight our way back to the island we had left, but found the storm equally violent on all sides, so that there was no hope of escape. But as we looked into the distance, we saw Father Ethelwald, the beloved of God, come out of his cell on Farne to watch our progress, for he had heard the roar of the gale and raging of the sea, and had come out to discover what would happen to us. When he saw us in distress and despair, he fell on his knees to the Father of our Lord Jesus Christ, and prayed for our safety. Directly his prayer was ended, the raging sea grew calm, the severity of the storm lessened on all sides, and a following wind bore us over the sea towards the land. As soon as we had reached the shore and dragged our small boat out of the water, the wind that had dropped awhile for our sakes at once began to blow again, and continued strongly all that day. So we realized that the short interval of calm had been granted by the mercy of heaven at the prayer of the man of God so that we might escape.'

The man of God remained on Farne Island for twelve years and died there, but he was buried on the island of Lindisfarne in the church of the blessed Apostle Peter next to the bodies of the above-mentioned bishops. These events took place in the time of King Alfrid, who succeeded his brother Egfrid as King of the Northumbrians, and reigned for eighteen years.

CHAPTER 2: *The blessing of Bishop John cures a dumb man*

AT the beginning of King Alfrid's reign Bishop Eata died, and was succeeded as Bishop of Hexham by a holy man named John.* Many miracles are told of him by those who knew him well, and in particular by Berthun, a most reverend and truthful man, formerly John's deacon and now abbot of the monastery known as Inderawood, which means 'In the wood of the Deiri'.[1] I have thought it fitting to preserve the memory of some of these miracles for posterity.

Whenever opportunity offered and especially during Lent, this man of God used to retire with a few companions to read and pray quietly in an isolated house surrounded by open woodland and a dyke. It stood about a mile and a half from the church at Hexham across the river Tyne, and had a

1. Now Beverley.

burial-ground dedicated to Saint Michael the Archangel. John once came to stay here at the beginning of Lent, and as was his invariable custom, told his companions to find some poor person who was either seriously infirm or in dire want, so that he might live with them during their stay and benefit from their alms.

In a village not far distant lived a dumb youth known to the bishop, who had often visited him to receive alms, and had never been able to utter a single word. In addition, he had so many scabs and scales on his head that no hair ever grew on the crown, but only a few wisps in a ragged circle. So the bishop ordered this youth to be fetched, and a little hut to be made for him in the enclosure round the house, where he could live and receive his daily allowance. When one week of Lent was past, on the following Sunday John told the poor fellow to come to him, and ordered him to put out his tongue and show it him; then he took him by the chin, and making the sign of the holy cross on his tongue, told him to retract it and speak. 'Pronounce some word,' he said: 'say *gae*,' which is the English word of agreement and assent, *i.e.* 'Yes'. The young man's tongue was loosed, and at once he did what he was told. The bishop then proceeded to the names of letters: 'Say A,' he said. And he said 'A'. 'Now say B,' he said, which the youth did. And when he had repeated the names of each of the letters after the bishop, the latter added syllables and words for him to repeat after him. When he had said all of them, he told him to repeat longer sentences, and he did so. All those who were present say that all that day and the next night, as long as he could keep awake, the youth never stopped saying something, and expressing his own thoughts and wishes to others, which he had never been able to do previously. He was like the cripple healed by the Apostles Peter and John, who stood up, leaped, and walked, entering the temple with them, *walking, leaping, and praising God*, rejoicing in the use of his feet, of which he had been so long deprived. The bishop was delighted at his cure, and directed the physician to undertake the cure of the youth's scabby head.

The physician did as he was asked, and with the assistance of the bishop's blessing and prayers, his skin healed, and a vigorous growth of hair appeared. So the youth obtained a clear complexion, readiness of speech, and a beautiful head of hair, whereas he had formerly been deformed, destitute, and dumb. The bishop was so pleased with his recovery that he offered to give him a permanent place in his household, but the lad preferred to return to his own home.

CHAPTER 3: *Bishop John heals a sick girl by his prayers*

BERTHUN described another miracle done by the bishop. When the most reverend Wilfrid became Bishop of Hexham after his long exile, and John became Bishop of York on the death of the holy and humble Bosa, he came one day to a convent of nuns at a place called Wetadun, ruled at the time by the Abbess Hereberge. 'When we had arrived and been welcomed with great joy, the abbess informed us that one of the nuns, her own daughter, was very seriously ill. She told us that the nun had recently been bled in the arm, and that while she was being treated, she was suddenly seized by a violent pain which rapidly increased, so that the wounded arm grew worse and became so swollen that it could hardly be encircled with two hands. In consequence, the nun was lying in bed in terrible pain and seemed likely to die. The abbess therefore begged the bishop to visit her and give her his blessing, being sure that she would improve if the bishop blessed or touched her. He enquired when the girl had been bled, and when he learned that it had been on the fourth day of the moon, he said: "You have acted most foolishly and unwisely to carry out blood-letting on the fourth day of the moon. I remember that Archbishop Theodore, of blessed memory, said that it was very dangerous to bleed at a time when the light of the moon and the pull of the tide is increasing. And what can I do for the girl if she is going to die?" But the abbess pressed him most earnestly on behalf of her daughter, who was very dear to her, and whom she intended to appoint abbess in her own place, and at length she prevailed on him to visit the sick girl. So he went in, taking me with him to see the girl who, as I have said, lay helpless and in great pain, with her arm swollen to such a size that she could not bend her elbow. The bishop stood and said a prayer over her, and having given her his blessing, went out. Some while later, as we were sitting at table, someone came in and asked me to come outside, saying: "Coenberg" – for that was the girl's name – "wishes you to come back to her room at once." I did so, and when I entered, I found her looking cheerful and apparently in sound health. And when I sat down by her, she said: "Would you like me to ask for a drink?" "Certainly," I replied, "I shall be delighted if you will." When a cup had been brought and we had both drunk, she began to tell me what had happened. "As soon as the bishop had blessed me and gone away, I began to feel better; and although I have not yet recovered my full strength, the pain has entirely left my arm where it was most intense, and from all my body. It was as though the bishop took it away with him entirely when he left, although the swelling on my arm seems to remain." When we left the convent, the disappearance of the pain in her limbs was followed by a subsidence of the swelling, and the girl, saved from pain and death, gave thanks to our Lord and Saviour with all the other servants of God in the place.'

CHAPTER 4: *The Bishop cures a thane's wife with holy water*

ABBOT BERTHUN told the story of another miracle not unlike the previous one performed by the bishop. He said: 'Not far from our monastery, about two miles distant,

stood the country house of a thane named Puch, whose wife
had been suffering from an acute complaint for forty days,
and for three weeks it had been impossible to move her from
the room where she lay. It happened at the time that the man
of God had been asked by the thane to dedicate a church, and
when he had done this, the thane invited him to dine in his
house. The bishop declined, saying that he must return to the
monastery, which was close by. But the thane pressed him
even more earnestly, promising to give alms to the poor if
only the bishop would consent to come into his house to
break his fast. I supported the thane's request, and also
promised to give alms to the poor if he would go in to have
a meal in the thane's house and give his blessing. After much
difficulty, we persuaded him, and went in for some food.
Meanwhile, at the hands of one of the brethren who had
come with us, the bishop had sent the sick woman some of
the holy water that he had blessed for the dedication of the
church, telling him to give her some of it to drink and to
wash the place where the worst pain lay with the water.
When this had been done, the woman immediately got up
cured, and finding herself not only relieved of her long illness but restored to her former strength, she brought a cup
to the bishop and us, and having performed this duty, she
continued to serve us with drink until the close of the meal.
In this she followed the example of Saint Peter's wife's
mother, who after being troubled by a burning fever, rose
at the touch of the Lord's hand, and, immediately restored to
health and strength, ministered to their needs.'

CHAPTER 5: *The Bishop's prayers recall the servant of a
thane from death's door*

O N another occasion, the bishop was asked to consecrate
the church of a thane named Addi, and when he had
completed the ceremony, the thane requested him to visit

one of his servants who was so seriously ill that he had completely lost the use of all his limbs, and now seemed about to die: indeed, a coffin had already been prepared to receive his corpse. The thane pressed him with tears, earnestly begging him to go in and pray for the man, saying that his life was of great concern to him. He was sure that, if only the bishop were willing to lay his hand on him and bless him, he would recover immediately. So the bishop went in and found the man at death's door, with the coffin in which he was to be buried lying beside him. All present were in tears. After saying a prayer and giving the man his blessing, the bishop went out with the usual comforting words: 'Hurry up and get well.' Later, while the company were sitting at table, the man sent to his master saying he was thirsty and asking if he might have a cup of wine. Delighted that he could drink, the thane sent him a cup of wine blessed by the bishop, and as soon as he had drunk it he got up, threw off his disease, and put on his clothes. Then he left his room and came in to greet the bishop, saying how glad he was to eat and drink with them. They were delighted at his recovery, and told him to sit down to dine with them; so he sat down, and made merry as one of the company. He lived for many years afterwards, and retained the good health that had been restored to him. Abbot Berthun says that he was not present when this miracle took place, but that he had an account of it from those who were.

CHAPTER 6: *By his prayers and blessing, Bishop John saves from death one of his clergy who had been bruised in a fall*

I CANNOT leave unmentioned a miracle that God's servant Herebald relates as having been performed for his benefit by Bishop John. At the time he was one of the bishop's clergy, but is now abbot of a monastery near the mouth of

the river Tyne. 'Living with him, and knowing his way of
life very intimately,' he says, 'I knew it to be wholly worthy
of a bishop, so far as it is permissible for a man to judge. But
many others beside myself amply experienced how great
his virtues were in the eyes of Him who sees the heart; for, as
I shall tell, he brought me back from death's door, and
restored me to life by his prayer and blessing. In the prime of
youth I lived among his clergy, occupied in reading and
singing, but my heart had not yet entirely abandoned youth-
ful follies. As we were travelling with him one day, we
happened to come to a level open road, well suited for gallop-
ing our horses. The young men with him, mainly layfolk,
began to ask the bishop's permission to gallop, and try out
their horses against each other. At first he refused their request, saying that it was an unprofitable occupation, but at
length he gave in to their unanimous wish, saying: "Do so if
you wish, but Herebald is not to take part in the race." I begged
him persistently to let me race with the rest, for I had confidence in an excellent horse he had given me, but I could not
obtain his consent.

'When they had galloped to and fro several times, and
came back spurring their horses in a race while the bishop and
I watched, my ill humour got the better of me, and I could
not restrain myself. Despite his prohibition, I rushed into
their contest, and began to race at full speed. As I did so, I
heard the bishop behind me say sadly: "Oh, how you grieve
me by riding like that!" But although I heard him, I went on
against his orders. Shortly afterwards, as my spirited horse
took off in a powerful jump across a hollow in the path, I fell,
and at once lost all feeling and power of movement as though
I were dying; for at the spot lay a stone, level with the ground,
lightly covered by turf, the only stone to be found in the
whole of that level plain. And it happened, either by chance
or by the disposition of divine providence as a punishment
for my disobedience, that as I fell, I struck my head and hand
which I raised to protect my head on this stone. As a conse-

quence, my thumb was broken and my skull cracked, and, as I said, I lay as though dead. As I was unable to move, they stretched an awning over me for protection, and from an hour after midday until evening I lay motionless as a corpse. When I revived slightly, my companions carried me home, where I lay speechless all night, vomiting blood as a result of some internal injury. The bishop was greatly distressed about my accident and possible death because he was especially fond of me, and he did not remain with his clergy that night as was his usual custom, but spent all night in vigil and prayer, as I understand, asking God of His mercy to restore me to health. Early next morning he came and said a prayer over me, calling me by name, and waking me out of what seemed to be a heavy sleep. "Do you know who it is speaking to you?" he asked. Opening my eyes, I replied: "I do. You are my beloved bishop." "Can you live?" he asked. "I can do so with the help of your prayers, God willing," I replied.

'Having laid his hand on my head and blessed me, he went away to pray. On his return after a short while, he found me sitting up, and well enough to talk. Then, inspired by God – as was soon evident – he asked me if I knew for certain whether I had been baptized. I answered that I was quite sure that I had been washed in the waters of salvation for the forgiveness of sins, and I told him the name of the priest who had baptized me. But he said: "If you were baptized by that priest, you were not validly baptized, for I know him, and when he was ordained priest, he was so slow-witted that he could not learn how to instruct and baptize. For this reason, I ordered him to cease presuming to exercise his ministry because he was too ignorant to carry it out properly." He then proceeded to instruct me on the spot, and when he happened to breathe on my face, I immediately began to feel better. He called the surgeon, and told him to close and bandage up the cracks in my skull; and after receiving his blessing, I was so much better next day that I mounted my horse and journeyed on with him to another town. I was soon completely recovered, and was cleansed in the lifegiving waters of Baptism.'

John remained in his bishopric for thirty-three years, and then entered the kingdom of heaven. He was buried in Saint Peter's porch in his own monastery of Inderawood in the year of our Lord 721. When his advanced years prevented him from administering his bishopric, he consecrated his priest Wilfrid to the See of York, and retired to his monastery to end his days in a manner pleasing to God.

CHAPTER 7: *Caedwalla, King of the West Saxons, goes to Rome for Baptism: his successor Ini also makes a pilgrimage of devotion to the shrine of the Apostles* [A.D. 688]

IN the third year of King Alfrid's reign, Caedwalla, King of the West Saxons, who had governed his people most ably for two years, abdicated from his throne for the sake of our Lord and his eternal kingdom, and travelled to Rome. For having learned that the road to heaven lies open to mankind only through baptism, he wished to obtain the particular privilege of receiving the cleansing of baptism at the shrine of the blessed Apostles. At the same time, he hoped to die shortly after his baptism, and pass from this world to everlasting happiness. By God's grace, both of these hopes were realized. Arriving in Rome during the pontificate of Sergius, he was baptized on Holy Saturday before Easter in the year of our Lord 689, and fell ill while still wearing his white robes.* He departed this life on the thirtieth of April, and joined the company of the blessed in heaven. At the time of his baptism, the aforesaid Pope had given him the name of Peter, in order that he might be linked by name to the most blessed Prince of the Apostles, to whose most sacred body the king's devotion had brought him from the ends of the earth. He was buried in the Apostle's church, and the Pope directed that an epitaph be inscribed on his tomb to preserve the memory of his devotion for ever, and inspire all who

read or heard of it to religious fervour. This inscription was
as follows:

> High rank and wealth, offspring, and mighty realms,
> Triumphs and spoils, great chieftains, cities, halls,
> His forbears' glories and his own renown –
> All these great Caedwal left for love of God.
> This royal pilgrim then sought Peter's Chair
> To slake his thirst at Peter's vital spring,
> And in his splendid, glowing light to bathe
> From whom life-giving radiance ever streams.
> Eager to win the prize of life renewed,
> Converted, he amends his former name
> With its barbaric sound to Peter's own
> At father Sergius' word, that at the font
> Christ's grace may wash him from all taint of sin,
> And bring him swiftly cleansed to heaven's gate.
> Great was his faith; Christ's mercy greater still
> Whose secret purpose mortals may not know.
> Safely he came from Britain's distant shores,
> Through many peoples, over land and sea,
> Bearing his mystic gifts, to visit Rome
> And in the shrine of Peter lay them down.
> Now, robed in white, he moves among Christ's sheep:
> His body rests in peace, his soul on high.
> Wise king, his earthly sceptre to resign,
> And win from Christ in heaven His promised crown.

Caedwalla, also known as Peter, King of the Saxons, was buried here
on the twelfth day of the Kalends of May, the second indiction. He
lived about thirty years, during the reign of our most devout lord
Justinian Augustus, in the fourth year of his Consulship, and in the
second year of the pontificate of our apostolic lord Pope Sergius.

On Caedwalla's departure for Rome, he was succeeded as
king by Ina, who was of the blood royal. Having ruled the
nation for thirty-seven years, Ina also abdicated, and handed
over the government to younger men. He then set out to
visit the shrines of the blessed Apostles during the pontificate
of Gregory (II), wishing to spend some of the time of his

earthly pilgrimage in the vicinity of the holy places, hoping thereby to merit a warmer welcome from the saints in heaven. At this period, many English people followed this custom, both noble and simple, layfolk and clergy, men and women alike.

CHAPTER 8: *On the death of Theodore, Berthwald becomes archbishop: among many others whom he ordained, he consecrated Tobias, a man of great learning, to be Bishop of the Church of Rochester* [A.D. 690]

IN the year after Caedwalla's death in Rome, that is, the year of our Lord 690, Archbishop Theodore, of blessed memory, died old and full of years at the age of eighty-eight. He had long previously told his friends that he would die at this age, which had been foretold to him in a dream. He had held the archbishopric for twenty-two years, and was buried in the church of Saint Peter, where all the bodies of the Archbishops of Canterbury are buried. It may be said of him, as of all his colleagues in the same dignity, that '*their bodies are buried in peace, but their names live from generation to generation.*' To summarize briefly; the English churches made greater progress during his pontificate than they had ever done before. His epitaph publicly and clearly describes his character, life, age, and death to all who visit his tomb. This consists of thirty-four heroic verses, the first of which runs:

> Here rests the holy Primate in his tomb –
> Great Theodore, a Greek by race and name.
> A prince of pontiffs, and a blest high priest
> Who taught to all his flock the light of truth.

And the last verse is:

> The nineteenth of September was the day
> That saw his spirit burst its earthly bonds,
> Rising in rapture to a newer life
> In sweet communion with the saints on high.

Theodore's successor in the archbishopric was Berthwald, Abbot of the monastery of Reculver, which stands on the north bank at the mouth of the river Genlade. Although he can hardly be compared with his predecessor, he was learned in the Scriptures, and well versed in ecclesiastical and monastic affairs. He was elected bishop on the first of July in the year of our Lord 692, when Witred and Swaebhard were kings of Kent: but he was consecrated on Sunday August the thirty-first by Godwin, Metropolitan of Gaul. Berthwald conse-crated many bishops, including Tobias, a man of wide learn-ing and a scholar of Latin, Greek, aad Saxon, who became Bishop of Rochester in place of Gebmund, who had died.

CHAPTER 9: *Egbert, a holy man, plans to travel to Germany and preach, but is prevented. Subsequently Wictbert goes, but meeting with no success, returns to his native Ireland*

AT this time, the venerable servant of Christ, Bishop Egbert, a man whose name deserves high honour, was living a life of exile in Ireland in order to attain his heavenly home, as I have already mentioned. He planned to bring bless-ings to many people by undertaking the apostolic work of preaching the word of God to some of the nations who had not heard it. He had learned that there were many such nations in Germany, of whose stock came the Angles or Saxons now settled in Britain, who are for this reason still miscalled Garmans by their neighbours the Britons. These nations include the Frisians, Rugens, Danes, Huns, Old Saxons, and Boructuars; there are also several races in that region who still observe pagan rites. So this warrior of Christ planned to sail around Britain, and attempt to snatch some of them from Satan and bring them to Christ. If this proved impossible, he proposed to travel to Rome, to visit and ven-erate the shrines of the blessed Apostles and martyrs of Christ.

Heavenly portents and occurrences, however, forestalled the execution of either of these projects. For when he had chosen the boldest of his companions, whose distinguished lives and learning rendered them well fitted to preach the Gospel, and when all preparations for the voyage were complete, early one morning one of the brethren came to him, who had formerly been a disciple and assistant to God's beloved priest Boisil in Britain, when the latter was Prior of the monastery of Melrose under the above Abbot Eata. This brother told him of a vision which he had seen that night: 'After the morning hymns,' he said, 'I had lain down on my pallet and fallen into a light sleep, when my old master and most loving teacher Boisil appeared to me, and asked whether I recognized him. "Of course I do," I said: "you are Boisil." He then said: "I have come to bring a message from our Lord and Saviour to Egbert, which you must deliver to him. Tell him that he is not to go on the journey that he has in mind, for it is God's will that he should go and instruct the monks of Columba." ' Now Columba was the first teacher of the Christian Faith to the Picts living north of the mountains, and founder of the monastery on the Isle of Iona, which long remained venerated by the people of the Picts and Scots. For this reason, Columba is known by some people as Columbkill, a name compounded from Columba and cell. When Egbert had heard about this vision, he ordered the brother who had related it not to tell anyone else, in case the vision were a delusion; but silently turning it over in his own mind, Egbert feared that it was true. But he did not abandon his preparations for his voyage to evangelize the nations.

After a few days, this brother came to him once more, saying that Boisil had again appeared to him in a vision after Matins, saying: 'Why did you convey the message that I gave you for Egbert in such a careless and offhand fashion? Now go and tell him that, whether he wishes it or not, he is to visit the monastery of Columba, because their ploughs do not run straight,* and it is his duty to recall them to the right way.' Hearing this, Egbert again enjoined the brother not to disclose the vision to anyone. But although he was now convinced of the vision's reality, he none the less attempted to carry out his projected voyage with the brethren. And when they had stored the ship with everything necessary for the voyage and had waited some days for a favourable wind, a storm of such violence arose one night that the ship was left lying on her side among the breakers, and part of her stores was lost. However, everything that belonged to Egbert and his companions was salvaged. Then, like the prophet Jonah, Egbert said: '*This storm has happened on my account*', abandoned his plan, and resigned himself to staying at home.

But Wictbert, one of Egbert's companions, was well known for his contempt for worldly things and for his knowledge of doctrine, having lived the life of a hermit in great perfection for many years as an exile in Ireland. He took ship and arrived in Frisia, where he preached the word of life constantly for two years to the people and their king Rathbed, but his great efforts produced no results among his barbaric hearers. He then returned to his beloved land of exile and began to give himself to our Lord in his accustomed silence. And since he had been unable to help foreigners towards the Faith, he sought to be of more help to his own people by setting them a holy example.

CHAPTER 10: *Wilbrord preaches in Frisia and converts many to Christ: his companions the Hewalds suffer martyrdom*
[A.D. 692]

So the man of God, Egbert, realized that he was not permitted to go and preach to the heathen, and that he was retained to be of some other service to Holy Church, as he had been forewarned by the vision. But although he knew that Wictbert had enjoyed no success when he visited those parts, he attempted to send other holy and zealous men for the work of preaching, among whom was an outstanding priest of radiant virtue named Wilbrord.* When he and his companions arrived, they made a detour to visit Peppin, Duke of the Franks, by whom they were graciously received. And since the latter had recently conquered Nearer Frisia and driven out King Rathbed, he dispatched them to preach there, supporting them with his imperial authority so that no one should interfere with their preaching, and granting many favours to those who wished to embrace the Faith. Consequently, aided by God's grace, they converted many folk in a short while from idolatry to belief in Christ.

Two other priests of English race, who had long lived as exiles in Ireland for the sake of the eternal kingdom, followed their lead and went to the province of the Old Saxons in order to try and win them for Christ by their teaching. They shared the same name and the same zeal, but with the distinction that, since their hair was of different colour, one was known as Hewald the Black, and the other as Hewald the White. Both men were devout and religious, but Hewald the Black was more learned in the holy scriptures. On entering the province, they were given hospitality by a certain steward, whom they asked to conduct them to his lord, as they had a message to his advantage which they were bound to communicate to him. For these Old Saxons have no king, but several chieftains who rule the nation. Whenever war breaks out, these cast lots impartially, and all follow and obey the man on whom the lot falls for the duration of the war; but as soon as the war ends, the chieftains revert to equality of status. So the steward received and kept them with him for some days, promising to send them to his master as they had asked.

Now the Hewalds devoted themselves to psalms and prayers, and daily offered the sacrifice of the saving Victim to God, having with them sacred vessels and a consecrated table for use as an altar. And when the barbarous people realized that they belonged to a different religion, they began to distrust them, fearing that if they went to their chieftain and spoke to him, they might turn him from his gods and convert him to the new religion of the Christian Faith, so that the whole province would gradually be compelled to change its old ways of life for new. So they suddenly seized them and put them to death; Hewald the White was killed outright with a sword, and Hewald the Black was put to lingering torture. And when they had torn them limb from limb, they flung the murdered men into the Rhine. When the chieftain whom they had wished to see heard of this, he was extremely angry that strangers desiring to see him had not been allowed to do so, and he sent and slew all the villagers, and burned down their village. These priests and servants of Christ suffered on the third of October.

Their martyrdom was not unmarked by heavenly signs, for when their bodies were thrown into the Rhine by the heathen as I have described, they were carried upstream against the current for nearly forty miles to the place where their companions were. And a great ray of light reaching high into the sky shone all night above the spot where the bodies had arrived, and was also seen by the heathen who had murdered them. Furthermore, one of them appeared by night in a vision to one of their companions, a distinguished man of noble family named Tilmon, a soldier turned monk, and told him that their bodies would be found at the spot where he saw the light shining from heaven to earth. This happened as he said, for their bodies were found and buried with the honour due to martyrs, and the day of their death, or of the finding of their bodies, is observed in those parts with fitting respect. When Peppin, the most illustrious Duke of the Franks, later heard of these events, he directed that the bodies be brought to him, and buried them with great splendour in the church of the city of Cologne on the Rhine. It is said that a spring bubbled up at the scene of the martyrdom, which affords a plentiful supply of water to this day.

ON their first arrival in Frisia, as soon as Wilbrord learned that the prince had granted him permission to preach, he hurried to Rome, where Pope Sergius then ruled the apostolic see, in order to obtain his approval and blessing on the evangelistic work he wished to undertake. He also hoped to obtain from him relics of the blessed Apostles and martyrs of Christ, so that when he had destroyed the idols and built churches among the people to whom he preached, he might have the relics of the saints ready to put in them. And when he had deposited them, he intended to dedicate these places fittingly in honour of each of the saints whose relics they were. He also wished to learn and obtain many other things required for carrying out so formidable a task. And having obtained all that he wanted, he returned to preach.

At this time the brethren who were engaged in the ministry of the word in Frisia elected one of their number named Suidbert, who was modest in his ways and humble-hearted, to be consecrated their bishop. And they sent him to Britain, where, at their request, he was consecrated by the most reverend Bishop Wilfrid, who happened to be driven out of his own country at the time, and was living in exile among the Mercians. For there was no bishop in Kent at this juncture, Theodore having died, and Berthwald his successor, who had crossed the sea to be consecrated, having not yet returned to his episcopal see.

When he had been made bishop, Suidbert returned from Britain, and shortly afterwards went to the Boructuars, many of whom he guided into the way of truth by his teaching. But after a short while, the Boructuars were defeated by the Old Saxons, and those who had accepted the word of God were scattered. The bishop himself went with certain others to Peppin, who at the request of his wife Blithryda, gave them a place of residence on an island in the Rhine, which in their language is called Inlitore.[1] Here he established a monastery, which is still occupied by his successors, and after leading a most austere life for some while, he ended his days there.

When those who had come over had taught in Frisia for a number of years, Peppin, with their unanimous consent, dispatched the venerable Wilbrord to Rome where Sergius still reigned as Pope, with the request that he might be consecrated Archbishop of the Frisian nation. His request was carried out in the year of our Lord 696, and Wilbrord was consecrated in the church of the holy martyr Cecilia on her feast day, when the Pope gave him the name of Clement, and quickly sent him back to his bishopric fourteen days after his arrival in the city.

Peppin assigned him a place for his see in his own famous castle, which is known in the ancient language, of that people as Wiltaburg, that is, the Town of the Wilts; but it is known in the Gallic tongue as Utrecht. Having built a church here, the most reverend prelate preached the word of God far and wide, recalling many from their errors, and establishing several churches and a number of monasteries in those parts. And not long afterwards he appointed a number of bishops, choosing them from among the brethren who had come with him to preach. Some of these have now fallen asleep in the Lord, but Wilbrord himself, surnamed Clement, is still living, and is much revered for his great age. He has been thirty-six years a bishop, and after the countless spiritual battles he has fought, longs with all his heart for the prize of a heavenly reward.

1. Kaiserswerth.

CHAPTER 12: *A man in the province of Northumbria returns from the dead and tells of the many dreadful and desirable things that he saw*

ABOUT this time, a noteworthy miracle, like those of olden days, occurred in Britain. For, in order to arouse the living from spiritual death, a man already dead returned to bodily life and related many notable things that he had seen, some of which I have thought it valuable to mention here in brief. There was a head of a family living in the area of Northumbria known as Cunningham, who led a devout life with all his household. He fell ill, his condition steadily deteriorating until the crisis came, and he died in the early hours of the night. But at daybreak he returned to life and suddenly sat up to the great consternation of those weeping around the body, who ran away; only his wife, who loved him more dearly, remained with him. The man reassured her, and said: 'Do not be frightened, for I have truly risen from the grasp of death, and I am allowed to live among men again. But henceforward I must not live as I used to, and must adopt a very different way of life.' Then he rose and went off to the church in the town, where he continued in prayer until daybreak. He then divided all his property into three parts, one of which he allotted to his wife, another to his sons, and the third he retained and distributed at once to the poor. Not long afterwards, he abandoned all worldly responsibilities and entered the monastery of Melrose, which is almost completely surrounded by a bend in the river Tweed. There he was given the tonsure, and entered a separate part of the house allotted him by the abbot, where he entered upon a life of such physical and spiritual penance to the day of his death that even if he had kept silence, his life would have witnessed that he had seen many dreadful and desirable things that remained hidden from others.

He described what he had seen as follows: 'A handsome

man in a shining robe was my guide, and we walked in silence in what appeared to be an easterly direction. As we travelled onwards, we came to a very broad and deep valley of infinite length. The side to our left was dreadful with burning flames, while the opposite side was equally horrible, with raging hail and bitter snow blowing and driving in all directions. Both sides were filled with men's souls, which seemed to be hurled from one side to the other by the fury of the tempest. When these wretches could no longer endure the blast of the terrible heat, they leaped into the heart of the terrible cold; and finding no refuge there, they leaped back again to be burned in the middle of the unquenchable flames. A countless host of deformed spirits were tormented far and wide in this wretched condition without any interval of respite as far as the eye could see, and I began to think that perhaps this was Hell, of whose intolerable torments I had often heard tell. But as if in response to my thoughts, the guide who preceded me said: "Do not think this, for this is not Hell as you imagine."

'When he had led me gradually to the further end, much alarmed by the terrible scene, I saw the place suddenly begin to grow dim, and darkness concealed everything. As we entered it, this darkness gradually grew so obscure that I could see nothing except it, and the outline and robes of my guide. And as we went on through the nocturnal gloom, frequent masses of black flame suddenly appeared before us, rising as though from a great pit, and falling back into it again. When my guide had brought me to this place, he suddenly disappeared and left me alone in the midst of the darkness before this horrible scene. Meanwhile these masses of flame continued ceaselessly leaping up and falling back again into the depths of the chasm, and I saw that, as the tongues of flame rose, they were filled with the souls of men which, like sparks flying up with the smoke, were sometimes flung high in the air, and at others, dropped back into the depths as the vapours of the fire died down. Furthermore, an indescribable stench welled up with these vapours, and filled the whole of this gloomy place.

'When I had stood there a long time terrified, not knowing what to do, where to turn, or what would happen to me, I suddenly heard behind me the sound of a most hideous and desperate lamentation, accompanied by harsh laughter, as though a rough mob were mocking captured enemies. As the noise increased and drew nearer, I saw a throng of wicked spirits dragging with them five human souls howling and lamenting into the depths of the darkness while the devils laughed and exulted. I saw among them one man tonsured like a clerk, a layman, and a woman. The wicked spirits dragged them down into the centre of the burning chasm, and as they descended deeper, I could no longer distinguish the weeping of the men from the laughter of the devils, but only a confused noise in my ears. Meanwhile, some of the dark spirits emerged from the fiery depths and rushed to surround me, distressing me with their glowing eyes and foul flames issuing from their mouths and nostrils. They threatened to seize me with the glowing forceps that they brandished in their hands, but although they frightened me, they did not dare to touch me. While I was thus beset about by enemies and black darkness and looked everywhere for some means of help to save me, there appeared behind me on the road by which I had come what seemed to be a bright star shining in the gloom, which grew in size and came swiftly towards me. As it approached, all the evil spirits who had tried to drag me away with their forceps, scattered and took to flight.

'The newcomer whose approach put them to flight was my former guide, who took a road to the right and began to lead me towards the south-east. He soon brought me out of darkness into an atmosphere of clear light, and as he led me forwards in bright light, I saw before us a tremendous wall which seemed to be of infinite length and height in all directions. As I could see no gate, window, or entrance in it, I began to wonder why we went up to the wall. But when we reached it, all at once – I know not by what means – we were on top of it. Within lay a very broad and pleasant meadow, so filled with the scent of spring flowers that its wonderful fragrance quickly dispelled all the stench of the gloomy furnace that had overcome me. Such was the light flooding all this place that it seemed greater than the brightness of daylight, or of the sun's rays at noon. In this meadow were innumerable companies of men in white robes, and many parties of happy people were sitting together. And as my guide led me through these crowds of happy citizens, I began to wonder whether this was the Kingdom of Heaven, of which I had heard so often. But in response to my thought, he said: "No, this is not the Kingdom of Heaven as you imagine."

'When we had passed through these abodes of blessed spirits and progressed further, I saw ahead of us a much more lovely light than before, and heard in it a sweet sound of people singing, while a scent of such surpassing fragrance emanated from the place that the earlier scent that I had thought so wonderful now seemed quite indifferent. And even the wonderful light that had flooded the flowery meadow seemed of small significance when compared with that now visible. As I was hoping that we should enter this delightful place, my guide suddenly halted, and without stopping, retraced his steps and led me back along the road by which we had come.

'When we returned to the happy dwellings of the souls robed in white, he asked me: "Do you understand all these things that you have seen?" "No", I replied. Then he said: "The valley that you saw, with its horrible burning flames and icy cold, is the place where souls are tried and punished who have delayed to confess and amend their wicked ways, and who at last had recourse to penitence at the hour of death, and so depart this life. Because they confessed and were penitent, although only at death, they will all be admitted into the Kingdom of Heaven on the Day of Judgement. But many are helped by the prayers, alms, and fasting of the living, and especially by the offering of Masses, and are therefore set free before the Day of Judgement. The fiery, noisome pit that you saw is the mouth of Hell, and whosoever falls into it will never be delivered throughout eternity. This flowery place, where you see these fair young people so happy and resplendent, is where souls are received who die having done good, but are not so perfect as to merit immediate entry into the Kingdom of Heaven. But at the Day of Judgement they shall all see Christ, and enter upon the joys of His heavenly Kingdom. And whoever are perfect in word, deed, and thought, enter the Kingdom of Heaven as soon as they leave the body. The Kingdom is situated near the place where you heard the sound of sweet singing, with the sweet fragrance and glorious light. You must now return to your body and live among men once more; but if you will weigh your actions with greater care, and study to keep your words and ways virtuous and simple, then when you die, you too will win a home among these happy spirits that you see. For when I left you for a while, I did so in order to discover what your future would be." When he told me this, I was most reluctant to return to my body, for I was entranced by the pleasantness and beauty of the place I could see and the company that I saw there. But I did not dare to question my guide, and meanwhile I suddenly found myself alive among men once more.'

This man of God would not discuss these and other things that he had seen to any apathetic or careless-living people, but only to those who were haunted by fear of punishment or gladdened by the hope of eternal joys, and were willing to take his words to heart and grow in holiness. But in the vicinity of his cell lived a monk named Haemgils, an eminent priest who adorned his office with good deeds: he is still living, and leads the life of a hermit in Ireland, supporting his latter years on a diet of bread and cold water. He often used to visit this man, and by repeated questioning, he learned from him what sort of things he had seen when freed from the body; and it is from his account that I have come to know these details that I have briefly described. He also related his visions to King Alfrid, a man of wide learning, who listened so readily and attentively to him, that, at his request, he was admitted to the above monastery and received the monastic tonsure. And whenever the king visited those parts, he frequently went to listen to him. At the time of these events, the ruler of the monastery was the religious and humble abbot and priest Ethelwald, who at present most worthily occupies the episcopal see of the church of Lindisfarne.

This man was given a more secluded dwelling in the monastery, so that he could devote himself more freely to the service of his Maker in unbroken prayer. And since this place stands on the bank of a river, he often used to enter it for severe bodily penance, and plunge frequently beneath the water while he recited psalms and prayers for as long as he could endure it, standing motionless with the water up to his loins, and sometimes to his neck. When he returned to shore, he never removed his dripping, chilly garments, but let them warm and dry on his body. And in winter, when the half-broken cakes of ice were swirling around him which he had broken to make a place to stand and dip himself in the water, those who saw him used to say: 'Brother Drycthelm (for that was his name), it is wonderful how you can manage to bear such bitter cold.' To which he, being a man of simple disposition and self-restraint, would reply: 'I have known it colder.' And when they said: 'It is extraordinary that you are willing to practise such severe discipline', he used to answer: 'I have seen greater austerity.' So until the day of his summons from this life he tamed his aged body by daily fasting, inspired by an insatiable longing for the blessings of heaven, and he helped many people to salvation by his words and life.

QUITE the reverse happened in the case of a man living in Mercia, whose visions and words – although not his way of life – benefited many others, but not himself. For in the reign of Coinred, Ethelred's successor, there was a layman who held a military command, and pleased the king as greatly by his public diligence as he displeased him by the carelessness of his private life. The king repeatedly warned him to confess and amend, and to abandon his wicked ways before a sudden death deprived him of any time for repentance and amendment. But although frequently warned, he rejected his salutary advice, and promised that he would do penance at some future date. Meanwhile he fell ill, and taking to his bed, began to suffer severe pains. The king, who was fond of him, visited him and urged him even then to repent of his sins before he died. But he answered that he did not wish to confess his sins at this time, but would do so when he recovered from his illness, for he did not wish his friends to accuse him of doing in fear of death what he had refused to do when he was well. He thought that he had spoken bravely, but it soon became clear that he had been deceived by the Devil's tricks.

As his illness grew more serious, the king again came to visit and reason with him, but the man at once cried out in a miserable voice: 'What do you want now? Why have you come here? There is nothing that you can do to help or save me now.' The king answered: 'Do not talk like that. Behave like a sensible man.' 'I am not mad', he replied, 'but I have the knowledge of my wickedness set clearly before my eyes.' 'What do you mean by that?' the king asked. 'A short time ago', the man said, 'two most handsome youths entered this house and sat down beside me, one at my head and the other at my feet. One of them produced a tiny but very beautiful book, and gave it to me to read. When I looked at it, I found all the good deeds that I had ever done recorded, but they were few and trifling. Then they took back the book, but said nothing to me. Suddenly there arrived a horde of wicked spirits with horrible faces, who surrounded the house and occupied the greater part of it. Then one, who from the blackness of his gloomy face and exalted position seemed to be their chief, produced a horrible-looking book of enormous size and almost unbearable weight, which he ordered one of his satellites to bring me to read. When I read it, I found all my crimes clearly recorded there in black letters, not only sins of act and word, but even of the least thought. And he said to the glorious white-robed men who were sitting beside me: "Why are you sitting here? You know very well that this man belongs to us." They replied: "You are right. Take him, and enrol him in your company of the damned." With these words, they immediately vanished, and two wicked spirits rose and struck me with the tridents in their hands, one on the head and the other on the foot. These blows are now penetrating the inmost parts of my body with awful agony, and when they meet, I shall die. The devils will be waiting to snatch me away, and I shall be dragged down through the gates of Hell.'

So spoke the wretched man in his despair, and died shortly afterwards, so he is now vainly undergoing everlasting torments because he refused to undergo penance for a short while to win the grace of pardon. In his case it is clear – as Pope Gregory writes of certain people – that he did not see these things for his own benefit, since they did not help him, but for the benefit of others. For when people learned of his death, they would fear to delay their penance while they still had time, lest the intervention of sudden death might cause them to perish unrepentant. When this man saw good and evil spirits offering him different records, this was done by divine providence in order that we should remember that our actions and thoughts are not scattered by the wind, but are all preserved to be examined by the Supreme Judge, and will be shown to us at the last either by our friends the angels or by our enemies. And whereas the white-robed angels first produced a white record, and the devils a black, the former tiny and the latter enormous, let it be noted that in his early years he did some good deeds which he completely obscured by his evil-doing as a young man. In contrast, if in his youth he had taken care to correct the errors of his childhood and cancel them in God's eyes by well-doing, he might have been assigned to the company of those mentioned in the psalm: '*Blessed are they whose unrighteousness is forgiven, and whose sins are covered.*' I have thought that this story should be told in a straightforward way as I heard it from the venerable Bishop Pecthelm, to further the salvation of those who may read or hear it.

CHAPTER 14: *Another man about to die sees the place of punishment reserved for him in Hell*

I KNOW a brother – Ah, how I wish I had never known him! – whose name I could mention were it desirable, and who lived in a noble monastery, but lived an ignoble life. He was often taken to task by the brethren and authorities of the house, and warned to adopt a more disciplined life; and although he refused to listen to them, they bore with him patiently because they had need of his manual labour, for he was a skilled smith. But he was much addicted to drunkenness and the pleasures of a loose life, and used to remain in his workshop day and night rather than enter the church to sing and pray, and to listen to the word of life with the brethren. So it happened to him that, as folk often say, whoever refuses to enter the church door humbly and willingly will certainly be damned and enter the gates of Hell unwillingly. Falling ill, he summoned the brethren to his death-bed, and sorrowing like one already damned, began to describe to them how he saw Hell open, and Satan in the depths of the abyss, with Caiaphas and others who had slain our Lord condemned like him to the avenging flames. 'Close to them, alas', he cried, 'I

see a place of eternal doom prepared for my wretched self!'
As the brethren listened, they began earnestly to urge him
to repent while he remained in the body, but he answered in
despair: 'There is no time left for me to amend my ways; I
have already seen my judgement pronounced.'

With these words, he died without receiving the saving
Viaticum, and his body was buried in the remotest part of the
monastery, nor did anyone dare to say masses or sing psalms
for him, or even to pray for him. Oh, how vast a distance has
God set between light and darkness! When the blessed Protomartyr Stephen was about to die for the truth, he *saw the
heavens open, the glory of God revealed, and Jesus standing at the
right hand of God*. And in order that he might die the happier,
he fixed his mental gaze before death on the place where he
hoped to be after death. In contrast the smith, a man of dark
thoughts and deeds, saw Hell open as death drew near, and
saw the damnation of the Devil and his followers. The unhappy man even saw his own place of punishment among
them, so that he might despair of salvation and die in greater
misery, but also that through his own perdition he might
bequeath a means of salvation to the living who learned of
his fate. This happened recently in the Province of Bernicia,
and was talked of far and wide, rousing many people to do
penance for their sins without delay. And may the reading of
this account have the same effect.

CHAPTER 15: *Under Adamnan's influence, many churches
of the Scots adopt the Catholic Easter. He writes a book on
the Holy Places* [c. A.D. 703]

A⊤ this period, by the grace of God, the majority of the
Scots in Ireland, together with some of the Britons in
Britain, conformed to the logical and canonical time of keeping Easter.* Adamnan, priest and abbot of the monks who
lived on the Isle of Iona, was sent by his nation on a mission

to Alfrid, King of the English, and remained in his province for some while, where he observed the rites of the Church canonically performed. He was earnestly advised by many who were more learned than himself not to presume to act contrary to the universal customs of the Church, whether in the keeping of Easter or in many other observances, seeing that his following was very small and situated in a remote corner of the world. As a result he changed his opinions, and readily adopted what he saw and heard in the English churches in place of the customs of his own people. For he was a wise and worthy man, excellently grounded in knowledge of the Scriptures.

On his return home, he tried to lead his own people in Iona and those who were under the jurisdiction of that monastery into the correct ways that he had himself learned and wholeheartedly accepted, but in this he failed. Then he sailed over to preach in Ireland, and by his simple teaching showed its people the proper time of Easter. He corrected their ancient error and restored nearly all who were not under the jurisdiction of Iona to Catholic unity, teaching them to observe Easter at the proper time. Having observed the canonical Easter in Ireland, he returned to his own island, where he vigorously pressed his own monastery to conform to the Catholic observance of Easter, but had no success in his attempts, and before the close of the next year he departed this life. For God in his goodness decreed that so great a champion of peace and unity should be received into everlasting life before the time of Easter returned once more, and before he should be obliged to enter upon more serious controversy with those who refused to follow him in the truth.

Adamnan also wrote a book about the Holy Places, which is most valuable to many readers. The man who dictated the information to him was Arculf, a bishop from Gaul who had visited Jerusalem to see the Holy Places. Having toured all the Land of Promise, Arculf had travelled to Damascus, Constantinople, Alexandria, and many islands; but as he was returning home, his ship was driven by a violent storm onto the western coast of Britain. After many adventures, he visited Christ's servant Adamnan, who, finding him learned in the Scriptures and well acquainted with the Holy Places, was delighted to welcome him and eager to listen to him. As a result, he rapidly committed to writing everything of interest that Arculf said that he had seen at the Holy Places. And by this means, as I have said, he compiled a work of great value to many people, especially those who live at a great distance from the places where the patriarchs and Apostles lived, and whose only source of information about them comes from books. Adamnan presented this book to King Alfrid, and through his generosity it was circulated for lesser folk to read. The writer himself was sent back to his own land richer by many gifts. And I think it will be valuable to readers of this history if I make some extracts from this book, and include them in this history.

CHAPTER 16: *Descriptions from this book of the sites of our Lord's Birth, Passion, and Resurrection*

ADAMNAN wrote about our Lord's birthplace as follows: 'Bethlehem, the city of David, is situated on a narrow ridge almost entirely enclosed by mountains. It is a thousand paces in length from east to west, and has a low wall without towers built around the circumference of the plateau. At the eastern corner is a kind of natural grotto, the outer part of which is said to have been the place of our Lord's birth, while the inner part is known as our Lord's manger. The interior of this grotto is entirely faced with precious marble over the exact spot where our Lord is said to have been born, and above it stands the lofty church of Saint Mary.'

On the site of Christ's Passion and Resurrection, he writes as follows:

'For those entering the city of Jerusalem from the northern

side, the lay-out of the streets makes the Church of Constantine, known as the Martyrdom, the first of the Holy Places to be visited. This was erected by the Emperor Constantine in a magnificent regal style, for this is the place where his mother Helena discovered the Cross of our Lord. To the west, the Church of Golgotha comes into view, where can be seen the rock on which once stood the Cross, with the Body of our Lord nailed to it: it now supports an enormous silver cross, over which hangs a great bronze wheel bearing lamps. Beneath the site of our Lord's Cross a crypt has been hewn out of the rock, and the Holy Sacrifice is offered for the honoured dead on an altar here, while their bodies remain outside in the street. To the west of this stands the Church of the *Anastasis*, which is the church of our Lord's Resurrection, circular in shape, surrounded by three walls, and supported on twelve columns. Between each of the walls is a broad passage, where three altars stand at three places against the central wall, to the north, south, and west. There are eight doors or entrances through the three walls, four facing east, and four facing west. In the centre is the circular Tomb of our Lord, cut out of the rock, and a man standing inside it can touch the roof with his hand. The entrance faces eastward, and against it stands the great stone, which still bears the marks of iron tools. The exterior is completely covered with marble to the top of the roof, which is adorned with gold, and bears a great golden cross. The Sepulchre of our Lord is cut out of the north side of the Tomb; it is seven feet in length, and raised three palms' breadth above the pavement. The entrance is on the south side, where twelve lamps burn day and night, four inside the sepulchre itself, and eight above it on the right-hand side. The stone that once formed the door of the Tomb has now been broken, but the smaller portion stands as a small square altar in front of the Tomb, while the larger portion forms another altar at the eastern end of the same Church, and is draped with linen cloths. The colour of the Tomb and Sepulchre is a mingled white and red.'

ON the site of our Lord's Ascension, Adamnan writes:
'The Mount of Olives is of the same height as Mount Sion, but is broader and longer. It is sparsely wooded, except for olives and vines, but grows corn and barley, for the soil is thin and suitable only for plants and flowers. On the very top of the hill, where our Lord ascended into heaven, stands a lofty circular Church, with three roofed-in porches on the outside. The interior of the building could not be roofed and vaulted because our Lord's body passed upwards, but it has an altar on the east side, protected by a narrow canopy. In the centre of the Church, where our Lord ascended, can be seen His last footprints, exposed to the sky above. And although the earth is daily removed by the faithful, it remains undiminished, and still retains these marks resembling footprints. Close by lies a bronze wheel, as high as a man's neck, with great lamps hanging above it on a pulley, and burning day and night. On the west side of the Church are eight windows, and as many lamps hanging opposite them on cords. These cast their rays through the glass as far as Jerusalem, and their light is said to evoke a feeling of ardour and penitence in the hearts of all who see it. Each year on the day of our Lord's Ascension, at the end of Mass, a powerful rush of wind is said to descend from above and throw to the ground all who are in the Church.'

On the situation of Hebron, and the tombs of the patriarchs, Adamnan writes:

'Hebron, once a city and the capital of David's kingdom, now only shows what it was by its ruins. In a valley one furlong to the east of it is a double cave, where the tombs of the patriarchs are enclosed in a square wall with their heads to the north. Each tomb is covered by a single stone slab, cut like those in a church: those of the three patriarchs are white, while that of Adam is of humbler and inferior workmanship,

and lies not far away at the northern extremity of the wall.
There are also three smaller and plainer monuments to three
women. The hill of Mamre rises a thousand paces away from
these monuments to the north, and is covered with grass and
flowers. There is a level plateau at the summit, to the north
of which stands Abraham's Oak – a trunk twice the height
of a man, enclosed in a church.'

I have thought it useful to include these extracts from the
works of the above author for the benefit of those who read
this history, and have retained the sense of his words, but
summarized them in a shorter form. Should anyone wish to
know more about his book, they may either study it in the
original form, or read the abridgement containing short
extracts which I have recently compiled.

CHAPTER 18: *The South Saxons receive Eadbert and Ealla,
and the West Saxons Daniel and Aldhelm as their bishops.
The writings of Aldhelm [c. A.D. 705]*

IN the year of our Lord 705, Alfrid, King of the Northumbrians, died after a reign of nearly twenty years, and was
succeeded on the throne by his son Osred, a boy of about
eight years of age, who reigned eleven years. At the com-
mencement of his reign, Bishop Hedda of the West Saxons
departed to the life of heaven. He was a good, just man, who
carried out his duties as bishop guided by an inborn love of
goodness rather than by anything learned from books. The
most reverend Bishop Pecthelm – of whom more will be
said in due course – who was a fellow-monk or deacon for a
long time with Hedda's successor Aldhelm, relates how many
miracles of healing occurred through his holiness at the place
where he died. He says that the people of that province used
to carry away earth from it to mix in water for the sick, and
that many sick men and beasts who drank or were sprinkled
with it were restored to health. In consequence, there was a

considerable pit created there by the continual removal of the hallowed soil.

At his death, the bishopric of the province was divided into two dioceses, one of which was assigned to Daniel,* who rules it to this day, and the other to Aldhelm,* who administered it with great energy for four years. Both bishops were well acquainted with church matters, and learned in the study of the Scriptures. While Aldhelm was still a priest, and abbot of the monastery known as Maildreib's Town,[1] he was directed by a synod of his own people to write a notable treatise against the errors of the Britons, who did not observe Easter at the right time, and did other things contrary to the orthodoxy and unity of the Church. By means of this book he persuaded many of those Britons who were subject to the West Saxons to conform to the Catholic observance of our Lord's Resurrection. He also wrote an excellent book *On Virginity*, which he composed in a double form in hexameter verse and prose in the manner of Sedulius. He also wrote other books, for he was a man of wide learning, with a polished style, and, as I have said, was extremely well-read both in biblical and general literature. At his death, Forthere, who is also a man of great learning in the scriptures, was appointed to the bishopric in his place, and is still living today.

During their episcopates, it was decided by synodical decree that the province of the South Saxons, which had hitherto belonged to the diocese of Winchester under Bishop Daniel, should have an episcopal see and bishop of its own. Eadbert, who was Abbot of Selsey, a monastery founded by Bishop Wilfrid of blessed memory, was consecrated its first bishop, and at his death, Ealla succeeded him in the office. After some years, he also departed this life, and the bishopric has fallen into abeyance to this day.

1. Malmesbury, Dorset.

IN the fourth year of Osred's reign, Coinred, who had ruled the kingdom of Mercia with great renown for some while, resigned his kingly sceptre for a yet more noble kingdom. During the pontificate of Constantine, he went to Rome, received the tonsure, and became a monk at the shrine of the Apostles, passing the remainder of his days in prayer, fasting, and acts of mercy. He was succeeded on the throne by Ceolred, son of Ethelred, who had ruled the kingdom before Coinred. With Coinred went Offa, son of Sighere the above-mentioned king of the East Saxons, a very handsome and lovable young man whom the entire nation greatly hoped would inherit and uphold the sceptre of the kingdom. But, fired by an equal ardour, he left his wife, lands, family, and country for the sake of Christ and his Gospel, hoping *to receive an hundred-fold in this life, and in the world to come life everlasting*. So when they had arrived at the holy places in Rome, he received the tonsure, entered upon the monastic life, and at last attained the long-desired vision of the blessed Apostles in heaven.

During the same year in which they left Britain, the renowned Bishop Wilfrid ended his days in the region of Oundle. The coffin containing his body was carried to his own monastery at Ripon, and buried in the church of the blessed Apostle Peter with the honours due to so eminent a prelate. I will now turn back and recall briefly some of the events of his life.* As a boy, he was of a good disposition and behaviour for his age, always bearing himself modestly and thoughtfully, so that he was deservedly loved, admired, and welcomed by his elders as one of themselves. When he reached the age of fourteen, he chose monastic life rather than secular, and when he informed his father – for his mother was dead – he readily agreed to his heavenly desires

and aspirations, and encouraged him to persevere in this
laudable decision. He therefore went to the Isle of Lindisfarne
and offered himself for the service of the monks, diligently
setting himself to learn and practise all that conduces to
monastic purity and devotion. Having a quick mind, he very
soon learned the psalms and certain other books, and even
before he received the tonsure, had become somewhat remarkable for the more important monastic virtues of humility and obedience, which made him rightly loved by the
older monks as well as his contemporaries. When he had
served God in that monastery for some years, being a shrewd
young man, he gradually came to realize that the way of life
taught by the Scots was very imperfect, so he decided to
visit Rome, and see what ecclesiastical and monastic customs
were in use at the apostolic see. When he acquainted the
brethren with his wish, they commended his proposal and
encouraged him to carry out whatever he had in mind.
Without further delay, he went to Queen Elfleda, who knew
him and at whose request he had been accepted into the
monastery, and told her of his desire to visit the shrines of the
blessed Apostles. The youth's plan pleased the queen, who
sent him to King Earconbert of Kent, her uncle's son, with
the request that he would send him honourably to Rome.
At this time Honorius, one of the disciples of blessed Pope
Gregory and a man of great experience in church matters,
was occupying the archbishopric with great distinction. And
while he was waiting there, Wilfrid, being an active-minded
young man, diligently set himself to study everything that he
saw. Another young man then arrived named Biscop, known
as Benedict, whom I have already mentioned: he came of
noble English family, and also wished to travel to Rome. So
the king gave Wilfrid to Benedict as his companion, with
instructions to accompany him to Rome. On their arrival at
Lugdunum,[1] Wilfrid was detained there by Dalfin, bishop of
the city, but Benedict continued on his journey to Rome

1. Lyons.

without staying. For the bishop took great pleasure in the young man's wise conversation, graceful appearance, and enthusiasm for action, as well as in his balanced and mature opinions. He therefore made ample provision for all the needs of Wilfrid and his companions for as long as they stayed with him, and offered to entrust to him, if he were willing, the administration of a considerable area of Gaul, to give him his young niece as wife, and make him his own adopted son. Wilfrid thanked him for the kindness that he had been pleased to show a stranger, but told him that he had in mind a somewhat different way of life, which was the reason why he had left his own country and set out on the journey to Rome.

Hearing this, the bishop sent him on to Rome, providing him with a guide, and generously supplying everything that the needs of the journey demanded. And he earnestly pressed him to remember to come that way on his return journey to his own country. When Wilfrid arrived in Rome, he devoted himself to constant prayer and study of church matters as he had intended, and by his daily attendance on him, won the friendship of the most holy and learned Archdeacon Boniface, who was also a Papal Counsellor. Under his guidance he learned each of the Gospels in turn and the correct method of calculating Easter, while through this tutor he came to understand many other things relating to church order about which he had known nothing in his own country; and having spent some months engrossed in profitable study, he returned to Dalfin in Gaul. He remained with him three years, received the tonsure at his hands, and so won his affection that the bishop considered making him his heir. But the bishop's cruel death intervened to prevent this, for Wilfrid was destined to become a bishop of his own people the English. For Queen Baldhilda sent soldiers with orders to kill the bishop, and, as his clerk, Wilfrid accompanied him to the place of execution, wishing to die with him, although the bishop strongly opposed this. But when the executioners learned

that he was a foreigner and an Englishman, they spared him
and refused to put him to death with his bishop.

On his return to Britain, Wilfrid was admitted to the
friendship of King Alfrid, who had learned to love and follow the Catholic laws of the Church; and when he found
Wilfrid to be a Catholic, he gave him ten hides of land at a
place called Stamford, and not long afterwards, a monastery
with thirty hides at Ripon. This place had been formerly
granted to monks who followed the Scots customs in order
to build a monastery there. But since, when offered the alternative, they had preferred to abandon the place rather than
adopt the Catholic Easter and other canonical rites in accordance with the usage of the Roman and apostolic Church, the
king gave it to one whom he knew to be trained in better
doctrines and customs.

At this time, under instructions from the king, Wilfrid was
ordained priest at this monastery by the above-mentioned
Agilbert, Bishop of the Gewissae, because the king wished to
retain a man of such great learning and devotion as a priest
and counsellor for his own court. Shortly after the exposure
and banishment of the Scottish sect that I mentioned, and
with the approval and advice of his father Oswy, the king
sent Wilfrid to Gaul, asking that he be consecrated as his
bishop, Wilfrid being at the time about thirty years of age.
And when Agilbert, then Bishop of Paris, and eleven other
bishops had gathered to make him a bishop, they carried out
the rite of his consecration with great splendour. But since
Wilfrid remained overseas for some while, a holy man named
Chad was consecrated Bishop of York at the orders of King
Oswy, as I have already described. And having ruled the
church very ably for three years, he resigned the see and
retired to his monastery of Lastingham, Wilfrid then becoming bishop of the whole province of Northumbria.

Subsequently, as I have already told, Wilfrid was expelled
from his bishopric during the reign of Egfrid, and other
bishops were consecrated in his place. Intending to travel to

Rome and plead his case before the apostolic Pope, he therefore took ship, but a strong westerly wind drove him to Frisia, where he was honourably received by the barbarous people and their king Aldgils. He preached Christ among them, teaching the word of truth to many thousands, and cleansing them from the guilt of their sins in the font of our Saviour. He was the first to attempt the work of their evangelization, which was later completed so zealously by the most reverend Christian Bishop Wilbrord. Having spent the winter happily there with God's new people, Wilfrid set out once more for Rome, and when his case was heard before Pope Agatho and several bishops, they were unanimous in acquitting him of the charges laid against him, and declared him worthy of his bishopric.

At this time Pope Agatho summoned an hundred and twenty bishops to a Synod in Rome in order to combat those who were teaching that there was only one will and action* in our Lord and Saviour. He ordered Wilfrid to be summoned to take his place among the bishops, and to state his own belief and that of the province or island whence he had come. And when both he and his nation were shown to be Catholic in their belief, it was thought fitting to include this among the other findings of the synod in the following form: 'Wilfrid, beloved of God, Bishop of the city of York, having brought his case before the apostolic see, has been acquitted by its authority from all charges against him, both definite and indefinite. Appointed to take his seat in consultation with one hundred and twenty-five bishops in synod, he affirmed the true and Catholic Faith on behalf of all the northern part of Britain, Ireland, and the islands inhabited by the English, Britons, Scots, and Picts, ratifying this by his own signature.'

After this, Wilfrid returned to Britain, and converted the province of the South Saxons from their idolatrous rites to the Faith of Christ. He also sent preachers to the Isle of Wight, and during the second year of King Alfrid, Egfrid's successor, he was restored to his own see and bishoprics at the king's invitation. But five years later he was again accused by the king and several bishops, and expelled from his diocese. He travelled to Rome, and was given opportunity to defend himself in the presence of his accusers before the apostolic Pope John (VI) and several bishops. It was unanimously decided that his accusers had brought partially false charges against him, and the Pope wrote to the English kings Ethelred and Alfrid that he had been unjustly condemned, and that they should restore him to his bishopric.

His acquittal was greatly forwarded when the transactions of the Synod held by Pope Agatho of blessed memory were read. This had taken place when Wilfrid visited the city on a former occasion, and sat at the council with the other bishops, as I have already described. For when, in connexion with the case and at the direction of the apostolic Pope, the transactions of this Synod were read for some days in the presence of the nobility and many of the people, they came to the passage where it is written: 'Wilfrid, beloved of God and Bishop of the city of York, having brought his case before the apostolic see, has by its authority been acquitted from all framed and unframed charges etc', as already recorded. When this was read, those who listened were surprised, and when the reader finished, they began to ask one another, 'Who was this Bishop Wilfrid?' Then Boniface, Counsellor to the apostolic Pope, and many others who had met him there in Pope Agatho's time, explained that he was the same bishop who had been accused by his own people and had recently come to Rome to be tried by the apostolic see. 'He came here long ago under a similar accusation,' they said, 'and the dispute between the two parties was quickly heard and decided. Pope Agatho of blessed memory showed that he had been unjustly expelled from his bishopric, and had so high a regard for Wilfrid that he ordered him to sit in the council of bishops which he had summoned, as a man of blameless faith and honest mind.' Hearing this, the Pope and all the assembly declared that a man of such authority, who had been a bishop for nearly forty years, should certainly not be condemned, but should be cleared of all the charges laid against him, and return home with honour.

As Wilfrid was crossing Gaul on his return to Britain, he was suddenly overtaken by an illness which grew so serious that he was unable to ride, and had to be carried by his attendants in a litter. He was brought to Maeldum,[1] a city of Gaul, where he lay four days and nights as though dead, and only his faint breathing showed that he was still alive. He remained like this for four days without food or drink, speech or hearing, but at daybreak on the fifth day he sat up as though waking from a deep sleep. When he opened his eyes and saw around him a crowd of brethren singing psalms and weeping, he sighed and asked for the priest Acca, who came in at once when summoned, and seeing Wilfrid better and able to speak, fell on his knees and thanked God with all the brethren present. And when they had sat down, and began with some hesitation to talk of the judgements of heaven, the bishop told the others to leave them for an hour, and said to the priest Acca:

'I have seen a momentous vision, which I want you to keep secret until I know God's will for me. There stood beside me a noble being in white robes, who told me that he was Michael the Archangel. "I am come to recall you from death," he said, "for our Lord has granted you life at the prayers of your brethren and the intercession of His blessed Mother the ever-virgin Mary. So I now pronounce that you shall be healed of this sickness: but be prepared, for I shall return to visit you after four years. When you return to your own country, you shall recover the greater portion of the possessions that were taken from you, and end your life in perfect peace."' And to the delight of all, who gave thanks to God, the bishop recovered, resumed his journey, and arrived in Britain.

1. Meaux.

When they had studied the letters that Wilfrid had brought from the apostolic Pope, Archbishop Berthwald and Ethelred very readily supported him. The latter, formerly king but now a monk, sent for Coinred whom he had appointed king in his own place, and asked him to be a friend to Wilfrid, to which he agreed. But Alfrid, King of the Northumbrians, refused to receive him; but he died shortly afterwards, and was succeeded by his son Osred. A synod was soon held near the river Nidd, and after some argument between the parties, it was generally agreed that Wilfrid should be restored to the bishopric of his own church. And so for four years, until the day of his death, he lived his life in peace. He died in his monastery in the region of Oundle during the rule of Abbot Cuthbald, and was carried by the brethren to his first monastery at Ripon, where he was buried in the church of the blessed Apostle Peter close to the altar on the south side, as already recorded, and the following epitaph was inscribed above him:

> Here Wilfrid, mighty prelate, lies at peace
> Who, spurred by love of God, this temple raised,
> And hallowed it in Peter's noble name
> To whom our Master Christ bequeathed the keys.
> Fair gold and purple vestments he bestowed,
> And noble cross of richly shining ore
> He placed aloft as sign of victory won.
> The four Evangelists he also caused
> To be inscribed in order, and each book
> He fitly cased in covers of red gold.
> The time of keeping Easter he set right
> In due conformity with canon law
> Determined by the Fathers, and our fault
> Corrected by his teaching of the truth.
> Here he established many bands of monks,
> And as a watchful shepherd bade them keep
> The Rule established by the saints of old.
> In his long life he weathered many storms,

Discords at home, and perils overseas.
He ruled as bishop five and forty years,
And passed away rejoicing to our God.
Grant us, O Jesus, his true flock to be,
And tread with him the road that leads to Thee.

CHAPTER 20: *Albinus succeeds the devout Abbot Hadrian,
and Acca succeeds to Wilfrid's bishopric* [A.D. 709]

IN the year following the death of the above Father Wilfrid,
that is, the fifth year of King Osred, the most reverend
father, Abbot Hadrian, fellow-worker in the word of God
with Archbishop Theodore of blessed memory, died and
was buried in the church of the blessed Mother of God in his
own monastery. This was the forty-first year after his dis-
patch by Pope Vitalian with Theodore, and the thirty-ninth
after his arrival in Britain. Among others testifying to his
learning and that of Archbishop Theodore is his disciple
Albinus, who succeeded him as abbot of his monastery, and
was so well grounded in the study of the Scriptures that he
had no small grasp of Greek, while he understood Latin as
thoroughly as his native English tongue.

Acca, Wilfrid's chaplain, who succeeded him as Bishop
of the church of Hexham, was a man of great energy, and
noble in the sight of God and man. He greatly beautified and
enlarged the structure of his church, which was dedicated in
honour of blessed Andrew the Apostle. He devoted much
care, as he still does, to obtaining relics of the blessed Apostles
and martyrs of Christ from various places, and builds altars
for their veneration, placed for this purpose in recesses within
the walls of his church. He also compiled accounts of their
sufferings, and collected books on church matters to form a
very complete and excellent library. And he was diligent in
providing sacred vessels, lights, and similar articles necessary
for the furnishing of God's house. He also invited a famous

singer named Maban, who had been trained by the successors of blessed Pope Gregory's disciples in Kent, to come and instruct him and his clergy. He retained his services for twelve years, to teach them whatever church music they did not know, and also to restore to their original form any familiar chants that had become imperfect through lapse of time or neglect, for the bishop himself was a singer of great experience. He was also most learned in the holy Scriptures, orthodox in his profession of the Catholic Faith, and well acquainted with the rules of church administration. Nor did he cease to maintain all these things until he received the reward of his piety and devotion, for he had been reared and trained from boyhood among the clergy of the most holy Bosa, God's beloved Bishop of York. He had later come to Bishop Wilfrid in the hope of improving himself, and remained under him continuously until the latter's death, travelling to Rome with him, and there learning many valuable things about the organization of Holy Church of which he had known nothing in his own country.

CHAPTER 21: *Abbot Ceolfrid sends church architects to the King of the Picts, and with them a letter about the Catholic Easter and tonsure* [c. A.D. 710]

At this time, Nechtan, King of the Picts living in the northern parts of Britain, convinced after assiduous study of Church writings, renounced the error hitherto maintained by his nation about the observance of Easter, and adopted the Catholic time of keeping our Lord's Resurrection with all his people. In order to do this more smoothly and with greater authority, the king asked help from the English people, whom he knew to have based their practice long previously on the pattern of the holy, Roman, apostolic Church. So he sent messengers to the venerable Ceolfrid, Abbot of the monastery of the blessed Apostles Peter and

Paul, which he ruled most illustriously as successor of the above-mentioned Benedict. This monastery stands at the mouth of the river Wear, and close to the river Tyne at a place called Ingyrum.[1] The king requested Ceolfrid to write him a letter of guidance that would help him to refute those who presumed to keep Easter at the wrong time, and although he was relatively well informed on these matters himself, he also required information about the form and reason for the tonsure that clergy should wear. In addition, he asked that architects be sent him in order to build a stone church for his people in the Roman style, promising that he would dedicate it in honour of the blessed Prince of the Apostles, and that he and his people would follow the customs of the holy apostolic Roman Church as far as they could learn them in view of their remoteness from the Roman people and language. The most reverend Abbot Ceolfrid complied with his devout wishes and requests, sending him the architects he asked for, together with the following letter:

'To the most excellent and illustrious lord, King Nechtan, from Abbot Ceolfrid – Greetings in our Lord.

'In response to your devout enquiries as a God-fearing king, I am most willing and ready to attempt to explain the Catholic observance of Easter in accordance with the rulings of the apostolic see, for we know that whenever Holy Church sets itself to learn, teach, or maintain the truth concerning our Lord, this truth is revealed to it from heaven. As a secular writer very truly said,[2] the world would be a very happy place if kings were philosophers, or philosophers were kings. And if a man of the world could make a true estimate of this world's philosophy and judge rightly about the state of this world, it is much more desirable, and sincerely to be prayed for by the citizens of our heavenly home who are pilgrims in this world, that the greater any man's position in this world, the more he should exert himself to obey the

1. Jarrow.   2. Plato, in *The Republic*.

commands of the Supreme Judge, and by his example and authority induce those committed to his charge to follow him in observing them.

'There are three rules in holy scripture that determine the time of keeping Easter, and which no human authority may change. Two of these are decreed by God in the Law of Moses, and the third is added in the Gospel as a consequence of the Passion and Resurrection of our Lord. For the Law directed that the Passover should be kept in the first month of the year, and in the third week of that month, that is, between the fifteenth and twenty-first days of the month. To this, the apostolic ordinance in the Gospels adds that we are to wait for the Lord's Day in this third week, and begin to observe Eastertide on that day. Whoever keeps this third rule correctly will never make a mistake in fixing the Feast of Easter. But if you wish to hear more clear and detailed information about this, it is written in Exodus, where the people of Israel, before their deliverance from Egypt, are directed to keep the first Passover, that " *The Lord said to Moses and Aaron: This month shall be to you the beginning of months; it shall be the first month of the year to you. Speak ye to all the congregation of Israel, saying, In the tenth day of this month every man shall take a lamb according to their families and households.*" And a little later, "*And ye shall keep it up until the four-teenth day of the same month: and the whole assembly of the congregation of Israel shall kill it in the evening.*" These words make it very clear that, in the paschal observance, the fourteenth day is mentioned not because it was the day on which the Passover is commanded to be kept, but because the lamb is commanded to be killed on the fourteenth day, that is, the fifteenth lunar day, which begins the third week when the moon shows her face in the heavens: and because it was on the night of the fifteenth moon that the Egyptians were slain, and Israel redeemed out of its long slavery. "*Seven days shall ye eat unleavened bread*", it is said. In these words, all the third week of the first month is directed to be solemnly observed.

But lest we should think that those seven days were to be reckoned from the fourteenth to the twentieth days, it is added: "*On the first day there shall be no leaven in your houses; whosoever eateth unleavened bread from the first day until the seventh day, that soul shall be cut off from Israel*" and so on, until he says: "*For in this selfsame day I will bring your army out of the land of Egypt.*"

'So the day on which God was to bring out their army from Egypt is called the first day. It is clear, however, that they were not brought up out of Egypt on the fourteenth day, on the evening of which the lamb was killed and which is properly known as the Passover or Phase, but on the fifteenth day, as is quite plainly recorded in the Book of *Numbers;* "*So they departed from Rameses in the first month, on the fifteenth day of the month*" – a different day to the Phase – "*and the children of Israel went out with a high hand.*" So the seven days of unleavened bread, on the first of which the Lord's people were led up out of Egypt, are to be reckoned from the beginning of the third week, as I have said: that is, from the fourteenth day of the month to the twenty-first day of the same month inclusive. But the fourteenth day is noted down separately from this number under the title of the Passover, as is clearly defined in the ensuing passage of *Exodus*, where it is said: "*For in that day I will lead your armies out of the land of Egypt,*" and immediately adds: "*And you shall keep that day in your generations by an ordinance for ever. In the first month, on the fourteenth day of the month at evening, ye shall eat unleavened bread, until the one and twentieth day of the month at even. Seven days there shall be no leaven in your houses.*" Who can fail to see that if the fourteenth day is included, there are not seven but eight days between the fourteenth and twenty-first days? But if, as careful study of the scriptures reveals the truth, we reckon from the evening of the fourteenth day to the evening of the twenty-first, we shall at once see that this fourteenth day gives its evening to the beginning of the Paschal feast, so that the entire sacred solemnity comprises no more than seven days and nights. Accordingly our definition is shown to be correct, in which we stated that it should be celebrated during the first month of the year and in its third week. For it is in fact the third week, because it begins on the evening of the fourteenth day, and closes on the evening of the twenty-first.

'The reasons for the Catholic practice are therefore evident: equally evident is the irrational error of those who presume to anticipate or exceed the periods prescribed in the Law without real necessity. Those who consider that the day of our Lord's Resurrection should be kept between the fourteenth day of the month and the twentieth day of the moon anticipate the time prescribed in the Law without any reasonable necessity; for when they begin to keep the vigil of the holy night from the evening of the fourteenth day, it is evident that they regard that day as the beginning of their Easter, and they cannot show any authority for this in the decrees of the Law. And when they refuse to keep the Lord's Easter on the twenty-first day of the month, they clearly exclude from their observance a day which the Law often recommends as suitable for the greater festival. Consequently, they disarrange the proper order, sometimes even placing Easter entirely in the second week, and never keeping it on the seventh day of the third week. Again, considering that Easter should be celebrated between the sixteenth day of the said month to the twenty-second, they no less incorrectly go to the opposite extreme, deviating from the correct course, and as though avoiding shipwreck on Scylla, they are sucked down and drowned in the whirlpool of Charybdis. For when they teach that Easter is to begin at moonrise on the sixteenth day of the first month, that is, from the evening of the fifteenth day, it follows that they entirely exclude from their solemnity the fourteenth day of the month, which the Law particularly recommends. Consequently, they hardly include the evening of the fifteenth day, on which God's people were redeemed from slavery in Egypt, and on which our

Lord redeemed the world from the darkness of sin by His
own Blood, and on which He was buried, bestowing on us
the hope of blessedness and peace after death.

'When they place the Lord's day of Easter on the twenty-
second day of the month, these people incur the penalty of
their error and openly violate the legitimate limits of Easter,
beginning it on the evening of the day on which the Law had
directed that it should be finished and completed. They also
appoint as the first day of Easter a day of which no mention
is made in the Law, that is, the first day of the fourth week.
Not only are they sometimes mistaken in defining and calculating the age of the moon, but even in discovering the
first month. However, this controversy is too lengthy to be
dealt with fully in this letter. I will say only that the first and
last months of the lunar year can always be accurately determined by reference to the vernal equinox. According to the
views of all the eastern nations, and in particular of the
Egyptians, who are especially skilled in such calculation, the
vernal equinox usually occurs before the Kalends of April, as
we can prove by horological observation. Therefore, whatever moon is at the full before the equinox, when it falls on
the fourteenth or fifteenth day, rightly belongs to the last
month of the preceding year, and consequently is not suitable for keeping Easter. But the full moon falling either on
or after the equinox itself certainly belongs to the first month;
on it the ancients used to keep the Passover, and when Sunday
comes, we should keep Easter. There is a very convincing
reason why this should be so, because it is written in *Genesis*:
"*God made two lights, a greater light to rule the day, and a lesser
light to rule the night.*" For, as the sun, moving from the centre
of the east, predetermined the vernal equinox by his rising,
and later the moon followed full from the centre of the east
after sunset in the evening; so the same first month of the
moon must be observed in the like order each year, and the
full moon must not fall before the equinox, but on the day
of the equinox itself as it was in the beginning, or else after it.

And if the full moon falls only one day before the time of equinox, the above reason shows that it may not be regarded as the first month of the new year, but as the last of the preceding year, and therefore not eligible for the observance of the Easter Festival.

'If it pleases you to know the symbolic reason in this matter, we are directed to keep Easter in the first month of the year, which is also known as the Month of New Fruit, because we should celebrate the mysteries of our Lord's Resurrection and our own deliverance with our minds refreshed to love of heavenly things. We are bidden to keep it in the third week of the month, because Christ, who had been promised before the Law and under the Law, came in the third age of the world to be sacrificed as our Passover. He also rose from the dead on the third day after the offering of His Passion, and wishes this to be known as the Lord's Day, bidding us keep this solemn Passover rightly, that is, His passing out of this world to the Father, if we are careful to do so with Him in faith, hope, and love. We are commanded to keep the full moon of the Paschal month after the equinox, so that the sun may make the first day longer than the night, for then the moon shows the whole of her light face to the world. This signifies how first "*the Sun of Righteousness with healing in His wings*", that is the Lord Jesus, overcame all the darkness of death by the triumph of His Resurrection, and having ascended into heaven, filled His Church, which is often symbolically described as the moon, by sending down the Spirit on her from above. This was the plan of our salvation which the prophet had in mind when he said: "The sun was exalted, and the moon stood still in her course."

'Whoever argues, therefore, that the Paschal full moon can occur before the equinox, disagrees with the teaching of the scriptures in the observance of our highest mysteries, and allies himself with those who believe that they can be saved without the assistance of Christ's grace. Such people presume to teach that they could have attained to perfect goodness even if the true Light had not overcome this world's darkness by His Death and Resurrection. So after sunrise at the equinox, and after the ensuing full moon of the first month – that is, after the close of the fourteenth day of that month, all of which should be kept in accordance with the Law – we still wait until the Lord's Day in the third week as the Gospel directs. Then at length we keep our proper Feast of Easter, and we show that we do not, like the ancients, celebrate the breaking of the Egyptian yoke of slavery, but that we venerate with faith and devotion the Redemption of the whole world, which was foreshadowed in the liberation of God's ancient people, and completed at Christ's Resurrection. In this way we show that we rejoice in the most certain hope of our own resurrection, which we believe will take place on the Lord's Day.

'This calculation of Easter which I have explained to you depends on a cycle of nineteen years, which began to be observed by the Church long ago in the time of the Apostles, especially in Rome and Egypt, as I mentioned earlier. But through the industry of Eusebius, who took his surname from the blessed martyr Pamphylus, it was reduced to a clearer system, so that whereas notification was formerly sent each year to all the churches by the Patriarch of Alexandria, thenceforward it could be easily understood by everyone, because the fourteenth day of the moon fell in a regular sequence. Theophilus, Patriarch of Alexandria, drew up an Easter table for the ensuing hundred years for the benefit of the Emperor Theodosius; similarly, his successor Cyril drew up a table for ninety-five years in five cycles of nineteen years. After him, Dionysius Exiguus added others in the same way which extend down to our own day. This table will soon expire, but today there are so many people able to calculate, that even in our own Church in Britain, there are many who understand the ancient rules of the Egyptians, and can readily compute the cycles of these paschal times for an indefinite number of years, even for five hundred and thirty-two years ahead if they so desire. After this period, all that concerns the sun and moon, month or week, recurs in the same order as before. But I do not propose to send you these cycles of times to come, because you only asked to be informed about the reasons for the time of Easter, and said that you were provided with Catholic Easter tables.

'Having written about Easter as you requested, albeit cursorily and briefly, I also urge you to make sure that the tonsure, about which you also asked me to write, is worn in accordance with Christian ecclesiastical practice. We know that the Apostles were not all tonsured in the same manner, and although the Catholic Church is united in one faith, hope, and love in God, it has not adopted one unvarying form of tonsure throughout the whole world. In short, looking back to the earlier days of the patriarchs, we find that Job, the pattern of patience, shaved his head in time of trouble, which shows that in times of prosperity he allowed his hair to grow. But Joseph, the famous follower and teacher of purity, humility, piety, and other virtues, shaved his head when about to be freed from slavery, which shows that while he was living in prison as a slave, he did not cut his hair. But notice how each of these men of God, while differing in their outward appearance, are alike in cherishing grace and virtue in their inmost hearts. But we may frankly admit that a variety in tonsure does no harm to those who have a pure faith in God and sincere charity towards their neighbour, especially since we do not read that there was ever any controversy about differences of tonsure such as there has been about Easter or diversity in matters of doctrine. Nevertheless, of all the tonsures to be found either in the Church or among the races of mankind, I consider none more worthy of being imitated and adopted than that worn on the head of the disciple to whose confession our Lord replied: *"Thou art Peter, and upon this rock I will build my church, and the gates of hell shall not prevail against it: and I will give unto thee the keys of the kingdom of heaven."* Nor do I consider any to be more

abhorrent and detestable to all the faithful than that worn by
the man to whom, when he wished to purchase the gift of
the Holy Spirit, Peter said: "*Thy money perish with thee,
because thou hast thought that the gift of God may be purchased
with money. Thou hast neither part nor lot in this matter.*" But
we are not shaven in the form of a crown solely because Peter
was shorn in this way, but because Peter was shorn in this
way in memory of our Lord's Passion. Therefore we who
desire to be saved by Christ's Passion, like Peter wear this
sign of the Passion on the crown of the head, which is the
highest part of the body. For as the Church came into being
through the Death of Him who gave it life, thus each member of it bears the sign of the Holy Cross on his forehead, so
that this emblem may afford constant protection against the
assaults of wicked spirits, and serve as a continual reminder
that he must crucify the flesh with all its vices and evil desires.
Similarly, those who have taken monastic vows or are in
Holy Orders should bind themselves to stricter self-discipline
for our Lord's sake, and wear their heads tonsured in the form
of the crown of thorns worn by Christ in His Passion, so that
Christ may bear the thorns and briars of our sins and take
them away from us, wearing them on His own head. In this
way they will openly show themselves willing and ready to
suffer ridicule and disgrace for His sake, always hoping to
receive "*the crown of everlasting life which God has promised to
those that love Him*", and to demonstrate that in order to win
this crown, they regard both adversity and prosperity as of
equal insignificance. As for the tonsure that Simon the magi-
cian is said to have worn, I ask what faithful Christian will not
instantly detest it, and reject it together with all his magic.
On the forehead it has indeed a superficial resemblance to a
crown, but when you look at the neck, you will find the
apparent crown cut short, so that you may fairly regard this
custom as characteristic of simoniacs, and not of Christians.
For in this life, deluded people thought such men worthy of
a lasting crown of glory, but in the life to come they are

not only deprived of all hope of a crown, but condemned to eternal punishment.

'Do not think that I have spoken in this way about those who wear this tonsure as though they are damned even if they maintain Catholic unity in belief and practice; on the contrary, I am sure that many of them were holy men and pleasing to God. Among them is Adamnan, a renowned priest and abbot, who when he was sent on an embassy from his nation to King Alfrid, wished to visit our monastery. He displayed such remarkable wisdom, humility, and devotion in his ways and conversation that, among other things, I said to him: "Holy brother, you believe that you are going forward to receive the crown of everlasting life. I beg you, why do you act contrary to this belief and wear an imperfect crown on your head? And if you seek the society of blessed Peter, why do you imitate the tonsure of the man whom Peter cursed? Why do you not do everything in this life to show that you love to imitate him with whom you desire to live in blessedness for ever?" He replied: "My dear brother, rest assured that although I wear Simon's tonsure after the custom of my country, I wholeheartedly abominate and reject all simoniacal wickedness. So far as my frailty permits, I wish to follow in the footsteps of the most blessed Prince of the Apostles." I then said: "I am sure that this is so. Nevertheless, you should give some indication of your inward esteem for whatever derives from the Apostle Peter by displaying openly whatever you know to be his. For I think that your wisdom clearly appreciates that it would be better for you, who are vowed to God, to alter your outward appearance from any resemblance to a man whom you wholeheardedly detest, and whose hideous face you would loathe to see. On the other hand, since you wish to follow the example and teachings of Peter, it would be fitting for you to conform to the outward appearance of him whom you desire to have as your advocate in the presence of God."

'Such, then, were my words to Adamnan, who showed

how greatly he had profited by seeing the observances of our Church, for after he had returned to Scotland, he won over large numbers to the Catholic observance of Easter by his preaching. But although he was their lawfully constituted head, he was unable to persuade the monks of Iona to adopt a better rule of life; for had his authority been sufficiently great, he would have taken care to correct the tonsure.

'I now beg Your Majesty in your wisdom, together with the nation over which the King of kings and Lord of lords has placed you, to set yourself to follow all that fosters the unity of the Catholic and Apostolic Church. In so doing, when the might of your earthly kingdom has passed away, the most blessed Prince of the Apostles will gladly open the gate of the heavenly kingdom to you and yours, and admit you to the company of God's elect.

'Most dearly beloved son in Christ, may the grace of God the everlasting King keep you in safety to reign many years, and preserve us all in peace.'

When this letter had been read in the presence of King Nechtan and many of his more learned men, and carefully translated into their own tongue by those who could understand it, he is said to have been so grateful for its guidance that he rose among his assembled chieftains and fell on his knees, thanking God that he had been accounted worthy to receive such a gift from England. 'I already knew that this was the true observance of Easter, but I now understand the reasons for it so clearly that I seem hitherto to have had very little knowledge about it. I therefore publicly proclaim in the presence of you all that I intend to observe this time of Easter with all my people for ever. And I decree that all the clergy of my kingdom shall adopt the tonsure of which we have now heard the full explanation.' The king at once enforced his statement with his royal authority. The nineteen-year cycles were immediately sent out under a public order to all the provinces of the Picts to be copied, learned, and adopted, and the erroneous eighty-four year cycles were universally abolished. All the ministers of the altar and monks adopted the circular tonsure, and the reformed nation was glad to be placed under the direction of Peter, the most blessed Prince of the Apostles, and secure under his protection.

CHAPTER 22: *The monks of Iona and the monasteries under its jurisdiction begin to adopt the canonical Easter at the preaching of Egbert* [A.D. 716]

NOT long afterwards, the Scottish monks who lived in the Isle of Iona, together with the monasteries under their jurisdiction, were led by God's providence to adopt the proper Easter and the canonical tonsure. For in the year 716, during which King Osred was killed and Coenred succeeded to the government of the Northumbrian kingdom, Egbert the beloved of God – a father and bishop to be mentioned with high respect, and of whom I have already spoken – came to them from Ireland and was welcomed with honour and great joy. Being a most persuasive teacher who most faithfully practised all that he taught, he was given a ready hearing by everyone, and by his constant devout exhortations he weaned them from the obsolete traditions of their ancestors, to whom the Apostle's description is applicable: '*they had a zeal for God, but not a zeal with knowledge.*' As I have said, he taught them to observe our chief solemnity in the Catholic and Apostolic manner under the analogy of an unbroken cycle. This seemed to happen by a wonderful dispensation of God's grace, in order that the nation which had willingly and ungrudgingly laboured to communicate its own knowledge of God to the English nation might later, through the same English nation, arrive at a perfect way of life which they had not hitherto possessed. In contrast, the Britons who had refused to share their own knowledge of the Christian Faith with the English, still remain obdurate and crippled by their errors, going about with their heads improperly tonsured, and keeping Christ's solemnity without fellowship with the Christian Church. But the English nation now believes rightly, and is fully instructed in the doctrines of the Catholic Faith.

Through Egbert's teaching, the monks of Iona under Abbot Dunchad adopted Catholic ways of life about eighty years after they had sent Aidan to preach to the English nation.* God's servant Egbert remained thirteen years on the island, where he restored the gracious light of unity and peace to the Church and consecrated the island anew to Christ. In the year of our Lord 729, during which our Lord's Easter was kept on the twenty-fourth of April, Egbert celebrated the solemnity of the Mass in honour of our Lord's Resurrection, and departed to him the same day. So he began to keep the greatest of all festivals with the brethren whom he had won to the grace of unity, and ended it with our Lord, the Apostles, and all the citizens of heaven, where he now keeps it for ever. And by a wonderful dispensation of divine providence, the venerable Egbert not only passed from this world to the Father on Easter Day, but when Easter was being kept on a day when it had never been kept before in those parts. So the brethren had the joy of a sure and Catholic knowledge of the time of Easter, and rejoiced in the protection of their father departed to our Lord, by whom they had been converted. Egbert himself showed great joy that he had been permitted to live until he saw his disciples accept and keep with him the Easter day that they had previously always rejected. So the most reverend father was assured of their conversion. *He rejoiced to see the Lord's Day: he saw it, and was glad.*

CHAPTER 23: *The present state of the English nation and the rest of Britain* [A.D. 725-731]

IN the year of our Lord 725, which was the seventh year of King Osric of Northumbria, the successor of Coenred, Wictred, son of King Egbert of Kent, died on the twenty-third of April, leaving the kingdom that he had ruled for thirty-four and a half years to be inherited by his sons Ethelbert, Eadbert, and Alric. In the following year Bishop Tobias of Rochester died. He was a very learned man, as I said earlier, and had been a disciple of Archbishop Theodore and Abbot Hadrian of blessed memory. Consequently, in addition to his knowledge of ecclesiastical and general literature, he understood the Greek and Latin languages so thoroughly that they were as familiar to him as his own native tongue. He was buried in the porch of Saint Peter the Apostle, which he had built within the church of Saint Andrew for his own burial place. And when he had been consecrated by Archbishop Berthwald, Aldwulf succeeded to the bishopric after Tobias.

In the year of our Lord 729, two comets appeared around the sun, striking terror into all who saw them. One comet rose early and preceded the sun, while the other followed the setting sun at evening, seeming to portend awful calamity to east and west alike. One comet was the precursor of day and the other of night, to indicate that mankind was menaced by evils at both times. They appeared in the month of January, and remained visible for about a fortnight, bearing their fiery tails northward as though to set the welkin aflame. At this time, a swarm of Saracens* ravaged Gaul with horrible slaughter, but after a brief interval in that country they paid the penalty of their wickedness. During this year the man of God Egbert departed to our Lord on Easter Day as I have mentioned, and immediately after Easter, on the ninth of May, King Osric of Northumbria departed this life after a reign of eleven years, having appointed Ceolwulf, brother of his predecessor Coenred, to follow him. Both the outset and course of Ceolwulf's reign were filled by so many serious disturbances that it is quite impossible to know what to write about them, or what the outcome will be.

On the ninth of January in the year of our Lord 731, Archbishop Berthwald died of old age, having held the see for thirty-seven years, six months, and fourteen days. In the same year Tatwin, from the province of Mercia, who had been a priest in the monastery of Bredon, was made archbishop in his place. He was consecrated in the city of Canterbury on Sunday the tenth of June by the venerable Bishops Daniel of Winchester, Ingwald of London, Aldwin of Lichfield, and Aldwulf of Rochester. Tatwin was a man distinguished for his religion and wisdom, and extremely learned in holy scripture.

At the present day* Tatwin and Aldwulf preside over the churches of Kent; Ingwald is Bishop of the East Saxons; Aldbert and Hadulac are Bishops of the East Angles; Daniel and Forthere are Bishops of the West Saxons; and Aldwin is Bishop of the Mercians. Walstod is Bishop of the folk who live in the west, beyond the river Severn; Wilfrid is Bishop of the Hwiccas; Cynebert is Bishop of the province of the Lindisfarnes. The bishopric of the Isle of Wight belongs to Daniel, Bishop of Winchester. The province of the South Saxons has now been without a bishop for some years, and obtains the offices of a bishop from the prelate of the West Saxons. All these provinces, together with the others south of the river Humber and their kings, are subject to Ethelbald, King of the Mercians.

In the province of Northumbria, ruled by Ceolwulf, four bishops hold office; Wilfrid in the church of York, Ethelwald at Lindisfarne, Acca at Hexham, and Pecthelm in the see known as The White House,* where the number of believers has so increased that it has recently become an episcopal see with Pecthelm as its first bishop.

At the present time, the Picts have a treaty of peace with the English, and are glad to be united in Catholic peace and truth to the universal Church. The Scots who are living in Britain are content with their own territories, and do not contemplate any raids or stratagems against the English. The Britons for the most part have a national hatred for the English, and uphold their own bad customs against the true Easter of the Catholic Church; however, they are opposed by the power of God and man alike, and are powerless to obtain what they want. For although they have a certain measure of self-government, they have also been brought to some extent under subjection to the English.

As peace and prosperity prevail in these days, many of the Northumbrians, both noble and simple, together with their children, have laid aside their weapons, preferring to receive the tonsure and take monastic vows rather than study the arts of war. What the result of this will be will be seen in the next generation.*

This, then, is the present state of all Britain, nearly two hundred and eighty-five years after the coming of the English to Britain, but seven hundred and fifty-one years since our Lord's Incarnation. May the world rejoice under his eternal rule, and Britain glory in his Faith. Let the countless isles be glad, and sing praises to the honour of his holiness!

CHAPTER 24: *A chronological summary of the whole book, and a note about the author*

To assist the memory, I have thought it helpful to make a concise summary of events already dealt with at greater length.

In the sixtieth year before the Incarnation of our Lord, Gaius Julius Caesar, the first of the Romans, made war on Britain and was victorious, but was unable to hold the kingdom.

In the year of our Lord 46, Claudius, the second of the Romans, came to Britain and received the surrender of the greater part of the island. He also added the Isles of Orkney to the Roman Empire.

In the year of our Lord 167, Eleutherius became Bishop of Rome, and ruled the Church most gloriously for fifteen years. Lucius, a king of Britain, sent him a letter asking to be made a Christian, and obtained his request.

In the year of our Lord 189, Severus became Emperor and reigned seventeen years. He fortified Britain with an earthwork stretching from sea to sea.

In the year 381, Maximus became Emperor while in Britain. He crossed into Gaul and killed Gratian.

In the year 409, Rome was taken by the Goths, and thenceforward Roman rule came to an end in Britain.

In the year 430, Pope Celestine sent Palladius to be the first bishop to the Christian Scots.

In the year 449, Marcian became co-Emperor with Valentinian. He reigned seven years, during which time the English came to Britain at the invitation of the Britons.

In the year 538, an eclipse of the sun occurred on the sixteenth of February, lasting from Prime to Terce.

In the year 540, an eclipse of the sun occurred on the twentieth of June, and the stars appeared for nearly half an hour after the hour of Terce.

In the year 547, Ida began his reign, and occupied the throne for twelve years. The royal family of Northumbria derives its origin from him.

In the year 565, the priest Columba came into Britain from Scotland to teach the Picts, and built a monastery on the Isle of Iona.

In the year 596, Pope Gregory sent Augustine and his monks to Britain, to preach the word of God to the English people.

In the year 597, these teachers arrived in Britain. This was about one hundred and fifty years after the coming of the English to Britain.

In the year 601, Pope Gregory sent the *pallium* to Britain for Augustine, who had already been made a bishop. He also sent several ministers of the word, including Paulinus.

In the year 603, the Battle of Degsastan was fought.

In the year 604, the East Saxons under King Sabert received the Faith of Christ through Archbishop Mellitus.

In the year 605, Pope Gregory died.

In the year 616, King Ethelbert of Kent died.

In the year 625, Archbishop Justus consecrated Paulinus as Bishop of the Northumbrians.

In the year 626, Eanfled, daughter of King Edwin, was baptized on Whitsunday with twelve others.

In the year 627, King Edwin and his people were baptized on Easter Day.

In the year 633, King Edwin was killed, and Paulinus retired to Kent.

In the year 640, King Eadbald of Kent died.

In the year 642, King Oswald was killed.

In the year 644, Paulinus, first Bishop of York and later Bishop of Rochester, departed to our Lord.

In the year 651, King Oswin was killed, and Bishop Aidan died.

In the year 653, the Middle Angles under Peada their prince accepted the mysteries of the Faith.

In the year 655, Penda was slain, and the Mercians became Christians.

In the year 644, an eclipse occurred. King Earconbert of Kent died, and Bishop Colman returned to his own land with the Scots. A plague came. Chad and Wilfrid were consecrated Bishops of the Northumbrians.

In the year 668, Theodore was consecrated bishop.

In the year 670, King Oswy of Northumbria died.

In the year 673, King Egbert of Kent died. A synod was held at Hertford in the presence of King Egfrid under the presidency of Archbishop Theodore. It was valuable, and enacted ten canons.

In the year 675, Wulfhere, King of the Mercians, died after a reign of seventeen years, and left the throne to his brother Ethelred.

In the year 676, Ethelred ravaged Kent.

In the year 678, a comet appeared. Bishop Wilfrid was expelled from his see by King Egfrid: Bosa, Eata, and Eadhed were consecrated bishops in his place.

In the year 679, Elfwin was killed.

In the year 680, a synod was held in the plain of Heathfield under the presidency of Archbishop Theodore to affirm the Catholic Faith: John, an abbot from Rome, attended. Abbess Hilda died at Whitby.

In the year 685, Egfrid, King of the Northumbrians, was killed. King Lothere of Kent died.

In the year 688, Cadwalla, King of the West Saxons, left Britain for Rome.

In the year 690, Archbishop Theodore died.

In the year 697, Queen Osthryda was killed by her own people, the Mercian chieftains.

In the year 698, Berctred, the royal commander of the Northumbrians, was killed by the Picts.

In the year 704, Ethelred became a monk after ruling the Mercians for thirty years, and resigned the kingdom to Coenred.

In the year 705, King Alfrid of Northumbria died.

In the year 709, Coenred, King of the Mercians, after a reign of six years, went to Rome.

In the year 711, Earl Berctfrid fought against the Picts.

In the year 716, Osred, King of the Northumbrians, was killed, and Ceolred, King of the Mercians, died. The man of God Egbert converted the monks of Iona to the Catholic Easter and the canonical tonsure.

In the year 725, King Wictred of Kent died.

In the year 729, comets appeared: the holy Egbert departed this life: Osric died.

In the year 731, Archbishop Berctwald died. In the same year, the fifteenth of the reign of King Ethelbald of Mercia, Tatwin was consecrated ninth Archbishop of Canterbury.

*

WITH God's help, I, Bede, the servant of Christ and priest of the monastery of the blessed Apostles Peter and Paul at Wearmouth and Jarrow, have assembled these facts about the history of the Church in Britain, and of the Church of the English in particular, so far as I have been able to ascertain them from ancient documents, from the traditions of our forebears, and from my own personal knowledge.

I was born on the lands of this monastery, and on reaching seven years of age, my family entrusted me first to the most reverend Abbot Benedict, and later to Abbot Ceolfrid for my education. I have spent all the remainder of my life in this monastery, and devoted myself entirely to the study of the scriptures. And while I have observed the regular discipline and sung the choir offices daily in church, my chief delight has always been in study, teaching, and writing.

I was ordained deacon at the age of nineteen, and priest at the age of thirty, receiving both these orders at the hands of the most reverend Bishop John at the direction of Abbot Ceolfrid. From the time of my receiving the priesthood until my fifty-ninth year, I have worked, both for my own benefit and that of my brethren, to compile short extracts from the works of the venerable Fathers on holy scripture, and to comment on their meaning and interpretation. These books include:

The Beginning of Genesis, up to the birth of Isaac and Ishmael's rejection: four Books.

The Tabernacle: its vessels and priestly vestments: four Books.

The First Part of Samuel, up to the death of Saul: three Books.

On the Building of the Temple: an allegorical interpretation like the others: four Books.

Thirty Questions on the Book of Kings.

On the Proverbs of Solomon: three Books.

On the Song of Songs: seven Books.

On Isaiah, Daniel, the Twelve Prophets, and part of Jeremiah, with chapter headings taken from blessed Jerome's Treatise.

On Ezra and Nehemiah: three Books.

On the Song of Habakkuk: one Book.

On the Book of the blessed father Tobias: an allegorical interpretation on Christ and the Church: one Book.

Chapters of Readings on the Pentateuch of Moses, Joshua, and Judges.

On the Books of Kings and Chronicles.

On the Book of the blessed father Job.

On Proverbs, Ecclesiastes, and the Song of Songs.

On the Prophets Isaiah, Ezra, and Nehemiah.

On the Gospel of Mark: four Books.

On the Gospel of Luke: six Books.

Homilies on the Gospel: two Books.

On the Apostle: in which I have carefully transcribed in order whatever I have found in the works of Saint Augustine.

On the Acts of the Apostles: two Books.

On the Seven Catholic Epistles: one Book on each.

On the Apocalypse of Saint John: three Books.

Also, *Chapters of Readings* from all the New Testament except the Gospel.

Also, a book of *Letters* to various persons, including one on the six ages of the world; on the dwellings of the children of Israel; on Isaiah's saying, '*And they shall be shut up in prison, and after many days they shall be visited*': on the reason for the bissextile year; and on Anatolius' explanation of the equinox.

Also, *The Histories of the Saints*. I have translated Paulinus' metrical work on the *Life and Sufferings of the confessor Saint Felix* into prose. And I have corrected, to the best of my ability, the sense of a book on *The Life and Sufferings of Saint Anastasius*, which had been badly translated from the Greek, and worse amended by some unskilful person. I have also written the *Life* of our father, the holy monk and Bishop Cuthbert, firstly in heroic verse, and later in prose.

I have written in two books *The History of the Abbots Benedict, Ceolfrid, and Huetbert*, rulers of this monastery in which I delight to serve the Divine Goodness.

The Church History of our island and people: in five Books.

The Martyrology of the feast-days of the holy martyrs: in which I have carefully tried to record everything I could learn not only of the date, but also by what kind of combat and under what judge they overcame the world.

A Book of Hymns in various metres or rhythms.

A Book of Epigrams in heroic, or elegiac, verse.

On the Nature of Things, and *On Times*: a book on each.

A Book on *Orthography*, arranged in alphabetical order.

A Book on *The Art of Poetry*, with a small work appended *On Tropes and Figures*; that is, the figures and manners of speech found in holy scripture.

*

I PRAY YOU, noble Jesu, that as You have graciously granted me joyfully to imbibe the words of Your knowledge, so You will also of Your bounty grant me to come at length to Yourself, the Fount of all wisdom,
and to dwell in Your presence
for ever.

NOTES

P. 33 King Ceolwulf, a man of considerable learning, resigned his throne in A.D. 737 and became a monk at Lindisfarne.

P. 33 Bede's authorities. Albinus succeeded Hadrian as Abbot of the monastery of S. Peter and S. Paul, Canterbury, *circa* A.D. 709. He died *c.* A.D. 732.

     Nothelm appears to have visited Rome to examine the papal archives during the pontificate of Gregory II (A.D. 715–731). As this pope had been librarian of the Roman Church prior to his elevation, he would have been well qualified to direct Nothelm's researches. Nothelm became Archbishop of Canterbury in A.D. 735, and died *c.* A.D. 736.

P. 37 In his early chapters, Bede quotes from earlier authorities such as Orosius and Tacitus. His statements are not based on his own observations.

P. 38 The Scots. When Bede refers to the Scots, it should be remembered that he is speaking of the people of Ireland (Hibernia). These emigrated in large numbers to the northern parts of Britain between the second and fifth centuries.

P. 41 Claudius' purpose in annexing the Orkneys was to counter attacks on the island of Britain from the north. In the ninth century, they were to become an important base of operations for the Scandinavian invaders.

P. 48 In brief, the Arian heresy denied the reality of the divine nature in Christ. It takes its name from Arius, its propagator, whose false teachings were condemned by the Church at the Council of Nicaea in A.D. 325.

P. 49 Pelagianism, 'the British heresy', denied the reality of original sin, and affirmed that man could attain perfection by his own efforts, unaided by the grace of God. This misconception is still strong today!

P. 53 Bede makes no mention of the mission of S. Patrick, who was also sent by Pope Celestine. The origins of Christianity in Ireland remain very uncertain.

Notes

P. 68 Indictions were cycles of fifteen years. Bede says elsewhere of this system: 'If you wish to find the indiction, take the year of our Lord, add three, and divide by fifteen: the remainder gives you the indiction of the current year.'

P. 68 The Anglo-Saxon 'hide' was originally the amount of land necessary to support one family. As the quality of land varied from place to place, the term was elastic, and there was no uniform measurement for the hide throughout England.

P. 72 Gregory refers to clergy in minor orders. Marriage was forbidden to those in major orders: i.e. subdeacon, deacon, and priest, although celibacy does not seem to have been enforced in the earlier centuries, viz., S. Patrick was son of a deacon.

P. 75 The *pallium*. An ornament granted by the Pope to archbishops as a mark of dignity and authority. It can be seen in the arms of the See of Canterbury, and takes the form of a circular white stole worn on the shoulders, with a pendant front and back, marked with four crosses. It is made of lamb's wool woven in the convent of S. Agnes at Rome. It was originally an Imperial mark of favour and adopted by the popes, who made it an essential mark of authority, without which no archbishop could exercise jurisdiction.

P. 86 Relics of the saints are sealed into the altar of a church during the ceremony of its consecration. Bede tells how many bishops were indefatigable collectors of relics for this purpose.

P. 90 Gregory is referring to the current expectation that the end of the world would come in the year A.D. 1000 (see *Revelation* xx. 2–7).

P. 91 Christ Church, Canterbury, predecessor of the present Cathedral. The Anglo-Saxon Chronicle records that it was consecrated on June 9, the feast of S. Primus and S. Felician, probably in the year A.D. 603.

P. 99 It is often forgotten that the Christian Church was firmly established in Britain several centuries before the mission of Augustine, and its bishops naturally looked askance at the newcomer's claim to supreme authority. The origins of the Celtic Church are veiled in the mists of antiquity, and offer a fascinating field for valuable research. Glastonbury claimed to have been founded by Joseph of Arimathaea, and the Celtic saints and bishops had certainly evangelized large areas of

Britain by an earlier date that is generally realized. But, as Augustine foretold, their refusal to attempt the conversion of the Saxon invaders resulted in the ultimate decay of Celtic influence and customs.

P. 101 The Paschal question long remained a matter of dispute between the Roman and Celtic Churches, and was finally settled in favour of the former at the Council of Whitby in A.D. 664. Bede often speaks with deep disapproval of Celtic obstinacy. While no fundamental doctrinal issues were at stake, these differences caused considerable confusion. Bede mentions (III. 25) how King Oswy of Northumbria was celebrating Easter in accordance with the Celtic customs, while his queen was still fasting and observing Palm Sunday.

P. 110 The Four Crowned Martyrs – *Quatuor Coronati* – were Severus, Severianus, Victorianus, and Carpophorus. Their church on the Caelian Hill, Rome, is mentioned as early as the time of Gregory I.

P. 124 The question of the national religion was evidently debated upon in the Witenagemot. Coifi's entirely materialistic reasons for a change of religion show that mass conversions were seldom sincere or lasting. This was borne out by the widespread apostasy which followed Edwin's death.

P. 126 All native buildings in Britain at this period were of timber or wattle. Building in stone was a craft learned mainly through Roman influence, and in many cases masons and architects were brought over from Gaul, as in the case of Benedict Biscop's church at Wearmouth.

P. 130 The *Tufa* was a standard of Roman origin, and took the form of a winged globe mounted on a spear. It was adopted as the personal standard of the Bretwalda or High-King of Britain.

P. 134 Most of the Scottish Church leaders to whom this letter was addressed can be identified: Tomianus (Tomene) was Abbot and Bishop of Armagh; Columbanus (Colman), Abbot and Bishop of Clonard; Cromanus (Cronan), Abbot of Nendrum; Dunanus (Duia), Bishop of Bangor; Baithanus (Baethin), Bishop of Tibohine; Cromanus (Cronan) of Movilla; Hermanus (S. Ernan), Abbot of Tory Island; Laistranus (Laisren), Abbot of Leighlin; Scellanus (Sillan), Bishop of Devenish; Segenus (Seghine), Abbot of Iona; Saranus. (Saran Ua Critain).

P. 135 Cadwalla, otherwise Cadwallon, was King of Gwynedd, the leader of the Welsh in the struggle against the Angles, and Edwin's most dangerous antagonist.

P. 142 The Scots monastery on the island of Hii (Iona) was founded by S. Columba, and became a centre of intense spiritual activity, from which the Celtic missionaries carried the light of the Gospel far and wide in Britain. It was often known as *I Columb-kill*, i.e. the Island of Columb's Cell.

P. 143 S. Ninian, a native of North Wales, was a redoubtable opponent of his fellow-countryman the heretic Pelagius. He was a great scholar and traveller, and corresponded with S. Martin of Tours, to whom he dedicated his church after the latter's death *c.* A.D. 400. According to Ailred, Martin sent him masons from Gaul to build his stone church at Whitherne in Galloway (*Candida Casa*). His diocese seems to have extended from the neighbourhood of Glasgow to the borders of Westmorland.

P. 143 The amazing life and labours of S. Columba were recorded sixty years after his death by Adamnan, Abbot of Iona from A.D. 657 to 669. Columba is said to have died on June 7, A.D. 597, the year of S. Augustine's landing in Kent.

P. 144 The Celtic Church was organized on a tribal and monastic basis rather than diocesan. The abbot of a monastery exercised ecclesiastical jurisdiction over the *provincia*, while the bishop, who was a member of the monastic community, exercised his episcopal functions at the behest of the abbot. The abbot himself – like S. Columba – was not of necessity a bishop, and did not exercise episcopal functions such as ordination. Bede, as a supporter of the Roman diocesan system, disapproved of the Celtic custom.

P. 148 Hedda was bishop from A.D. 676 to 703. The original cathedral at Winchester was built by Cenwalh, and was consecrated in A.D. 648.

P. 150 Faremoûtier-en-Brie, founded by S. Fara, a disciple of S. Columba, in A.D. 617.

P. 150 Those already established included Canterbury, Lindisfarne, Bury St Edmunds, Melrose, and Malmesbury.

P. 151 This was a double monastery of monks and nuns, each living in their own enclosure. The arrangement was later adopted in Britain in such houses as Ely and Whitby, but fell into disuse after the Danish invasions.

P. 158   In A.D. 875 the monks, fearing the Danes, abandoned Lindisfarne, and took away with them the body of S. Cuthbert and the head of King Oswald. After a series of temporary resting-places, these were eventually deposited at Durham.

P. 158   Acca, who became Bishop of Hexham in A.D. 709, was a close friend of Bede, and several of the latter's books are dedicated to him.

P. 166   This has sometimes been claimed as the origin of the University of Cambridge, but the school was probably at Dunwich. The schools at Canterbury were probably founded by S. Augustine, and were the predecessors of those established by Theodore.

P. 167   Bury St Edmunds.

P. 168   Burgh Castle, near Yarmouth.

P. 171   Lagny, on the Marne.

P. 172   The Gyrwas province included parts of Northants, Hunts, Lincoln, and Cambridge. The Book of Ely says: 'The Gyrwas are all the southern Angles living in the great fen in which lies the Isle of Ely.'

P. 173   At-Wall: probably Walton, near Newcastle.

P. 174   The see was first established at Repton. S. Chad later moved it to Lichfield, where it remains to this day.

P. 175   Ythancestir was probably Othona, a Roman military settlement in Essex.

P. 180   Whitby was a double foundation for monks and nuns, ruled by an abbess. The princess became co-abbess with her mother Queen Eanfleda, who probably retired here soon after Oswy's death. Aelffleda was a friend of S. Cuthbert. Wilfrid owed much to her support in his troubles, and Eddius describes her as 'a very wise woman, the best of comforters and counsellors in the whole province.'

P. 188   S. Aldhelm employs the same argument with King Gerontius of Cornwall. 'If the keys of the kingdom of heaven were entrusted to Peter, how can anyone who disregards the laws of the church hope to enter the gates of paradise?'

P. 189   The case for the Roman style of tonsure is presented in Ceofrid's letter to King Nechtan (Bede, V. 21). The claim that it originated with S. Peter is, of course, unhistorical. It seems to have been adopted as a sign of monastic profession in the early centuries, and in the fifth century it became also the mark of all clerics. The Roman clergy shaved the crown, and left a circle of hair around the head above the temples, in memory of our Lord's crown of thorns. The Celtic clergy shaved the front of the head, and allowed the hair to grow at the back. Their Roman opponents denounced this as the tonsure of Simon Magus.

P. 192   Egbert became Abbot of Iona in A.D. 716. See Bede. V. 22.

P. 193   Clothair III, King of Neustria.

P. 193   These bishops were probably Cornish. This fact is of interest, as it indicates the beginning of co-operation between the Celtic and English bishops. Hitherto their relations had been distant and strained by the mutual hostility between the two races, and by the refusal of the British bishops to submit to the claims and customs of the Roman Church.

P. 198   Not far from S. Benedict's Abbey of Monte Cassino.

P. 201   This statement is incorrect. Prior to Wilfrid's consecration, there had been five bishops of English birth whose orthodoxy was unquestioned – Ithamar, Thomas, Boniface, Deusdedit, and Damian.

P. 202   On his reconsecration, Chad was translated to Mercia. The grounds of Theodore's doubt on the validity of Chad's consecration appear to have been (1) That he had been consecrated to a see that was not vacant. (2) That two British bishops not in communion with Rome had taken part in his consecration.

P. 207   In A.D. 1148, the relics of S. Chad were translated to Lichfield.

P. 208   Mayo. Alcuin later wrote to these monks as 'exiles for love of Christ's Name' and said: 'The great light of your learning has spread far and wide throughout the land ... let your light shine among that barbarous nation like a star in the western skies.' It is noteworthy that, whereas the Irish had formerly taught the English, the roles now seem to be reversed. Up to a late date, Mayo was known as *Magheo na Saxan* – Mayo of the Saxons.

P. 208   This refers to the abandonment of Celtic customs, and the adoption of Roman.

Notes

p. 212 Aecci was appointed to the original See of Dunwich *c.* A.D. 673; Bedwin to the See of Elmham in Norfolk.

p. 213 The morning Offices of Matins and Lauds were sung before dawn.

p. 220 St Paul's, London.

p. 221 That is, those Picts north of the Forth who were tributary to the kingdom of Northumbria. In 585 they repudiated their allegiance, and Bishop Trumwin had to abandon his see at Abercorn and retire to Whitby.

p. 222 The eastern part of Hampshire: the name is preserved in Meonstoke.

p. 229 The heresy of Eutyches was Monophysite, i.e., a denial of the co-existence of two perfect natures, divine and human, in our Lord. This heresy, together with Monthelitism, was finally condemned by the sixth General Council at Constantinople, A.D. 680–681. To prepare for this Council, Pope Agatho called a synod in Rome in A.D. 680, to which Archbishop Theodore was invited. In his absence, Wilfrid, already in Rome on his personal affairs, vouched for the orthodoxy of the northern provinces.

p. 230 The first Lateran Council, A.D. 649.

p. 233 S. Etheldreda (Audrey). Her life is included in Thomas of Ely's *Historia Eliensis*. Her feast day is Oct. 17.

p. 234 Sexburga had received the veil from Archbishop Theodore in Sheppey, where she founded a large convent of nuns.

p. 234 Grantchester, near Cambridge, was a Roman settlement, and this sarcophagus was doubtless of Roman origin.

p. 238 Blood-feuds could be averted by the payment of compensation (*wergeld*) by the offending party to the family of the deceased. The sum payable was based on a recognized scale, and depended on the status of the dead man, whether royal, noble, free, or slave.

p. 239 A similar story is told in the *Life of S. Cadoc*.

p. 248 The Holy Sacrament was evidently reserved for the use of the sick in the Infirmary of the monastery.

p. 252 The Battle of Nechtansmere (Dunnichen Moss, Forfar), A.D. 685.

p. 266 Later known as S. John of Beverley. He ordained Bede deacon and priest.

P. 274 Among other rites at Baptism, which was normally administered at Easter and Whitsun, the newly baptized was given a white robe, which symbolized his purification. This was worn until the Sunday after Easter, known as *Dominica in albis depositis* – i.e. the Sunday when the white robe is laid aside.

P. 278 Meaning that they had turned aside from the true faith.

P. 280 Wilbrord was born in Northumbria *c.* A.D. 657. His father became a hermit near the mouth of the Humber, and entrusted the child to the monks of Ripon. In A.D. 677, Wilbrord crossed to Ireland, and remained with Egbert and Wigbert for twelve years. In A.D. 690, he landed at the mouth of the Rhine, and travelled to Utrecht, where he found all the Frisians heathen. After an arduous and successful apostolate, he died and was buried at Echternach in A.D. 738.

P. 293 Adamnan was ninth Abbot of Iona, which he ruled A.D. 679–704. He wrote the famous *Life of S. Columba*.

P. 299 Bede mentions Daniel in his Preface as the source of his information about the growth of the Church in Wessex, Sussex, and the Isle of Wight.

P. 299 S. Aldhelm, a learned writer and an energetic missionary, was connected with the royal family of Wessex. He became a monk at Malmesbury, a bishop in A.D. 705, and died in A.D. 709. He is said to have been a talented harpist, and to have composed sacred songs to interest and instruct the simple people, which King Alfred considered the best extant English poetry.

P. 300 Bede had plenty of material to draw upon for the life of Wilfrid. Aedde (Eddius), one of Wilfrid's cantors, had already written his life, while Bede himself had personal acquaintance with Wilfrid, and had doubtless learned much from him. Bede evidently has the warmest admiration for Wilfrid's zeal and courage, but less for the autocratic and uncompromising spirit that involved him in so many quarrels.

P. 304 In preparation for the sixth General Council which took place at Constantinople from Nov. A.D. 680 to Sept. 681, Pope Agatho summoned the leaders of the Western Church to a synod in Rome in March A.D. 680. Archbishop Theodore did not attend, but held a council at Hatfield, which re-affirmed the loyalty of the English Church to the Catholic Faith. Meanwhile Wilfrid, who was already in Rome to appeal for the Pope's support against his expulsion from his bishopric, was invited to sit at the synod and to vouch for the orthodoxy of the English Church.

P. 322   Aidan's mission probably began in A.D. 635, so the Iona monks adopted Catholic practices about A.D. 716.

P. 323   The Saracens or Moors overran Spain between A.D. 710 and 713, and crossed the Pyrenees to plunder the rich provinces of France. They suffered a severe defeat at the hands of Charles Martel at the battle of Tours, and were thus prevented from establishing a grasp on France such as they had on Spain. In his theological works, Bede regards the Saracens as the type of all enemies of the Christian Faith – 'sons of Ishmael, whose hand is against every man.'

P. 324   When Bede completed his history in A.D. 731, there were seventeen Saxon sees: In the Kingdom of Kent; Canterbury and Rochester. In Northumbria: York, Lindisfarne, Hexham, and Whitherne. In Mercia: Lichfield, Worcester, Hereford, Dorchester, Lindsey. In the East Saxon Kingdom: London. In East Anglia: Dunwich and Elmham. In Wessex: Winchester and Sherborne. In Sussex: Selsey.

P. 324   The White House, or *Candida Casa*, was at Whitherne in Galloway. Pecthelm, who had been one of Aldhelm's monks, became the first bishop under a Saxon dynasty. But, as Bede himself mentions (III. 4), the see had been founded by S. Ninian in A.D. 412. Tribal wars and the Saxon invasions, however, probably caused several interruptions in the succession of bishops between Ninian and Pecthelm.

P. 325   Bede had become alarmed at the large numbers of men and women entering monasteries for unworthy or improper reasons (see IV. 25). In a letter to his friend Bishop Egbert, he calls attention to the fact that some did so in order to evade their proper obligations to the community, and not to live a life of religion. He suggests that any houses where this abuse was countenanced should be suppressed as 'useless to God and man', and their endowments diverted to increase the inadequate number of bishoprics.

*Some other books
in the Penguin Classics
are described on the
following pages*

CHAUCER
THE CANTERBURY TALES
Translated by Nevill Coghill

L22

The Canterbury Tales is one of the great books of the world and is certainly the liveliest, wisest, wittiest presentation of the human comedy in our language. The passage of time has, however, obscured it a little from us, and what were once the freshest colloquial Chaucerisms seem at times archaic, quaint, and even difficult to understand. Notes and glossaries are necessary, yet they impede the eager reader plunging for pleasure among the tales. And pleasure there is in plenty, whether in the sharp portrayal of a lively and varied human nature that does not seem to have changed much since the fourteenth century, or in the tales that are told; tales that range from noble romances of love and warfare to the ruderies of millers and cooks. Nevill Coghill's translation, passages from which have been read and later dramatized on the B.B.C.'s Third Programme, has given the easy fluency of a modern conversational idiom to Chaucer's work, while remaining faithful in scholarship to the original texts, without expurgation.

WILLIAM LANGLAND
PIERS THE PLOUGHMAN

Translated by Frank Goodridge

L87

This great epic poem was in its day possibly more popular than *The Canterbury Tales*. Latterly, it has been relegated to a dusty corner of anthologies dealing with early English poetry somewhere between *Sir Gawain* and Chaucer. Every serious student knows it from excerpts, yet hardly anyone has ever tackled the work as a whole. This translation should go a long way to remedying this injustice. It is a simple translation into clear modern English prose which, oddly enough, enhances the poetic force of the original, and reveals Langland not only as a brilliant satirist but as a great Christian thinker.

SIR GAWAIN AND THE GREEN KNIGHT

Translated by Brian Stone

192

Sir Gawain and the Green Knight, a poem of 2,500 lines, is the masterpiece of medieval alliterative poetry and was the first poem of the age outside Chaucer's works. In fact, neither Chaucer nor any succeeding poet wrote a narrative poem of such richness. The background is the medieval court and it tells of the adventures of a Christian Knight, although in all probability the origin of the poem was in pagan ritual. Brian Stone's translation is the only easily available complete version in modern English in the original metre.

THOMAS À KEMPIS
THE IMITATION OF CHRIST
Translated by Leo Sherley-Price

L27

After the Bible itself, probably the best-known and best-loved book in Christendom is *The Imitation of Christ*, Thomas à Kempis's guide towards Christian perfection, which for over five hundred years has continued to exercise a widespread influence over Christians of every age and race. Unfortunately most English translators have tended to misrepresent this book – either by making alterations in the text to accord with their personal views, or by presenting it in a pseudo-Jacobean style. Thus many would-be readers have missed the advantage of Thomas's profound wisdom, his clarity of thought and vision, his wide knowledge of the Scriptures and Fathers, and his clear understanding of human nature and its needs. It was time for a new translation, and L. Sherley-Price, a senior Chaplain of the Royal Navy, has provided it for the Penguin Classics series.

THE LADDER OF PERFECTION

Translated by Leo Sherley-Price

L74

Walter Hilton is probably the most influential of the English fourteenth-century mystics. He was a Canon Regular of S. Augustine, and belonged to the community of Thurgarton Priory, near Southwell, where he probably died in 1395. His work, which is in two parts, deals with the vital matters of man's spiritual development and destiny.

Today there is a widespread interest in the lives and writings of great men and women of prayer, and this is due to the instinctive recognition by thoughtful people that, by itself, the rapid advance in scientific knowledge cannot secure man's peace or happiness unless accompanied by a change of heart in man himself. It is this vital need for self-discipline and the substitution of holiness for indifference and mediocrity, which provides for the modern reader the supremely relevant theme of *The Ladder of Perfection*.

BEOWULF

Translated by David Wright

L70

Beowulf is the most famous and impressive long poem in Old English, and one of the finest literary products of the Dark Ages in Europe. Composed about the eighth century in England during the zenith of Anglo-Saxon civilization and culture, *Beowulf* is a highly sophisticated poem: heroic in temper, elegiac in mood, it is at the same time the work of a Christian poet and an expression of the older and grimmer pagan outlook. There have been many translations of *Beowulf*, but this is the first time it has been rendered into contemporary English prose. Based on the latest editions and readings of the text, this new rendering avoids the archaic diction generally adopted in other translations, and is designed for the enjoyment of the general reader as well as the student.

THE LITTLE FLOWERS OF
ST FRANCIS

Translated by Leo Sherley-Price

191

For centuries this little book has been one of the best known and loved in Christendom, and in its pages the unique personality of St Francis of Assisi comes to life. It is not a formal biography, but was compiled in the fourteenth century from various earlier sources, and presents a series of intimate glimpses into the life of the Seraphic Father and his first companions. It captures the simplicity and zeal of the friars in the springtime of the Franciscan movement, and reveals the inner spirit and ideals of the 'little poor man' who has been universally hailed as the most Christ-like of the Saints, and in whose life the graces of humility, love, and joy are shown to be the only solvents for hatred and tensions with which the twentieth century is afflicted. It is a book to be read and pondered.

GOTTFRIED VON STRASSBURG
TRISTAN
Translated by A. T. Hatto

L98

The story of Tristan and Isolde constitutes one of the most famous romances of all time. The *Tristan* of Gottfried von Strassburg, who lived in the thirteenth century, has every right to be considered the classic form of the romance. This is the first unabridged edition of Gottfried's *Tristan* and indeed of any masterpiece of the medieval generation of German poets to be offered to English readers together with the surviving fragments of Thomas's version, *Tristran*.